Civil War Ghosts of Virginia

by L. B. Taylor, Jr.

*Photographs by the Author
Illustrations by
Brenda Goens*

ISBN: 0-9628271-2-6

Contents

Dedication
This book is for my cousin, Layton
Taylor — the brother I never had.

LBT

Author's Note and Introduction

How and why did I come to write this book? As some readers may know, I have previously written seven books on Virginia ghosts; regional books on Williamsburg, Richmond, Tidewater, Fredericksburg and Charlottesville-Lynchburg, and two volumes covering the entire state. Over the past year, a number of additional accounts of ghostly experiences and psychic phenomena came my way. People called and wrote about encounters they had, and others provided leads and material as I traveled about the Commonwealth — at book signings, craft shows, and on research trips.

I began to write a volume III of "The Ghosts of Virginia." As time went on, I noticed that I had accumulated a fair amount of data regarding Civil War spirits. I had about a dozen chapters. There was: the apparitional march of Robert E. Lee's army toward Appomattox; the spectral return of Stonewall Jackson's surgeon; an account involving Confederate President Jefferson Davis' young son; and battlefield haunts at Cold Harbor, Sailor's Creek, and Manassas.

I then went back to my previous books and discovered I had already written of about 25 separate occurrences related to the War Between the States. I asked around. When I gave a talk on the subject of ghosts, I asked if there was interest in a book of such entities tied to the 1860s era. I was surprised, though I shouldn't have been, at the high level of positive response. I was encouraged by friends, by my companion and illustrator Brenda Goens, and by my printer, Danny Thornton of Progress Printing in Lynchburg, and others, to proceed. They all thought it was a good idea. There is, as I have learned, an incredible, almost insatiable interest in the Civil War among many Virginians.

And so, I went back to the libraries, back to the archives, and dug some more. I pored over dozens of books and leafed through thousands of magazine pages to add to the verbal interviews I conducted. I also visited a number of battlefields and witnessed reenactments of the past, to get a feel, to lend an atmosphere.

Historically, allusions to phantom armies that have been heard or seen to be engaged in battle date to ancient times. In 490 B.C., the

Greeks reported hearing the sounds of the battle of Marathon 400 years after the fighting had ended! This included "the whistle of spears, and the screams of dying men." In Roman times, Pliny recorded that during the war of the Romans against the Cimbrians, "the clash of arms and the sound of trumpets were heard as if coming from the sky." It has been written that during the Crusades, several apparitions made their appearance on the battlefields and many strange visions were seen. At the siege of Antioch, "a celestial troop of warriors" was declared to have descended from heaven and to have been led to the assault by St. George. During the siege of Jerusalem, Crusaders stated they saw a ghostly knight "appear upon the Mount of Olives, waving his buckler and giving the Christian army the signal for entering the city." In 1750, a Scottish farmer and his son observed "a large number of phantom troops of which they counted 16 pairs of columns." Further, they saw a mounted officer on a gray dragoon horse and wearing a gold-laced hat and a blue hussar cloak.

In the book, "Travels in North America," the author tells of being mesmerized by a scene while observing Niagara Falls. He tells of a vapor appearing that resembled "an army climbing to storm some citadel on the summit. We thought, as it shone in the setting sun, that we could perceive the glistening of armour and in the prismatic colours we fancied to ourselves the military uniforms of our countrymen."

As a result of my research, I pulled the related chapters from my own past writings, dusted them off, and updated and expanded some of them. Then I screened the "new" material I had assembled for "Volume III," and excerpted some of this. From all this effort, I came up with 35 chapters covering Civil War ghost incidents in all parts of the state. They cover famous houses as well as sites with names only the most serious of Civil War scholars would know.

As past readers will recognize, I have tried, where possible, to tie in the legends, lore, and psychic happenings with historical fact, vignettes and anecdotes. There is a curious, interesting, and little-known evil omen associated with Jackson's untimely death, for instance. There is an unexplained premonition Robert E. Lee had before the Battle of Spotsylvania. There are other twists of fate, and eerie incidents. But, in fact, the history of the men, women and sites involved is fascinating enough in itself. I found it compelling.

I was, in a strange way, somewhat surprised at the lack of ghosts in certain places.

• Why, for instance, are there no spirits, or at least more evidence of spirits at Malvern Hill, off Route 5 in Charles City County. It was here, on July 1, 1862, that thousands of Confederates charged up a long, gently-sloping hill in the face of murderous cannon and musketry fire. Many were killed. The dreadful carnage was described by Union Colonel William W. Averell, who, as the foggy dawn broke the next morning, wrote: "Our ears had been filled with agonizing cries from thousands before the fog was lifted, but now our eyes saw an appalling spectacle upon the slopes down to the woodlands half a mile away. Over 5,000 dead and wounded men were on the ground in every attitude of distress. A third of them were dead or dying, but enough were alive and moving to give to the field a singular crawling effect." Yet despite the agony of such a disaster, there have been only a couple of vague reports of witnesses who, more than a century later, told of hearing strange noises and moans across the fields, and of catching fleeting glimpses of distant disembodied figures at Malvern Hill where blood once dyed the ground red.

• Why is there no ghost of Dr. David Minton Wright of Norfolk. A highly respected and beloved physician, Dr. Wright challenged a Yankee officer as he marched through the city in 1863. When the officer told Wright he was under arrest, the overwrought doctor pulled out a pistol and shot the officer dead. He was subse-

Malvern Hill

quently tried for murder and found guilty. While in prison his daughter visited him, and exchanged clothes with him, enabling Wright to escape. He was caught, however, and hanged in the middle of the race track at the Norfolk fair grounds in October 1863, before a crowd of thousands. It is said that he went to the gallows "touched with inner serenity . . . in an indescribable sense the victor over his own destiny." His shocking death, however, cast a pall over Norfolk for years.

• Why are there no accounts of the spectral return of the heroic teenage cadets of the Virginia Military Institute reported on the sacred battlefields of New Market? Many of them were slain or grievously wounded here. Wouldn't they have cause to haunt, having been struck down at such a tender age?

(There possibly could be some inexplicable phenomena associated with these courageous young men. There are still a few old-timers left in Lexington who will tell you — in absolute sincerity — that they have heard Sir Moses Ezekiel's statue of "Virginia Mourning Her Dead" *moan* on certain evenings at dusk, and they have seen *real tears* streaming down the bronze chiseled face. They say 'she' mourns above the graves of six teenagers who died in the Battle of New Market.)

• Why are there no wraiths wandering over the huge crater at Petersburg — the site where the Union forces blew a tremendous hole in the earth, sending Southern soldiers, horses, caissons, artillery guns, and gigantic clods of clay blasting hundreds of feet in the air; and, also, where hundreds of Federal troops later were pinned in the same crater and slaughtered in the furious crossfire of Rebel rifles?

• Why are there no hauntings at the notorious Libby prison in Richmond, where many Union soldiers died of disease, hunger and neglect as the war waged on around them? Wouldn't one think the dungeon cells would be rife with distraught and restless spirits?

• Why does one not hear of cries from the graves of hastily buried soldiers, their bodies in some cases lying hundreds of miles from their homes? And what of the bodies that were looted, desecrated, and brutalized? After the second Battle of Manassas, for example, William F. Swalm, assistant surgeon of the Fourteenth New York regiment, gave evidence at a hearing of the "careless, heartless and cruel manner in which the (Confederate) surgeons operated upon our men." He also testified that those wounded who died in Richmond "were put into the earth in the most unfeeling manner."

Civil War soldiers kneel at mass grave site at the Manassas Battlefield. Photo taken in 1862.

The list could go on. One can only wonder why a particular site yields apparitions from 130 years ago while another remains deathly quiet.

Still, there seems to be plenty of Civil War ghosts in Virginia — probably far more than any other state.

Why?

For one thing, the Old Dominion was the most exposed geographically in all of Dixie, hence it became *the* major battleground. As James Robertson, Jr., author of "Civil War Sites in Virginia," has pointed out, "The bitterest and bloodiest fighting in the history of the Western Hemisphere took place in a narrow band of land extending from Manassas to Petersburg."

Of the 620,000 men who died during this horrible period, more of them perished in Virginia than anywhere else. There were more battles, more skirmishes, more actions here than anywhere else. According to Robertson, 26 major battles were fought in the state, and there were over 400 smaller engagements. Virginia lost more than 17,000 sons during the war, and the count of those from other states who lost their lives here — both Northern and Southern — is enormous.

At Cold Harbor alone, 7,000 Union soldiers fell in less than half an hour. Tens of thousands of others lost their lives at Fredericksburg, Chancellorsville, the Wilderness, Spotsylvania, Manassas, New Market, Cedar Creek, Gaines Mill, Malvern Hill, Petersburg, and at a host of other sites.

The horrors of war were sometimes so graphically shocking as to defy imagination. One contemporary author managed to capture the vivid scene at one site as follows: "Ghastly spectacles were abundant, as the eye ranged over this scene of mortal strife; for the ground was in many places red with frozen blood, and the snow which lay under the pine thickets was marked with crimson streams. There were two miles of dead strewn thickly, mingled with firearms, artillery, dead horses, and the paraphernalia of the battlefield.

"Many of the bodies were fearfully mangled, and the ponderous artillery wheels had crushed limbs and skulls. The dead were promiscuously mingled, sometimes grappling in the fierce death-throe, sometimes facing each other as they gave and received the fatal shot or thrust, sometimes huddled in grotesque shapes, and again heaped in piles which lay six or seven feet deep."

"I could imagine," says an eye-witness of the field of carnage, "nothing more terrible than the silent indications of agony that marked the features of the pale corpses which lay at every step. Though dead and rigid in every muscle, they still writhed, and seemed to turn to catch the passing breeze for a cooling breath. Staring eyes, gaping mouths, clenched hands, and strangely contracted limbs, seemingly drawn into the small compass, as if by a mighty effort to rend asunder some irresistible bond which held them down to the torture of which they died.

"One sat against a tree, and, with mouth and eyes wide open, looked up into the sky, as if to catch a glance at its fleeting spirit . . . Great numbers lay in heaps, just as the fire of the artillery mowed them down, mangling their forms into an almost undistinguishable mass."

Is it thus any wonder that a number of ghosts have arisen from such indescribable scenes of horror?

Parapsychology experts say most ghosts appear if a person has been suddenly killed, tragically and/or traumatically. Such was the case with many Civil War casualties. Men were struck down in the flash of a bullet, in the prime of their lives. They were not ready to die. In the natural course of events, notwithstanding the war, it would not have been their time. Many others died under the knives of overworked surgeons desperately trying to save them. Thousands did not survive the terrible storms of disease which ran rampant through both sides of the conflict.

Of the nearly 360,000 Union deaths in the war, about 224,000 were attributed to such diseases as typhoid, typhus, continuous fever, typho-malarial fever, acute and chronic diarrhea, chronic dysentery, syphylis, gonorrhea, scurvy, delerium tremens, insanity, and paralysis. Of 264,000 Confederate deaths, 164,000 were caused by such diseases. Many of these men died, neglected, in enemy prisons, far from their homes.

That may be why there are so many Civil War ghosts in the Commonwealth.

That Virginia has not forgotten its heroic sons is evidenced in a number of ways. As Robertson has said, "the graves of Civil War soldiers have the aura of shrines." There are hundreds of Confederate monuments throughout the state, as well as nearly 500 official highway historical markers. There are, too, many well-preserved battlefields and cemeteries, and a host of museums dedicated to the remembrance of the "Lost Cause." In Richmond alone there is: the Museum of the Confederacy; the White House of the Confederacy, where Jefferson Davis resided; and several towering statues, to Lee, Jackson, and others, on Monument Avenue, plus many battlefields and graveyards.

As I have repeatedly said, throughout this series of books, it is not my intention to persuade one to believe or not believe in the existence of ghosts. That is up to each individual. My intention is to entertain, and in so doing, to hopefully bring to the reader's attention, sidelights of colorful history.

For my part, it has been a thoroughly absorbing and fascinating venture. My hope is that the reader may find it interesting and enjoyable as well.

L. B. Taylor, Jr., April 1995.

THE BIVOUAC OF THE DEAD

by Colonel Theodore O'Hara, CSA

The muffled drum's sad roll has beat
 The soldier's last tattoo;
No more on Life's parade shall meet
 That brave and fallen few.
On Fame's eternal camping-ground
 Their silent tents are spread,
And Glory guards, with solemn round,
 The bivouac of the dead.
No rumor of the foe's advance
 Now swells upon the wind;
No troubled thought at midnight haunts
 Of loved ones left behind;
No vision of the morrow's strife
 The warrior's dream alarms;
No braying horn nor screaming fife
 At dawn shall call to arms.
Their shivered swords are red with rust,
 Their plumed heads are bowed;
Their haughty banner, trailed in dust,
 Is now their martial shroud.
And plenteous funeral tears have washed
 The red stains from each brow,
And the proud forms, by battle gashed,
 Are free from anguish now.
The neighboring troop, the flashing blade,
 The bugle's stirring blast,
The charge, the dreadful cannonade,
 The din and shout, are past;
Nor war's wild note nor glory's peal
 Shall thrill with fierce delight
Those breasts that never more may feal
 The rapture of the fight.

* * * * * * * * * *

Full many a mother's breath has swept
    O'er Angostura's plain, —
And long the pitying sky has wept
    Above its mouldered slain.
The raven's scream, or eagle's flight,
    Or shepherd's pensive lay,
Alone awakes each sullen height
    That frowned o'er that dread fray.
Sons of the Dark and Bloody Ground,
    Ye must not slumber there,
Where stranger steps and tongues resound
    Along the heedless air.
Your proud land's heroic soil
    Shall be your fitter grave:
She claims from war his richest spoil —
    the ashes of her brave.
Thus 'neath their parent turf they rest,
    Far from the gory field,
Borne to a Spartan mother's breast
    On many a bloody shield;
The sunshine of their native sky
    Smiles sadly on them, here,
And kindred eyes and hearts watch by
    The heroes' sepulchre.
Rest on, embalmed and sainted dead!
    Dear as the blood ye gave;
No impious footstep here shall tread
    The herbage of your grave;
Nor shall you glory be forgot
    While Fame her record keeps,
Or honor points the hallowed spot
    Where valor prouldy sleeps.
Yon marble minstrel's voiceless stone
    In deathless song shall tell,
When many a vanished age hath flown,
    The story how ye fell;
Nor wreck, nor change, nor winter's blight,
    Nor Time's remorseless doom,
Shall dim one ray of glory's light
    That glids your deathless tomb.

Psychic Preludes
to the War?

as the Civil War inevitable? Did fate intervene to set brother against brother in the bloodiest fighting in American history? There were a number of ominous "signs" of the pending battle in the form of curious "incidents." Were they psychic-related?

* * * * * * * * * *

OMINOUS OMEN NUMBER 1

here are several references, if one digs deep enough, to the belief that George Washington may have had a foreboding psychic vision when he was encamped at Valley Forge during the bitter winter of 1777. According to the editor of a paper known as "The National Tribune," he had an interview with an elderly surviving veteran of the Revolutionary War — a man named Anthony Sherman — in 1859. Sherman, who was at Valley Forge with Washington, said the Commander in Chief allegedly said he saw the figure of a "singularly beautiful being" in his tent one night.

According to Sherman, Washington said: "Gradually, the surrounding atmosphere seemed to fill with sensations, and grew luminous. Everything about me seemed to rarify, the mysterious visitor also becoming more airy and yet more distinct to my eyes than before. I began to feel as one dying, or rather to experience the sensations which I have sometimes imagined accompany death."

Sherman then said Washington told of witnessing "dark manifestations inside the tent, including black clouds, lightning bolts, the light of a thousand suns . . . the thundering of the cannon, clashing of swords, and the shouts and cries of hundreds of thousands in mortal combat." The figure then vanished.

Some have interpreted this vision as being a startling premonition of the American Civil War.

OMINOUS OMEN NUMBER 2

pparently, as the war clouds gathered, a brilliant, fiery comet could be seen in the skies over northern Virginia and Washington in April 1861. Since colonial times, many viewed such spectacular phenomena as ill omens which signalled impending disaster. One family in the area had an old slave named Oola. She was a native African with gray-black skin wrinkled yet drawn tight over her forehead and cheek bones. It was said her eyes were so piercing that they sent shivers through anyone who stared into them. Other servants were afraid of her "evil eye," and her apparent ability to "conjure spells."

Of the blazing comet, Oola had a dire prediction. She viewed it as a "great fire sword," and said it warned of a great war coming with the handle toward the North and the point toward the South, and the North would take the sword and cut the South's heart out! Then she added that if Lincoln took the sword, he would perish by it.

Word of her foreboding prophecy spread, and it was reported that Abraham Lincoln's sons told him of it. He seemed strangely interested, and it was noted that he stared intently out a window at the comet, deep in thought.

* * * * * * * * * *

OMINOUS OMEN NUMBER 3

friend of the Lincolns told of an incident which occurred on June 29, 1861, at a ceremony where a new Union flag was to be raised at the White House. Attendees included a number of Federal generals and their aides, members of the cabinet, and other guests.

The Marine band began the national anthem and everyone rose. As the officers saluted, Lincoln pulled the cord to raise the flag. It stuck. He pulled harder, and suddenly the upper corner of the Union flag tore off and hung down.

One witness said that when this happened, "a gasp of surprise and horror at the sinister omen" was heard, and one general was "much disturbed" by the unfortunate accident.

A PROPHETIC QUOTE

"I . . . am now quite *certain* that the crimes of this guilty land . . . will never be purged away, but with Blood."

(John Brown, just before he was hanged, December 1859.)

FACT

More Americans died in the Civil War than the combined total of the nation's dead in the Revolutionary War, the War of 1812, the Mexican War, the Indian Wars, the Spanish-American War, World Wars I and II, and the Korean Conflict.

John Brown's Body Lies A Moldering . . .

(Harper's Ferry, West Virginia)

(Author's note: Granted, Harper's Ferry, 30 miles north of Winchester, today is in West Virginia. But it originally was a part of Virginia's Jefferson County, and therefore a slight literary license is being taken to include it in this work. It is one of the most scenic and unusual towns in America. It is also one of the most haunted, and includes several separate sites that are frequented by a variety of ghosts. And, too, of course, Harper's Ferry is where abolitionist John Brown staged his famous raid on the Federal arsenal in 1859, and was hanged for his efforts.)

In describing the natural beauty of Harper's Ferry, Thomas Jefferson, as he so often did, may well have said it best: "The passage of the Potomac through the Blue Ridge is, perhaps, one of the most stupendous scenes in nature. You stand on a very high point of land; on your right comes up the Shenandoah (River), having ranged along the foot of a mountain a hundred miles to seek a vent. On your left approaches the Potomac, in quest of a passage also; in the moment of their junction, they rush together against the mountain, rend it asunder, and pass off to the sea . . .

"This scene is worth a voyage across the Atlantic."

In his classic "History of the Valley," written in the 1830s, author Samuel Kercheval wrote: "It is scarcely necessary to inform the reader that this (Harper's Ferry) is the location of the United

States armory, and in the several shops are generally employed about 300 first-rate mechanics, engaged in the manufacture of arms for the purpose of war. There are annually made about six or seven thousand muskets, two or three thousand rifles, besides an immense number of swords, pistols and other side arms . . . A vast number of strangers annually visit this place to gratify their curiosity in seeing and inspecting the public works and great mechanical operations, so extensively carried on." Kercheval added, "This site for the public works, it is said, was first marked out or recommended by the immortal Washington, and is certainly evidence of his superior skill and judgment in all military matters."

It is somewhat ironic, amidst all this scenic splendor and colorful history, that Harper's Ferry is possibly best known for the notoriety of being the site where a madman went amok prior to the Civil War, resulting in a number of murders and hangings, and maybe even providing the cause for some ghostly presences who have lingered there over the decades.

His name was John Brown.

Above all else, Brown was a true enigma. He was hero to many, a devil incarnate to some, loved, hated, and most of all, feared. It is said his steel-cold gray eyes could look straight through a man; they had a magnetizing, hypnotizing effect. Ralph Waldo Emerson once called him "a new saint." A Kansas minister who knew him well described him as "impressed with the idea that God had raised him up on purpose to break the jaws of the wicked."

Brown himself once declared, "I am an instrument in the hands of Providence! God told me what to do!"

What Brown did was create chaos virtually everywhere he went. A hardened abolitionist who deplored slavery, he was a deeply religious man who used violence as a key tool to force his ideology on others. This penchant for fighting for "his cause," wracked the young nation, not once, at Harper's Ferry, but twice. In May 1856, as America was being torn apart over the slavery issue, a pro-slavery mob descended upon Lawrence, Kansas, and wantonly destroyed the town, smashing newspaper presses, setting fire to the state governor's home, and stealing everything that was not nailed down.

The sack of Lawrence aroused the fanatical Brown. Two days later he set out with his four sons and three other men toward Pottawatomie Creek, site of the pro-slavery settlement, where they killed five men in cold blood, ostensibly as revenge for Lawrence. This massacre led to a running guerilla war in the territory which lasted through most of the year, causing more than 200 deaths and $2 million in property damage.

Three years later, Brown concocted a diabolical plan which he believed would eventually free the slaves throughout the South. He would lead a group of his faithful followers, heavily armed, into Harper's Ferry and storm the Federal arsenal there. Once he had established his authority, slaves would rise up from the farms and plantations of the Shenandoah Valley, race to the armory, arm themselves into a veritable army, and rise up in rebellion.

And so it was on Sunday, October 16, 1859, that Brown and his motley crew of 15 White recruits, including his sons, and four Blacks, loaded a wagon full of arms — nearly 400 rifles and pistols and 950 iron-tipped pikes — and headed toward Harper's Ferry. There, under the cloak of a cold, wet darkness, the raiding party surprised the few defenders of the arsenal. They commandeered several buildings, traded shots with a few townspeople, and took a number of hostages. Brown set up headquarters in a brick fire engine house and waited for the slaves to come to him seeking their freedom.

Instead, he was met by a Federal force of Marines commanded by none other than Colonel Robert E. Lee. After Brown refused to negotiate a surrender with one of Lee's officers — J.E.B. Stuart — the troops stormed the buildings and quickly overpowered Brown's men. Brown, however, held out in the fortified firehouse. One of the hostages later reported that "Brown was the coolest and

3

John Brown

firmest man I ever saw. With one son dead by his side and another shot through, he felt the pulse of his dying son with one hand and held his rifle with the other and commanded his men with the utmost composure, encouraging them to sell their lives as dearly as they could."

The Marines soon overran the firehouse and captured Brown, who had been wounded in the fighting. He was turned over to Virginia authorities and tried for treason against the state and conspiracy to incite insurrection. But Brown, in a sense, won his day in court. That is, as the country watched, he used the courtroom as a platform to denounce the cruelties of slavery, and in so doing stirred the national conscience. Some historians believe this was one of the most important incident-causes which helped lead to the Civil War. Brown was convicted of his crimes, however, and was hanged, at age 58, on December 2, 1859, at Charles Town.

He rode to the site in a wagon, sitting on his own coffin. He climbed 13 steps up a platform to reach the noose. Among the more than 1,500 witnesses was a young professor from the Virginia Military Institute in Lexington — Thomas J. Jackson.

There is a curious footnote to John Brown's hanging. It is told by Shirley Dougherty, author of "A Ghostly Tour of Harper's Ferry," although this particular incident does not appear in her book. According to the legend that Shirley retells on her weekend ghost tours, when they took Brown's body down from the gallows, those present were frightened by his eyes. They were said to shine with an eerie luster, as if they could still see! In fact, Shirley says, the doctors examined him three different times after declaring him dead, and the eyes continued to almost glow. Finally, candle wax was poured over them.

Brown's body was then carted back to Harper's Ferry, where his wife was waiting to take it to Elba, New York. It is said that when they prepared the corpse for interment the candle wax was removed from its eyes — and the eyes continued to appear incredibly life like!

If ever there was reason for a ghost to return to the site of its mortal death, certainly John Brown might be expected to reappear on the streets of Harper's Ferry.

And perhaps he did!

While there have been no reported reappearances of Brown's apparition in the fire house, the armory, or anywhere else for that matter, a strange and curious thing happened a few years ago. A man closely resembling Brown appeared in the town, the likeness so startling that people's heads would turn when he passed. It was reported that a few visitors asked the stranger to pose for pictures with them.

When the photos were developed, however, the John Brown look-alike was mysteriously missing in the prints!

* * * * * * * * * *

THE DEMISE OF DANGERFIELD NEWBY

side from this rather odd occurrence, the only other ghostly phenomenon tied to the John Brown raid centers around a man named Dangerfield Newby — a former slave who had tried to buy the freedom of his wife and seven children, then still on a farm near Warrenton, Virginia. Newby had raised the money but when he confronted the slave owner, he had been rebuffed. Incensed, he joined Brown's group, hoping this might lead to his family's freedom.

But during the sometimes fierce street fighting that ensued that grim October in Harper's Ferry, Newby, who wore baggy trousers and an old slouch hat, was killed at the arsenal gate on Monday, October 17, 1859. There is some confusion as to just how he was killed. One writer said he was shot through the neck by a bullet, another said he was slain with a six-inch spike. In either case, the shot left a gaping hole in his neck, and the townspeople were so upset at the raiders, that his body was left on the street where he fell for more than 24 hours.

Then, gruesomely, it was dragged to a nearby alley and dumped in a spot where hogs roamed. Author Joseph Barry was a witness to what happened next. He wrote: " . . . A hog came up, rooted around the spot where the body lay and, at first appeared to be unconscious that anything extraordinary was in its way. After a while, the hog paused and looked attentively at the body, then sniffed around it and put its snout to the dead man's face. Suddenly, the brute was apparently seized with a panic, and, with bristles erect and drooping tail, it scampered away, as if for dear life. This display of sensibility did not, however, deter others of the same species from crowding around the corpse and almost literally devouring it.

"This writer (Barry) saw all this with his own eyes, and at the risk of further criticism, he will remark that none of the good people of Harper's Ferry appeared to be at all squeamish about the quality or flavor of their pork that winter."

Ever since that time this spot, between High and Potomac Streets, has been known as Hog Alley. And, according to a newspaper report some years ago, visitors have told of periodically seeing a man wandering about there . . . a man wearing baggy trousers and an old slouch hat . . . a man with a deep, ugly scar across his throat! The chilling vision is seen but a few brief seconds, and then vaporizes.

CHAPTER 2

Strange Occurrences in Harper's Ferry

trange. For a town that was described as unimportant from a military standpoint, Harper's Ferry figured prominently for nearly four years during the Civil War. It was Confederate General Joseph Johnston who noted that because of the town's unique setting, flanked by mountains, it was therefore virtually impossible to defend. "So," Johnston said, "it is anything but an important position." The area, in fact, was referred to as a "blind alley."

Yet, from the very onset of the action in Virginia, through the summer of 1864, Harper's Ferry was the site of nearly constant action in one way or another. It changed hands between Union and Confederate forces a number of times, and in between there was a steady stream of skirmishes, shellings, and firings from snipers and sharpshooters. As one example of the overall confusion that pervaded the area during this period, the railroad bridge was destroyed and rebuilt no less than nine times between 1861 and 1865.

Local citizens evacuated the town so many times they lost count; Harper's Ferry was torched at least twice; everything not nailed down was stolen and confiscated, including, at one point, a cemetery tombstone!; and there were several cruel and unusual occurrences from which ghosts often arise.

Perhaps all this was destined, for it is recorded that John Brown, before his death by hanging, prophesied the destruction of Harper's Ferry, and, as author Joseph Barry later pointed out, in a little more than two years, to all intents and purposes, the town was destroyed! Barry wrote: "Who will say that these were merely coincidences and who will not rather suspect that there were in these affairs something like a true spirit of prophecy and a divine retribution?" By the winter of 1861-62, Barry said, "Harper's Ferry presented a scene of the utmost desolation. All the inhabitants fled, except a few old people . . ."

It all began in the earliest days of the war — in April 1861. It was then that a hastily gathered troop of Virginia militia began marching northward toward Harper's Ferry in hopes of capturing the poorly guarded armory there. This force of about 2,000 men included units from Staunton (artillery), Charlottesville, Culpeper, and the already-famous Black Horse cavalry from Fauquier County.

Their mission was secret, but apparently word leaked out, because the small Union contingent in the town set fire to the armory early on the morning of April 18. By the time Major General Kenton Harper (note the coincidence of the name) marched in, nearly 20,000 rifles and pistols had been destroyed. Still, much of the machinery and a large number of gun and pistol barrels and locks were saved when Southern sympathizers working at the armory wet down the gunpowder which had been spread about the complex.

The Virginians didn't stay long, however, and the Union retook the region. More than a year later, Stonewall Jackson, enroute to the invasion of Maryland, stormed Harper's Ferry and took 12,000 prisoners, 13,000 arms, 73 pieces of artillery, and several hundred wagons. By this time Jackson's reputation was already so revered it is said that the captured Union soldiers lined the streets trying to catch a glimpse of him.

Later, the Union moved in again, only to be rooted out in 1863 when Lee's army was moving toward Gettysburg. Once more the Union took control of Harper's Ferry, and were driven out still another time in July 1864, when Confederate General Jubal Early attacked.

With all the fighting and shelling that took place during the war, only one building in the armory enclosure escaped destruction. It was the old engine house which John Brown had commandeered in 1859.

There were, during these eventful years, many strange occurrences, which would possibly be just cause for spirits to return to haunt. Consider:

— The saga of a Federal spy named Rice. In February 1862, he was spotted by Confederate soldiers and fired upon as he and

Harper's Ferry

another spy named Rohr tried to escape across the river to Maryland. Rohr was killed, but Rice got away by throwing himself into the water and keeping under the cover of his skiff. A few nights later, Rice, acting as a guide, and five other men tried to cross the river again, this time with the purpose of laying a pontoon bridge. It was a stormy night with a strong gale blowing down the river through the gorges of the Blue Ridge. The boat overturned and the men were thrown into the icy waters. Rice once more escaped the Grim Reaper by swimming to one of the buttresses of the bridge, but the five soldiers with him drowned.

Rice, in fact, survived the war and became a railroad engineer. He was killed one day when he fell from his engine and was cut to pieces by it.

— A Federal spy named Law was captured by a band of motley guerrillas. According to author Barry, he was taken to a lonely part of Loudoun Mountain, laid flat on his back, and fastened to the ground with switches twisted around his arms and legs and driven into the earth with mauls. There, "he was left to perish of hunger, thirst, cold, and any more speedy death from the fangs of wild animals that Heaven might mercifully vouchsafe for him."

— In July 1864, as the Union forces were retreating under Jubal Early's attack, a Federal soldier, probably intoxicated, shot and killed a 13-year-old girl standing in the window of a store. He was arrested, but escaped and was never seen again. The girl's mother died soon after from "great sorrow and broken-heartedness." The girl's father "became dissipated and a wanderer until he lost his mind, and it is supposed that he ended his days in some asylum for the insane."

— Sometime after this, a Confederate officer "of high rank" was found dead under mysterious circumstances near the armory yard. No one knew how or when he was killed, and since the Rebels had by then retreated, the officer was hastily buried by townspeople under a railroad trestle. Union cavalry then entered the scene and tramped the ground so hard with their horses, all traces of the grave were obliterated. After the war the officer's family came to Harper's Ferry to retrieve the body, but eventually had to abandon the search.

Any, or all of these incidents, one might think, would be just cause for spectral returns to the scenes. But such is not the case.

There are, however, at least a few sites in and around Harper's Ferry that are haunted by ghosts from the Civil War. One is told by the redoubtable Shirley Dougherty during her weekend ghost tours. It occurred in an old building known as the Town House, used during the war to house Union troops. Shirley says they captured a young Confederate drummer boy, probably then in his early teens. Instead of sending him to prison, they decided to keep him around, and made him do various chores, such as washing their clothes and cleaning their rooms.

The boy, distraught and obviously homesick, began to cry and beg for his mother. This infuriated his captors, and one night after much drinking, when the lad started to cry, the soldiers grabbed him and began tossing him from one to another. One man missed catching him, and the drummer boy plunged through a window and fell to his death on the hard surface below.

According to Shirley, a number of people working around the Town House in recent years have told her of hearing the sound of a young boy crying and begging for his mother.

Another ghostly phenomenon relates to a tragic incident which occurred in July 1861. It involved a group of Union volunteers from Ohio. These raw recruits had signed up for a 100-day enlistment in the army and were stationed on Maryland Heights overlooking Harper's Ferry. According to author Barry, they "had little or no conception of the military appliances which they were expected to use with some degree of intelligence."

It was July 4, 1861. It had been raining hard all day. Barry: "A company of them were preparing dinner, and, not having anything else convenient on which to build their fire, they procured from an ammunition wagon several large shells on which they piled their wood which was soon ablaze. 'Round the fire they all squatted, each intent on watching his kettle or saucepan.

"Soon a terrific explosion shook the surrounding hills, sending all the culinary utensils flying over the tree tops, and, unfortunately, killing or wounding nearly every man of the group."

According to Shirley, "Mysterious fires are frequently seen on Maryland Heights, but when investigated, there are no signs of fire. Those who know the story shake their heads — knowing that the One Hundred Day Men are again fixing their dinner . . . The light from that faraway campfire continues to glow from time to time even though 130 years have passed since those poor young recruits tried to fix what turned out to be their last meal on earth!"

And, finally, there are the dual spirits at St. Peters Catholic Church located at the top of some old stone steps on the way to Jefferson's rock, high above the town. St. Peters was the only church in the area to survive the war intact. It was saved, it is said, by the attendant priest at the time, a Father Costello. According to reliable accounts, each time the town was being shelled, by one force or the other, he would raise a British flag from the steeple, causing the artillery men to divert their fire so as not to cause an "international incident."

During the conflict the church served for a time as a hospital. According to one legend, a young Catholic soldier — it is not specified whether he was Yankee or Rebel — lay wounded in the churchyard. As his wounds were at first diagnosed as not being as severe as those of others, he was left unattended for most of the day. All the while, he was slowly bleeding to death.

At last, attendants reached him and as he was carried by stretcher over the threshhold of the church, he was heard to whisper, in a weak voice, "Thank God, I'm saved." These were his last words. He passed away almost immediately afterward.

Shirley Dougherty notes, "People say that on misty nights they will see a golden glow on the threshhold of the church and hear a weak voice whispering, "Thank God, I'm saved!"

Shirley says she can understand why he returns still to seek medical attention, but she isn't sure why or for what purpose a second spirit occasionally is sighted at St. Peters. "Many visitors tell us," she says, "that about six o'clock in the evening on their way to

Jefferson Rock, as they pass the church they meet an old priest coming from the rectory and wearing a black friars hat.

"Since his appearance is so quaint they stop to speak, but Father never returns their greetings. The visitor will stop to watch this odd-looking priest only to stare in disbelief as he turns and walks right through the doorless wall — into the church!"

CHAPTER 3

The Restless Casualties of Ball's Bluff

(Loudoun County)

I t was Murphy's law carried to the extreme. Everything that could go wrong, did, and then some!

It was October 21, 1861. The Union army had amassed a large force on Harrison Island, in the middle of the Potomac River separating Maryland and Virginia. They had spotted Confederate troops a few hundred yards away, on the Virginia side, in the woods surrounding a point called Ball's Bluff, a few miles from Leesburg.

The orders from General Charles P. Stone, a distinguished Federal officer, graduate of West Point, and veteran of the Mexican War, had been somewhat vague to start with (as had Stone's orders from his commander.) Colonel Edward D. Baker had been told to advance his men across the river, scale the bluff, and move on toward Leesburg if conditions warranted. Baker had left his position as United States Senator from Oregon to join the Union army. Although he was a brilliant and energetic legislator, well admired and respected by his peers, his enthusiasm and unabashed zeal far outweighed his meager military experience.

And, so, on the night of October 20, he assembled his men for the crossing. This was complicated from the start by the fact that there were only two small boats available to ferry the men, and only about 30 at a time could be carried. Captain Francis J. Young, of Baker's staff, recalled the scene: "The river was swollen and the current rapid, and there was much labor and delay making use of

the boats. . . The bank (at the base of Ball's Bluff) is a miry clay, and the heights almost precipitous (about 70 feet high), with fallen trees and rocks, making it very difficult to get up the artillery."

To this description, U.S. Colonel Milton Cogswell added: "Arrived at the landing opposite Harrison's Island, I found the greatest confusion existing. No one seemed to be in charge, nor any one superintending the passage of the troops, and no order was maintained in their crossing."

Further, the Union forces had no idea of the strength or location of the Confederates, or even if there were any troops there at all. One early report had it that a "row of tents" had been sighted by scouts, but once atop the bluff, this was determined to be a "row of trees" instead. The ground Colonel Baker and his men ascended to was open and vulnerable, and he was warned by more seasoned officers that the surrounding woods offered a perfect cover for Southern infantry.

This and other suggestions went unheeded, and Baker decided on his own to press forward. It was ill-advised. What followed was a tragic fiasco. The Confederates, massed in the woods, began a furious onslaught. Union soldiers, trapped in the open, were backed to the edge of the bluff. Their artillery was rendered useless by sharpshooters who picked off the cannoneers as quickly as they took their places. Charging to the front to encourage his troops, Colonel Baker was killed.

By dusk, the Federal forces had been badly beaten, and were ordered to retreat in any way possible back across the river to Harrison's Island. They were told to toss their rifles into the water so they would not be confiscated. As the men scampered down the steep bluff they became ready targets for the advancing Rebels. About 35 or 40 men leaped onto an old barge that had been found, but in mid-stream it overturned and sank, and most of the unfortunate soldiers drowned. Others swam as best they could. Some made it, others were carried away by the swift currents.

The extent of the disaster was described by author E. A. Pollard in his classic work, "The Lost Cause," published in 1866: "Such slaughter, such havoc, such mangling of living men was scarcely ever seen before. A whole army was retreating, tumbling, rolling, leaping down the steep heights. Hundreds plunged into the rapid current; many were shot in the act of swimming; and others were drowned in the water, choked with the wounded and dead. Large flats had been used to bring over reinforcements. They now attempted to return with the wounded; but such was the consternation among the troops that large numbers rushed on board, trampling upon the bleeding men until they all sank together, amid frightful screams.

"There were men in that agonized mass of fugitives who had never seen the field of battle. They had been sent over while the contest was in progress; they had climbed the mud of the bluff expecting to find before them a scene of victory. But before them glared a victorious and vengeful foe; and behind them rolled the deep river. All was consternation and dismay. A thousand men ran up and down the banks . . . Others rushed wildly into the stream; and the shrieks of the wounded and drowning mingled with the shouts of the victors and the rattle of musketry."

More than 900 Union troops were killed in the disastrous movement, and many others wounded or taken prisoner. The death of Colonel Baker shocked the young nation, and, eventually, and inexplicably, the blame for the ignominious defeat was placed on General Stone, although he actually had little to do with what went wrong. The following February he was placed under arrest and imprisoned at Fort Lafayette in New York Harbor. He was held there for five months, under guard, although no charges were ever filed against him! He finally was released, and later served credibly under General Ulysses Grant, although, some said, he was a broken man, his honor wrongfully tarnished.

Many of those who fell at Ball's Bluff are buried in a national cemetery there. It is from this graveyard that stories of strange happenings have emanated over the past 40 or more years; stories that have been told and retold by townspeople. The most prevalent account occurred sometime around 1950, when a group of teenagers drove out to the bluff one evening. As they walked around the perimeter of the otherwise deserted cemetery, they heard "terrible screams," for which no mortal source could be ascertained.

Frightened, they ran back to their car. The driver started it, but, mysteriously, it wouldn't move forward. The teens said it seemed as if some "unseen hands" were holding the car back. Amidst their panic, the force, or whatever it was, held them for several minutes, then suddenly released them. The car lurched forward and they sped to Leesburg, running both stop signs and red lights along the way. When they finally arrived home, still wondering what had happened, they got out and inspected the car. They found two huge gloved handprints of recently dried clay on each side of the trunk! As one chronicler of the event later noted, "It appeared that someone using these hands had been holding the car back."

One of the young men told his parents about the scary episode and showed them the handprints. His mother and father then got in their car and drove back to Ball's Bluff to investigate. It was a windless, moonlit night. All was quiet and eerily still. They heard no screams.

There are three grave sites outside the wall-enclosed cemetery. Two were believed to contain Federal soldiers, the other a Confederate. Beside this grave stood a small tree. Suddenly, the tree began to shake violently. Although there was no breeze at all, the small tree swayed back and forth, bending and dipping almost to the breaking point. No other tree in the area was so affected, not even a leaf elsewhere fluttered. The man and woman, shaken themselves, drove off without going nearer to the site.

One might well speculate about a number of supernatural sources for the extraordinary psychic occurrence. Would not Colonel Baker be justified in returning to the scene? Certainly, General Stone's spirit might be expected to assert itself in seeking vindication for his unwarranted punishment. Or might it well be one of the hundreds of Union soldiers who either were shot from ambush, or drowned in their desperate attempt to escape?

But, in time, local historians offered a more plausible explanation. They said, the grave over which the small tree shook so madly, was, in fact, not a grave at all. It rather was a marker signifying where a Virginia soldier had fallen. The word was this unidentified man's family had wanted him buried in the county's cemetery, but "because his religious faith frowned on participation in war," burial there was denied, and he was laid to rest elsewhere. And so, the belief persists that it was his spirit that psychically screamed and shook the tree, letting it be known that he would not be happy until he was buried with his fellow countrymen who died in the Battle of Ball's Bluff.

FOOTNOTE: Colonel Edward Baker, the brilliant young U.S. Senator who died tragically in the Battle of Ball's Bluff, has also made his ghostly presence known — but this time on the other side of the river. In Annington, Maryland, at seven miles distance from Ball's Bluff, within earshot of the muskets that fired during the fighting, there is a three story brick building on the promontory with the Potomac sweeping before it in a crescent, that is "the eternal home" of Baker.

His spirit has appeared there many times over the years to the James Caywood family. Both the Caywood daughters, Beth and Lin, recall often hearing, in the 1980s, the "stomp of the colonel's heavy military boots overhead in the house." Once, they said, Baker yelled down the stairs, calling someone's name, although the girls couldn't make it out. During house renovations one year, two workmen became alarmed when they ran into "an odd-looking guy in a Union uniform who just crossed the field in front of them and went into the woods."

Baker on the eve of the battle at Ball's Bluff is said to have boasted, "On the morrow I'll be in Leesburg or hell."

CHAPTER 4

The Lost Yankee
at Willis House

(Fredericksburg)

f John Allan, the Scottish merchant who built a small house at 1106 Princess Anne Street — considered to be the second house built in Fredericksburg (circa 1740s) — were to transcend time and come back today to view his abode, he doubtless would not recognize it. Two extra stories, an entire new wing and a spacious back porch have been added over the past 200 years. However, he probably would be pleased at the loving care successive owners have given it, including thorough renovations and the addition of handsome period furniture, antiques and family heirlooms.

It is called the Willis house today, and is presently owned by Judge Jere Willis and his wife, Barbara. It has been in the Willis family for more than a century. Flanked by no less than seven chimneys, the house features a large dining room, living room, music room, foyer, one bedroom and kitchen. From the sheltered porch, which the Willis family added, there is a pleasant view across a half-acre garden with old brick walls and a patio built with millstones found on the property. A pecan tree, dogwoods, daffodils, tulips and azaleas add color, fragrance and spice.

Remarkably, the house withstood ferocious Union army shelling, preceding the great battle of Fredericksburg during the bitter winter of 1862. It is remarkable because 181 guns, spaced along Stafford Heights from the Washington farm to Falmouth, opened up at dawn on December 11th, and all the fire was concentrated on the town. At times during the bombardment, 100 guns a minute were fired — round shot, case shot and shell.

One Civil War historian wrote: " . . . the guns opened, and a tremendous cloud of smoke came rolling down . . . to cover the river and the open plain and the tormented town, and presently tall columns of blacker smoke from burning buildings went up to the blue sky, and the waiting Federals saw walls and roofs collapse and bricks and timbers fly through the air, while men who had lived through Malvern Hill and Antietam said this was the most thunderous cannonade they had ever heard."

Of the awful shelling, John Goolrick, author of the book, "Historic Fredericksburg," published in 1922, added: " . . . walls toppled, fires sprang up and chaos reigned." One survivor described the scene: "Men, women and children were driven from town. Hundreds of ladies and children were wandering homeless over the frozen highways, with bare feet and thin clothing."

If anything, the awesome artillery blitz was overkill of historic proportions. Here, on the north side of the Rappahannock River, was Union General Ambrose Burnside with a force of more than 110,000 soldiers. General Robert E. Lee had set himself comfortably, and well protected, in the hills overlooking Fredericksburg with an army of about 75,000, waiting patiently for Burnside to cross the river.

But meanwhile, as the Union set about building a pontoon bridge to span the Rappahannock, a single brigade of approximately 1,500 Southerners, mostly from Mississippi, fired away at the advancing Yankees, killing a number of bridge engineers in the process. Here was a veritable handful of sharpshooters, hiding in and behind houses and buildings, holding off the vast Union forces.

And that was why and how the town of Fredericksburg came to be brutally destroyed. Burnside was so infuriated at the firing from the lone brigade that he turned loose all the artillery in his power.

Even so, the Confederates continued to plague their adversaries until the Federals were able to land enough men by boat to challenge them. There followed a bitter, fierce, door-to-door fight through the town's streets and alleys. The Willis House stood directly in the line of fire throughout the day.

Eventually, the greatly outnumbered Rebels retreated to the outskirts of Fredericksburg. Historian Bruce Catton summed up the action: "So the long day ended, and men remembered afterward that a strange golden dusk lay upon the plain and the surrounding hills, as if a belated Indian-summer evening had come bewildered out of peacetime autumn into wintry wartime. There was a haze on the horizon, and the western sky was scarlet and purple as the sun went down, and most of Fredericksburg seemed to be burning."

It was from the furious skirmishing that day that the Willis House became, for a time, haunted with the ghost of a young soldier from the North; a soldier who died prematurely and unexpectedly that day, and apparently was not ready to yet pass on to the Beyond.

Barbara Willis tells the story: "Our house is directly opposite to where the Union Army crossed the Rappahannock River on pontoon bridges, and there was house-to-house combat. Apparently, a young Union soldier was in the house, and was standing behind one of the double doors in the back hall, using the doors as a shield. A bullet ripped a splinter through the door at chest-high level, killing the soldier, and leaving blood stains on the floor. He was buried in the garden. The door was never fully repaired. It was plugged, and the plug remains there to this day. In the 1920s, a Mrs. Marian Carrie Willis was living in the house and she had a cook named Nannie. Carrie used to call the Union soldier 'Yip the Yank.' According to the legend that has been passed down, Nannie saw a young man come into the house by the side porch door, dressed in a Union uniform of the Civil War era. He went upstairs. She thought it might be Carrie's younger brother, and she told Carrie about it. But when they went upstairs to investigate, they found no one there."

This must have happened on more than one occasion, Barbara says, because Nannie finally said one day that she was going to "lay his soul to rest." She went out in the garden, kneeled, and said something over his grave. There have been no sightings of the apparition since. It appears that even though the Yankee soldier died far from home, Nannie persuaded him that Fredericksburg wasn't such a bad resting place after all.

CHAPTER 5

Kindred Spirits at Kenmore

One of the truly unsung heroes of the American Revolutionary War was an aristocratic gentleman not necessarily noted for his physical appearance but more so for his courtly bearing and great dignity. Though his name may be unfamiliar to high school history students, he was a close and respected associate of such noble patriots as Edmund Pendleton, Francis Lightfoot Lee, Richard Henry Lee, George Wythe and many others. He also was a lifelong intimate friend and brother-in-law of George Washington. His name was Fielding Lewis.

Perhaps his greatest measurable contribution to the cause of American freedom was the sacrifice of his personal wealth — and possibly of his health as well — to launch and operate a gun manufactory during the war, which provided arms for the colonial troops. He literally threw everything he had, materially, physically and otherwise, to keep this factory going during the darkest years of the fighting. And when the war ended with no proper compensation, as promised, from the Continental Congress, Lewis went broke. With less patriotic creditors pressing him, he suffered serious lung trouble — then called consumption — and died after a lingering illness in December 1781.

Among his other notable accomplishments was the building of a mansion and estate in Fredericksburg which came to be known as Kenmore. After his first wife died in February 1750, Lewis married Betty Washington, the only sister of the first President of the United States, in May of that year.

Construction of the house began in 1752 and evolved into what architects consider to be one of the most beautiful colonial mansions in America. The walls of the elegantly simple exterior of

Kenmore

Kenmore are two feet thick, fashioned of Flemish bond brick. Inside is an exceptionally elaborate interior containing what the Virginia Landmarks Register calls "the finest 18th century plasterwork and chimneypieces in the country."

Following Fielding Lewis' death in 1781, Betty Lewis maintained the 1,100 acre estate, raising her three youngest sons, for 15 years before moving to a farm south of town. The mansion passed through the ownership of several families during the 19th century and into the 20th, and after suffering relatively little damage through the Civil War, fell on hard times by the 1920s. When plans were announced to subdivide the property and dismantle the great house, a movement began to save it. This led to the formation of the Kenmore Association and fostered a nationwide preservation effort which, as any visitor to the site today will readily attest, has been highly successful.

It is now a museum open to the public, complete with period furniture, a beautifully restored garden, a gift shop, and a kitchen dependency in which old fashioned gingerbread is served. The recipe is said to be the same as that used by Mary Ball Washington, George Washington's mother. There are many special exhibits illustrating the history of Kenmore and the colonial period, and the Association calls it a house that "belongs to the nation."

It also has been said that when in the mansion one becomes conscious of the "brooding presence" of Fielding Lewis. And there are many people — both tourists and Association employees and volunteers alike — who have sworn they have seen and heard the ghost of this refined gentleman at Kenmore. The most common manifestation is the sound of his heavy tread in an upstairs bedroom as he paces back and forth.

He has been sighted a number of times, too, and the descriptions vary little. Often in broad daylight, witnesses have reported seeing a man with a "worried expression" on his face dressed in clothes of the Revolutionary War period. Some have claimed to have seen him poring over a sheaf of papers, which they have speculated were the bills of creditors he could not pay.

At times, the Kenmore Association hostesses have tried to discourage the stories of psychic experiences in the house, saying, appropriately, that the beauty and history of Kenmore are far more interesting. Still, the legends abound. Door knobs turn when no one is at the door. Doors have stuck shut for days at a time, but when a carpenter is called, they mysteriously open. Guests have felt inexplicable cold drafts "blowing on their heads" in the dead of summer. A visitor standing in the Betty Washington Lewis chamber with two friends in the 1920s remarked, "I think this is a haunted room." As she did, to their astonishment, they heard a "click" and the wardrobe door slowly swung open.

In fact, the tabloid newspaper, "The National Enquirer," has called Kenmore one of "America's 5 Most Haunted Houses." And, according to Gary Norman, chief archeologist at the mansion, a number of the suspected ghosts are of Civil War vintage. "There has been a surge in reported incidents of unexplained and unexplainable things happening here," Norman told Fredericksburg Free Lance-Star staff reporter Mike Zitz, in an interview.

According to Zitz, Norman says a series of recent events could be interpreted as paranormal activity:

• At a reenactment just before Christmas 1994, for example, Norman says, "We had the great room set up as an operating room. Four reenactors, all professional men, witnessed a candle elevate off a portable desk, move, fall, and go out."

• A housekeeper pointed out that a tall, heavy chest had been moved. "It would require at least two people to move it," Norman points out.

• A gift shop clerk, described as "very reliable" by Norman, reported seeing a dark, shadowy, caped figure.

One person who has had a number of psychic encounters at Kenmore over the past couple of years is a young lady named Evelyn Kealey, a volunteer who works on the archeological digs that take place on the mansions's grounds. "I definitely think I have more psychic powers than the average person," she says. "That may explain why I was the only one who saw some of the things I did."

Several of the "occurrences" take place around Labor Day and in the fall and winter, when Evelyn and her associates spend a lot of time in the basement sifting through, cleaning and cataloguing the artifacts found in the diggings. These have included animal bones and teeth, apothecary weights, Civil War buttons, shards of 18th century ceramic and glass, nails and other items. "I've said the more they dig, the more it will stir up the restless spirits," she laughs. She may be right.

Evelyn says some of the more common manifestations have included "someone fooling with the light. You have to flip the lights on and off or trip the circuit box," she points out. "The lights have gone out for no reason on more than one occasion, and no one working in the basement was anywhere near the switch.

"Sometimes 'it,' locks the door to the basement. Again, you would have to latch it, or lock it with a key, and sometimes when we try to get through the door, it's like someone is holding it, and then all of a sudden it releases." On another occasion, Evelyn set a pail of silty water down to open the door. She was taking it outside to dump the water which had been used to wash off the artifacts. She opened the door and turned back to get the pail only to find that it had been "knocked over" by unseen hands or feet, and the water spilled down the stairs.

Evelyn also has seen two apparitions in the basement, although she doesn't know if it was same entity or two different ones. "Once, I saw a big willowy outline of a person move from one room to another. It had a cloudy, billowy shape. I had had the feeling that day that something was going to happen. I don't know why but I did. There was not a whole lot of shape to what I saw, but it definitely was moving. Shortly after that, the lights went out."

The second sighting proved to be more frightening. "It was about four in the afternoon in the fall, and I was taking a bucket of water out to empty it. I felt very strange. I was getting spooked out.

As I got to the area I call 'mortuary wall,' I stopped. Against the wall I saw a dark outline. This is the darkest part of the basement, but I saw a tall figure that I estimated to be about six feet tall, draped with a cape around its shoulders.

"It was just standing there looking at me. I assumed it was a man, possibly a military officer in some kind of uniform. I could see the outline of his head, neck and shoulders, but when I looked down, I couldn't see any boots or footwear.

I just stood there. I froze. I was stunned. I could feel goose bumps. I know there was no way what I was looking at was mortal! Nor could it have been my shadow. The sun doesn't get to this part of the basement. When I couldn't see his feet or legs, a thought struck me that maybe they had been amputated. Kenmore had been used as a hospital during the Civil War and I had a theory that when any soldiers died, they stacked them up against this particular wall, because it is the coolest place in the entire house in the summer.

"Anyway, I stood there for what seemed like an eternity. I guess it was only a few seconds. Then I went outside and dumped the water and when I came in again, the figure was gone. It was very eerie. No one else has seen anything like it, but as I said, I believe I am more psychically sensitive than most. I can tell you this, though. There are people who work here who won't come into the basement.

"They are afraid."

CHAPTER 6

The Ghostly Reenactment of Jeb Stuart's Ride

(The Chickahominy River)

He was charismatic, flamboyant, dashing, daring, debonair — the living embodiment of Southern pride and spirit. If Robert E. Lee exemplified the dignity and integrity of "The Cause," he typified the flair and savoir faire.

He dressed for the part. His uniform included a gold-braided jacket with a yellow sash and a red-lined cavalry cape, knee-high jack boots, and a felt hat with pinned up brim and ostrich-feather plume. He wanted to be, and, in fact, was known to be — the last cavalier. He was the Sir Lancelot of the Civil War.

His exploits were of the nature of which legends are made. For three years, he dashed and slashed his way in and out of enemy lines, causing both embarrassment and dread. He himself was without fear. He was brave, courageous, and outrageously defiant. He veritably thumbed his nose at his adversaries and challenged them to catch him if they were good enough. They couldn't. In a war full of gigantic heroes, he stood among the tallest.

Perhaps no more accurate and personal description of this man could be made than that recorded by his own staff officers. One wrote: "One of the marked traits of this *preus chevalier* was his indifference to danger, which impressed everyone. It would be difficult to imagine a coolness more supreme. It was not that he seemed to defy peril — he appeared unconscious of it.

" . . . It is almost impossible to separate the man from the soldier. He was ready for a 'fight or a frolic,' and gifted by nature with

26

an enormous animal physique, which enabled him to defy fatigue, whether produced by marching night and day, or dancing until dawn. Ambitious, fond of glory, and sensitive to blame or praise, he was yet endowed with a bold and independent spirit which enabled him to defy all enemies.

"He was warm-hearted, and never did man love friends more dearly. He always seemed to be a perfect embodiment of the traits generally attributed to the English cavaliers. There was in him a rollicking love of frolic, a gallantry towards ladies, a fondness for bright colors, brilliant spectacles, and gay adventure, which made him resemble strongly the class of men who followed the fortunes of Charles the I., and at Naseby died rather than retreat or surrender.

"His nerve was of stern stuff, and under all that laughter there was a soul that no peril could touch. That bright blue eye looked into the very face of death without a quiver of the lid, and dared the worst. A man more absolutely indifferent to danger, I believe, never lived; and, like some chevalier of olden days, he rode to battle with his lady's glove upon his helm, humming a song, and determined to conquer or fall."

There was never a dull moment under his command. He was revered by his men and loved by Southerners with an adulation on a level with that accorded only to two other men — Robert E. Lee and Stonewall Jackson. To some, he was a swashbuckling rebel who often took unnecessary chances and "bent" orders in an effort to enhance his own status. Maybe he did, on occasion. But he backed up such endeavors with consummate skill. It has been written that, "No intelligence source surpassed his eye for seeing and evaluating a military landscape or an enemy's strengths and dispositions." CSA General Joseph Johnston once said of his reconnaissance abilities: "I know no one more competent than he to estimate the occurrences before him at their true value." Lee called him: "A skillful soldier of splendid courage and energy, and a hearty, joyous, loving friend."

Confederate General W. B. Taliaferro may have put it best when he said, "He was the best cavalryman America ever produced."

This was James Ewell Brown Stuart!

Though he was only 31-years-old when a Union sharpshooter's bullet struck him down, his exploits during the war have filled books. And the colorful anecdotes attributed to Jeb Stuart have made such volumes a course of excitement and entertainment for more than a century and a quarter. Consider:

- After the bloody debacle of the Battle of Malvern Hill in

Charles City County in July 1862, in which the Confederates suffered appalling losses, Union General George McClellan, instead of pressing his advantage, retired to regroup his enormous Army of the Potomac — 100,000 strong — at Harrison's Landing. To the complete surprise of just about everyone, Stuart led his band of cavalrymen around and to the rear of the Federal encampment, and with a single cannon, began firing on the startled Yankees. While the shelling caused more damage to Union pride than physical harm, it was Stuart's way of taunting his foes.

J. E. B. Stuart. (Photo courtesy Museum of the Confederacy.)

• Stuart's obvious delight in harassing his enemies may have reached a peak in December 1862, when he captured a supply depot at Burke Station in northern Virginia. On a commandeered telegraph, he wired Washington, tweaking President Lincoln with the following: "The last draw of wagons I've just made (in his raid) are very good, but the mules are inferior stock, scarcely able to haul off the empty wagons; and if you expect me to give your lines any further attention in this quarter, you should furnish better stock, as I've had to burn several valuable wagons before getting them in my lines."

• A humorous incident occurred in October 1862, when Stuart rode into Stonewall Jackson's camp late at night after everyone had retired for the evening. Stuart unbuckled his saber and climbed into bed with Jackson. The next morning Jackson admonished his friend by saying, "General Stuart, I'm always glad to see you here. You might select better hours sometimes . . . but General, you must not get into my bed with your boots and spurs on and ride me around like a cavalry horse all night!"

Jeb Stuart was mortally wounded at the Battle of Yellow Tavern near Ashland, north of Richmond on May 11, 1864. The circumstances of this sad event were described by a courier under Stuart's command in the September 1864 issue of "The Southern Bivouac." The report is excerpted as follows:

"Pretty soon, from the enemy came lively volleys whistling through the trees and starting the dust in the road. In a few minutes I saw two horsemen approach from the Confederate side. As they drew near, I recognized General Stuart. They halted nearby in the road and Stuart, taking out his field-glass, deliberately watched the maneuvers of the enemy though balls were whizzing past him . . . The enemy confidently pressed forward with exultant shouts, delivering tremendous volleys. The Confederates returned their fire with yells of defiance. Stuart (mounted), with pistol in hand, shot over the heads of the troops, while, with words of cheer, he encouraged them. He kept saying 'Steady, men, steady. Give it to them!'

"Presently, he reeled in his saddle. His head bowed and his hat fell off. (At this point, Stuart was taken in an ambulance to Richmond.) . . . He lay without speaking as it went along, but kept shaking his head with an expression of the deepest disappointment."

The general was brought to the home of his brother-in-law, Dr. Charles Brewer, on West Grace Street, where he was visited by Confederate President Jefferson Davis. One of his last requests was for the group surrounding him to sing his favorite hymn, "Rock of

Ages." Consoled with the thought of being reunited with his daughter, Flora, who had died in 1862, he passed away at 7:30 p.m. on May 12, 1864.

He was buried the next day in Hollywood Cemetery. The funeral was attended by President Davis and hundreds of local residents. It was said that "not since the death of Stonewall Jackson in 1863 had the South felt such a blow."

Does Stuart's ghost — and the apparitional spirits of his cavalrymen — occasionally return to relive some of his legendary charges? Possibly. There is at least one recorded account of his spectral return at the site of perhaps his most famous feat of all.

It was June 1862. Union General George McClellan, with an army of more than 100,000 men and an enormous arsenal of weapons and supplies, was plodding westward across Charles City County bordering the James River, toward Richmond. General Lee was deeply concerned about the size, strength, and strategy of McClellan's command. He was considering a strong frontal attack. He called on Stuart to lead a reconnaissance mission to gather such vital information. Lee deemed it necessary for Stuart only to go far enough to assess the situation, and then report back of him.

But the dashing cavalier saw in this probing operation an opportunity to again humiliate his opponents. Instead of parrying, thrusting and then retreating, he decided not only to reach the enemy lines, but to *ride completely around them*!

From a point north of Richmond, Stuart assembled 1,200 of his best horsemen and began his movement at 2 a.m. on June 12, 1862. He told no one of their mission or destination. As they moved eastward on the second day, Stuart's men encountered some resistance from a Yankee picket post shortly after crossing the Totopotomoy Creek.

Here, Captain William Latané of the 9th Virginia led a charge directly into the enemy. With a slash of his saber, he wounded a Union officer, but he was then killed by two pistol shots. He was the only man to die during this extraordinary ride.

He was buried on a nearby plantation by a group of women. A poem — an elegy — was written for the occasion:
"No man of God might say the burial rite
Above the 'rebel' — thus declared the foe
But woman's voice, in accents soft and low,
Trembling with pity, touched with pathos, read
Over his hallowed dust the ritual for the dead."
After routing the remaining forces, Stuart's men moved on. By

the time they reached a place called Old Church, Stuart had gathered all the data he needed to brief Lee. But instead of turning homeward, he then, characteristically, chose to keep moving east, sweeping around behind McClellan's forces, and then going south to the James River and north back to Richmond, past the entire army; a once-in-a-lifetime chance to thrust the ultimate defiant taunt at the Yankees.

J. E. B. Stuart display at the Museum of the Confederacy, Richmond. (Photo taken with permission of the museum.)

It was Friday the 13th. Jeb Stuart viewed it as his destiny.

He pressed forward. By now, the Federals knew he was in their midst, and they sent forces after him. The Confederates destroyed supplies, burned a 75-wagon supply train, and took prisoners as they went. On the morning of June 14, they reached the Chickahominy River.

Here, they faced a problem. The river was swollen and running high and fast from heavy storms over the past several weeks. It was too dangerous to be forded. The Forge Bridge had been destroyed a month earlier when General Joseph Johnston's men had retreated through the area. Union forces were now in full pursuit. Ever resourceful, Stuart ordered a makeshift bridge to be built, using timbers from a nearby barn.

It was during the construction of this bridge that Jeb Stuart may have lain down on the banks of the river, to repose. He and his men had had little rest and practically no sleep since they had begun their journey.

The long column of men crossed the bridge and then set it afire. Their timing couldn't have been better. As the bridge was burning, the first Federal forces reached the Chickahominy. All they could do was look on in chagrined admiration as the last of the Rebels waved at them from the other side.

Stuart then, unthreatened, rode 35 miles west back to Richmond and reported to Lee. When his men followed, intact except for Captain Latané, they received a rousing hero's welcome. As one writer described the scene, "There was an air of romantic adventure to Stuart's exploit which touched every Southerner who read of it . . . this acted as a tonic for the nation's spirit . . . Captain Latané became a martyr to the cause and Jeb Stuart's ride around McClellan became one of the "lasting legends of the Confederacy."

A century later, to the day, June 13, 1962, two Virginia couples picnicked at the site of Stuart's historic crossing of the Chickahominy. One of the men was named Edmund Farley. The other man was Bill Latané, the great, great grand nephew of Captain William Latané! What happened to them on that warm spring day was recorded by the noted author, Nancy Roberts, in her book on Civil War ghosts.

Farley, Roberts wrote, wandered off from the others and walked along the banks of the river searching for a clue as to where the old Forge Bridge may have stood. After a while he lay down to take a nap. When he awoke, a strange thing happened. He heard men's voices and the sounds of "pounding hammers and the sharp

crack of planks striking one another." But he could see nothing. It was, he felt, as if an invisible team were building a bridge!

Farley then noticed "a bearded sleeping figure lying on the ground near him." The figure was dressed in the uniform of a Confederate officer, complete with a bright yellow sash. Beside him was a black felt hat with a long plume tucked under its band, and a beautiful sword. Farley wondered if the man was dead. Then he saw that the figure was breathing. He reached down and touched the figure. Its blue eyes opened, and it spoke. "It's all right. Get some rest." The figure then smiled. "Don't worry," it said, "my cavalry will get the bridge built in time, and, if not, we will all have plenty of excitement when the Yankees catch up with us."

It was already enough excitement for Farley. He was dumbfounded, speechless. For a fleeting moment he wondered if he had somehow stumbled into some sort of historic time warp . . . the sounds of hammering, the voices of the men . . . the figure of the Confederate officer lying on the ground. How does one explain this? As he walked back to the picnic area, his only rational explanation was that a reenactment of some kind was going on, and the figure was an actor in it, who had stopped, as he had, to rest. It had to be. There could be no other answer. Or could there be?

Meanwhile, Bill Latané and the two ladies had encountered another phenomenon. As they neared the road which led back to the highway, they saw an entire troop of mounted Confederate soldiers led by a cavalry officer. The officer was wearing the same uniform the figure wore that Farley had seen; thigh-length black leather boots, yellow sash, and a hat with a brilliant feather!

Latané immediately assumed he was viewing a reenactment. As he stood watching, his eye caught "a small splash of white in the carpet of leaves. He reached down and picked it up. It appeared to be a handkerchief, a very old handkerchief. On it were embroidered initials, "W. L." They were *his* initials!

As Latané looked up, he saw the Confederates charge off toward Union cavalrymen. They were led by a captain. He struck a Federal officer in the neck with the blade of his sword, and at the same instant was shot by the officer. He fell to the ground. It was, young Latané believed, the most realistic reenactment he had ever witnessed. Then he was struck by an awesome thought: was this the spot where his ancestor, Captain William Latané, had been killed?

He was visibly shaken. He then realized that the handkerchief he had picked up seemed wet. He looked at it. His fingers seemed to be wet, stained with what appeared to be blood! What was going on?

Noise broke the spell. Latané looked up and saw a convoy of modern military vehicles on the road. When he looked back towards the site of the "reenactment," the Civil War soldiers had vanished!

Sometime later, Bill Latané had the strange handkerchief he had found that day analyzed. It was authenticated by a museum curator as a genuine Civil War relic!

Edmund Farley, who had seen the vision of the Confederate officer that same day, checked with authorities about the reenactment. He was told that one had been planned, but it had, at the last moment, been canceled because a military convoy was to move through the area!

C H A P T E R   7

Return of the Female Phantom

(Shenandoah Valley)

"She was a mystery while she lived, and she remains a mystery today."

— *The Washington Star*

alk about a spirited woman! Both in life and *afterwards*!

Her name has been coated over in the dusty annals of history, yet in her time, and for years afterwards, Belle Boyd was the talk the Commonwealth. She gained a well-deserved reputation for daring and heroism under fire that earned undying respect from her friends and followers . . . and grudging admiration from her enemies. Her exploits spanned the Civil War years.

There seems to be some controversy among writers and historians as to just how attractive, or unattractive, Belle Boyd really was. Descriptions pretty much run the gamut. Take your pick. She was:

— "Not beautiful, but she was attractive and fascinating to a degree that would charm the heart out of a monk and cause him to break his vows of celibacy."

— "A tall, somewhat long-faced brunette with prominent teeth."

— "Attractive in manner, appearance and personality, she possessed dash, energy, and courage; and she was a skilled rider."

— "Flirtatious and manipulative."

— "Pretty, fair-haired and blue eyed."

— "Irrepressible, allegedly pretty, on her record, fascinating."

— "A wildly romantic tomboy."

— "One who thrived upon the stir of war, (and) saw herself as the beautiful female spy of the Confederacy."

Whatever conclusion one may draw, it is a general consensus that Belle fairly well gushed a youthful exuberance and disarming charm which was, to most Yankees she dealt with, somewhat intoxicating, if not downright spellbinding. She had a flair about her that captivated men, old and young, experienced and immature alike. And she used this homespun, backwoods charisma to fullest advantage.

Belle Boyd's legend began in the early months of the War between the States, at her parents' home in Martinsburg, West Virginia. A troop of northern soldiers appeared at the house one day and insisted that a Union flag be raised on the grounds. Belle's mother said the family would rather die first. At this point, one of the men "spoke insultingly" to Mrs. Boyd, and, impulsively, Belle allegedly drew a pistol from her bosom and shot him dead. Amazingly, when officers heard the story later, they let the young girl go. She was then 16.

Shortly afterwards, Belle moved to Front Royal to live with an aunt, and began gathering information on Federal troop movements and strategies. On May 18, 1862, for instance, she overheard plans for the destruction of munitions and structures in the town, and for the retreat of Union forces as the Confederate army was approaching. She overheard this conversation taking place in her aunt's parlor between General James Shields and his staff through a peephole she had cut in the attic floor.

She then mounted her horse, Fleeta, as darkness fell, and rode 15 miles to the nearest Southern camp to relay her intelligence. For the better part of the next two years, she continued her covert actions, by cajoling information out of Yankees, and then braving bullets and swords as she dashed southward to deliver her secret messages. On one occasion she arrived at a Stonewall Jackson camp so breathless she couldn't speak for several minutes. Then she informed the assembled staff officers where the Union soldiers were and what they were up to. This helped lead to a Jacksonian rout. Afterwards, Jackson sent her a note saying, "I thank you, for myself and for the army, for the immense service that you have rendered your country . . ."

One of Belle Boyd's many dramatic exploits is documented in a book, "I Rode with Stonewall," written by Confederate Major

Belle Boyd

Henry Kyd Douglas and published in 1940. Following is one episode recorded by Douglas: "In the early afternoon (of May 22, 1862, General) Ewell struck the pickets of the enemy within sight of and negligently near to Front Royal. They were driven in and the small body of infantry supporting them easily routed. We stopped to form on a hill overlooking the small town of Front Royal and the hurried movement of blue-coats and the galloping of horsemen here and there told of the confusion in the enemy's camp. General Jackson, not knowing the force of the enemy there was so small or so unprepared by reinforcements for his approach, was endeavoring to take in the situation before ordering an advance.

"I observed, almost immediately, the figure of a woman in white, glide swiftly out of town on our right and, after making a little circuit, run rapidly up a ravine in our direction and then disappear from sight. She seemed, when I saw her, to heed neither weeds nor fences, but waved a bonnet as she came on, trying, it was evident, to keep the hill between herself and the village. I called General Jackson's attention to the singular movement just as a dip in the land hid her, and at General Ewell's suggestion, he sent me to meet her and ascertain what she wanted.

"That was just to my taste, and it took only a few minutes for my horse to carry me to meet the romantic maiden whose tall, supple, and graceful figure struck me as soon as I came in sight of her. As I drew near, her speed slackened, and I was startled, momentarily, at hearing her call my name. But I was not much astonished when I saw that the visitor was the well-known Belle Boyd whom I had known from her earliest girlhood. She was just the girl to dare to do this thing.

"Nearly exhausted, and with her hand pressed against her heart, she said in gasps, 'I knew it must be Stonewall, when I heard the first gun. Go back quick and tell him that the Yankee force is very small — one regiment of Maryland infantry, several pieces of artillery and several companies of cavalry. Tell him I knew, for I went through the camps and got it out of an officer. Tell him to charge right down and he will catch them all. I must hurry back. Good-by. My love to all the dear boys — and remember if you meet me in town you haven't seen me today.'

"I raised my cap, she kissed her hand and was gone. I delivered her message speedily, and while Jackson was asking me questions about her — for until then he had never heard of her — I saw the wave of her white bonnet as she entered the village and disappeared among its houses."

Belle Boyd herself told of one of her daring rides in a newspaper interview with reporter Charles Archer. The account was later published in a book in 1893. Said Belle: "It was at the time of (Nathaniel P.) Bank's retreat (from Strasburg to the Potomac), that I took a midnight ride of 54 miles over the mountains to find Jackson. He was at Luray. The Federals were round Front Royal. I had all the dispositions from Harper's Ferry down.

"There was a young Federal officer at our house who I knew had the countersign. He fell in love with me, and I was engaged to him to be married, but I had always refused to kiss him good-night. I wanted his papers, and so this night when he pressed me for a kiss I saw these papers sticking from his pocket. Here was the opportunity, and have them I must. I kissed him and at the same time deftly removed the packet of letters. He never missed them until long after I had gone.

"So you see it was the kiss of Judas after all.

"Fortune favored me. Those papers were more valuable than I had imagined. In the garb of a boy, I mounted my horse that evening and started on my journey. It was not a moonlight night, though the stars were out at the commencement of my weird journey, but soon became obscured.

"Ah, that was a wild ride that we took — Fleeta and I. I will never forget it. With only a general conception of the way, oftentimes I got off my course. At the best, there was only a bridle path. For much of the route, not even that, and here and there, rough, hard climbs up the stony beds of the brooks, with stiffish ledges and rocky barriers to leap in the gloomy and precipitous ravines and gorges.

"I found Jackson and delivered my dispatches. Coming back in the gray of the morning, I was overtaken by a thunderstorm. I dared not stop, so kept straight on, wet to the skin, 'mid the gloom of the storm and the blinding glare of the lightning.

"In one vivid flash there stood revealed the Federal guard with rifle poised.

"'Who comes there?' rang out his challenge.

"For the moment I forgot the countersign, when luckily, kind fate produced the corporal standing close beside the sentry. The friendly lightning gave him a glimpse of me.

"Said he, 'Let the boy pass; I know him.' "I was awfully glad he thought he did, and dashed by the picket with a lightened heart. Fleeta soon bore me to my father's door."

Just how many missions Belle carried out between 1862 and 1864 is not known, but in time her nocturnal journeys between enemy and friendly lines became well known to both sides, and eventually she was arrested and imprisoned. She was tried, found guilty of spying, and sentenced to hard labor in the Fitchburg jail where she nearly died of typhoid fever. Her father somehow managed to free her from prison.

Toward the end of the war, this energetic and totally dedicated young woman set off by sea with important Confederate dispatches for London. The vessel was captured, however, and sent to Boston under guard of a Lieutenant Harding of the United States Navy. Belle worked her magic again, and by the time they docked, she not only had converted the lieutenant to the southern cause, she also had become engaged to him!

He helped her escape to Canada and then to London and married her! They were divorced in 1868. Belle, in fact, went through several husbands, and wound up writing her memoirs of the war, and then touring the states giving lectures on her many adventures. She billed herself as the "Confederate Heroine Belle Boyd of Stonewall Jackson and Shenandoah Valley fame," and called her dramatic narrative, "North and South - Or the Perils of a Spy." Audiences loved it.

Belle Boyd died, of all places, in Wisconsin, in 1900 at the age of 56. She was buried in an area known as Wisconsin Dells. Of her passing, a local newspaper editor wrote: "She who sleeps today in that lovely cemetery is a link with that grave in another section of the Union. For Belle Boyd, 'the Spy,' was associated with 'Stonewall' Jackson, the General. No reader of the history of that memorable conflict, where one family fought among themselves, where the heroism of either side reflects the glory of the other, will ever stand beside the grave of Belle Boyd in the Kilbourn Cemetery without thinking sympathetically of the grave of 'Stonewall' Jackson, or the graves of the dead of both the Blue and the Gray in the cemeteries of America."

An obituary in the New York Times recalled "the thrill, the danger, the triumphs, the reverses, the many ups and downs, in the life of the most determined woman foe the United States ever had."

Perhaps because she is interred so far away from her home, or perhaps otherwise, Belle's spirit seems to live on.

Her wraithlike figure on horseback has allegedly been seen many times in the region around Winchester and Front Royal, gliding effortlessly across the hills and through the woods — her chestnut curls flying. As one writer put it, "she rushes with messages to a ghostly army commanded by Stonewall Jackson."

CHAPTER 8

Psychic Imprints on the Battlefield

(Manassas)

n late August 1862, Union General John Pope believed he could do what no one had done before — or would ever do for that matter; he thought he had trapped Confederate General Thomas J. "Stonewall" Jackson, and was about to destroy his army at a point south of Fairfax, near Manassas. But as Pope and many other Federal generals were to learn, to their dismay, he was chasing a phantom; a deadly phantom who exacted an awesome price for each mistake of his enemies.

Pope felt he had pinned Jackson and his men down along an unfinished railroad grade, and he launched numerous assaults at his adversary. But he failed to take into account three vital elements. One was the fighting ferocity and the courageous valor of the Southerners. Second was the inherent strength of Jackson's position. Third was the brilliant counter-strategy the Confederates were to employ.

When Pope launched another attack on August 30, it was said Jackson's lines "shook," under the heavy fire. But the Union forces had not reckoned with the incredible spirit of the men they were attacking. When a portion of the Southern troops ran out of ammunition, for example, they held off their attackers with *a barrage of rocks*!

But the real surprise came when General James Longstreet's troops appeared on Pope's left flank. Robert E. Lee and Longstreet

Stonewall Jackson monument at the Manassas Battlefield.

had moved under cover of the Bull Run Mountains to join Jackson.

According to Civil War historian Peter Lockwood, Pope, while chasing Jackson, had neglected to account for the other, and larger, part of Lee's army under Longstreet. Of this extraordinary maneuver, Lockwood wrote: "To unite separate forces (Jackson's and Longstreet's) without modern communications is recognized as one of the greatest feats of past warfare . . . Longstreet's wing came up on Jackson's right as if the units had spent weeks in dress rehearsal."

The result was a resounding victory for the Confederates. State marker C-33 says, of the Second Battle of Manassas: "Stonewall Jackson held position, August 29-30, 1862, repulsing all of Pope's assaults. . . Late in the afternoon of August 30, when Longstreet (counter) attacked, Jackson swept southward, completing the victory."

Of this action, Longwood wrote: "Once again the Northern 'invaders' were retreating pell-mell over Bull Run. Only a rear guard action on the Henry House Hill prevented the withdrawal from becoming a total rout; but, still, the field was surrendered in such disorder that more than 4,000 prisoners, dozens of artillery pieces, and thousands of small arms were captured."

One Yankee unit suffered a tremendous loss. Historian Bruce Catton wrote about it. "The 5th New York were dressed as Zouaves — bright red baggy pants, white canvas leggings, broad red sash at the waist, short blue jacket, tasseled red caps . . . They hung on long enough to let the regulars get the guns away, and then they retired — what was left of them anyway. In their brief fight they had lost 117 men killed and 170 wounded, out of 490 present — the highest percentage of loss, in killed, suffered by any Federal regiment in one battle during the entire war."

According to some visitors at Manassas, one or more Zouaves *still wander the battlefield*!

Writing in the Washingtonian Magazine a few years ago, Diana McLellan noted: "Less attractive is the scent of black powder and burning flesh, accompanied by sudden, highly localized drops in temperature, experienced by some visitors to the Manassas Battlefield in Northern Virginia. There, at dusk, images of members of the 5th New York Zouaves — who were cut to pieces during the Second Battle of Manassas — have been seen beckoning by the woods at the western end of the park, clad in their red pantaloons, white leggings, and nightcap hats."

According to Jim Burgess, curator at the Manassas National Battlefield Park, there not only have been numerous "sightings" of the ill-fated Zouaves, but there also have been a number of other accounts of unusual phenomena occurring here, some ghost-related, some otherwise. "Most of the reports of the reappearance of a Zouave apparition or apparitions took place before I came here in 1980," Burgess says. They were generally seen around dusk in the vicinity of the New York monuments. Some said they saw a headless spirit wandering about.

One of the most recent sightings occurred on Halloween about 1985 and involved a park ranger who was giving a tour of the second Manassas battlefield to a college group. They had stopped near the unfinished railroad site, and as the ranger was describing the action that had taken place there, he noticed out of the corner of his eye that the professor with the group seemed to be distracted. He was staring off into the distance.

The group then moved on to the next stop near the monuments marking the place where the Zouaves were struck down. Before concluding his lecture, the ranger mentioned, probably because it was Halloween, the legends of the Zouave ghosts. At this, the professor turned white as a sheet and appeared visibly shaken. When asked if anything was wrong, the professor said that at the previ-

Cannon at the Manassas Battlefield.

ous stop, he had seen a figure dressed in a Zouave uniform across the field! He said the soldier had either vanished, or disappeared by a tree. The man truly believed he had seen a ghost.

There is , too, according to several different witnesses who claim to have seen it, the specter of a headless Civil War soldier who roams the battlefield on occasional moonlit nights, searching either for his lost head or a fallen comrade. Reporting a decade ago in the Manassas Journal Messenger, staff writer Diane Hartson chillingly set the scene for this ethereal recurrence: "A shadow emerges from among the trees bordering the barren field. The sky is black and clouds are scudding across the face of the moon. But the moon provides enough light to make out the figure of a man in loose pantaloons scouring the battlefield, searching for something. In a moment, fleetingly, the field is bathed in light as the face of the moon clears. A chill runs down your spine as you realize the man appears to have no head!"

According to Hartson, the apparitional soldier was a member of the famed New York Zouaves, and he appears generally around Halloween each year in a section of the battlefield known as New York Hill. He allegedly has been seen "by several people," sometimes with a head, sometimes without, "always poring over the ground, as though looking for something."

Burgess tells a funny story about the monument dedicated to the fallen Zouaves of the 5th New York that was erected on the battlefield in 1906. Several years ago the monument was in need of some restoration. A numeral "5" was missing from the upper part of the monument and members of the 5th New York (Duryee Zouaves) reenactment unit volunteered to replace it and perform other work.

"To replicate the missing numeral, dimensions were needed of the monument and I went out one afternoon with a member of the 5th New York named Jack to take measurements," Burgess recalls. "Jack had been doing 'living history' interpretation at the park that day and was still wearing his distinctive Zouave uniform. We had taken a ladder with us and Jack climbed up to measure the space for the missing numeral.

"Meanwhile, Dave, a seasonal ranger, was conducting a tour on a bus stopped a short distance away. While addressing the tour group, Dave had his back to the monument and did not see us arrive but everyone else on the bus faced in our direction. As Dave described the unique appearance of the Zouaves, one on the bus, seeing Jack on the monument, asked, 'Is that one over there?' Turning, Dave was completely dumbfounded at the sight and later confessed thinking for a moment that he was actually seeing the fabled Zouave ghost. We all had a good laugh over that afterwards."

Burgess confirms the report in the Washingtonian Magazine that visitors on occasion said they smelled the odor of gunpowder and burning flesh while touring the park. He offers a possible explanation for this. "We know there were some unspeakable atrocities committed here during the war," he says. "The Public Broadcasting System's airing of Ken Burns' series on the Civil War, included the poignant last letter written by Major Sullivan Ballou of the Second Rhode Island regiment who was killed in the first battle.

"What wasn't mentioned was the fate of Major Ballou's body afterward. Major Ballou and Colonel John Slocum of the Second Rhode Island were carried back to Sudley Church, one of the Union field hospitals, where they both died from their wounds. With too few ambulances to evacuate even the wounded, there was little alternative but to bury the dead officers in shallow graves not far from the church.

"In March 1862, after the Confederate army vacated Northern Virginia, the governor of Rhode Island led an expedition to recover the remains of the two Union officers and return them for a proper burial in their home state. As the men began digging at the site of the makeshift graves, a Black girl came over and asked them what they were doing. Upon being told, the girl said the body of Colonel

Slocum had already been dug up by the Southerners. She said they had taken the body to a nearby ravine, decapitated it and then burned the remains, possibly to use the bones for souvenir rings. The Southerners apparently were seeking revenge for the damage inflicted on their unit during the battle by the Second Rhode Island.

"The men found charred remains where the girl had indicated, but further investigation proved them to be Major Ballou's. Slocum's body had not been disturbed. The remains were gathered up, taken back to Rhode Island and reinterred," Burgess says, "and perhaps this incident accounts for the smell of burning flesh some visitors have sensed. Judge for yourself."

Burgess says that other strange phenomena have included the feeling by some of cold spots on the battlefield. "This has happened even in the hot, humid heat of July. People have said they have been chilled." He adds that motorists driving through the park at night have occasionally told of seeing lights in houses which no longer exist! "They come back the next day and see no house at the spot where they said they saw the lights, and they ask what happened to the house."

In his book, *"Bull Run Remembers,"* Joseph Mills Hanson, the park's first superintendent, alludes to how certain parts of the battlefield can have a strange, chilling effect. Referring to the woods along the unfinished railroad, Hanson writes: "Many Union soldiers had fallen among those thickets, and it's an eerie kind of place

Battle scene at Manassas, from a contemporary sketch.

if you are tramping around by yourself toward twilight and get to thinking of things that have happened there. Something like old Mr. Jim Rowzie used to tell about the woods in back of the Conrad house where you find little piles of stones that once were chimneys of Confederate winter huts. He would hint darkly that hound dogs won't trail a fox into those woods after daylight dwindles. They'll whimper and slink off."

THE STONE HOUSE

O f all the sites across this great battlefield, certainly one of the most haunted is an old structure known as the Stone House. It is one of only two original buildings still on the grounds today. It is believed to have been built in 1828, and served as a tavern at the crossroads for the cattlemen and wagon teamsters coming down the Warrenton pike from the west with supplies for Alexandria and Washington. Here was where they spent the night and fed their horses.

According to a National Park Service brochure, the Stone House, even in its heyday, was "never a fancy hotel noted for fine food. The place sold hard liquor to hard men. Its success was short-lived, however, as railroads in the 1850s replaced wagons as the principal means of transportation. As the turnpike era ended, the house and its owners . . . seemed to slip into obscurity.

"But it was not to be. Twice, the determined armies of a divided nation would clash on the fields near Bull Run. Both times, Stone House would be brought into the mainstream of battle, its significance marked in blood. In this house, and others like it, many soldier's dreams of heroism and valor were forgotten in the nightmare of pain and agony experienced within its walls."

During the Second Battle of Manassas nearly 20,000 men fell. Surgeons worked around the clock, but haste and neglect were inherent. Many suffered for days on the field without any attention. The utter horror of this situation was graphically recorded in official Civil War documents. Consider the following testimony of Dr. J. M. Homiston, surgeon of the Brooklyn regiment captured at Bull Run.

He said that when he "solicited permission to remain on the field and to attend to wounded men, some of whom were in a helpless and painful condition, and suffering for water," he was brutally refused . . . He and his companions "stood in the streets of

Stone House at the Manassas Battlefield.

Manassas, surrounded by a threatening and boisterous crowd, and were afterward thrust into an old building, and left, without sustenance or covering, to sleep on the bare floor. It was only when faint, and without food for 24 hours, that some cold bacon was grudgingly given to them.

"When, at last, they were permitted to go to the relief of our wounded, the secession surgeon would not allow them to perform operations, but intrusted the wounded to his young assistants, some of them with no more knowledge of what they attempted to do than an apothecary's clerk." And further, "that these inexperienced surgeons performed operations upon our men in a most horrible manner, some of them were absolutely frightful.

" . . . The same witness describes the sufferings of the wounded after the battle as inconceivably horrible; with bad food, no covering, no water. They were lying upon the floor as thickly as they could be laid. There was not a particle of light in the house to enable us to move among them.

" . . . It is not a wonder that next morning we found that several had died during the night. The young surgeons, who seemed to delight in hacking and butchering those brave defenders of our country's flag, were not, it would seem, permitted to perform any operations upon the rebel wounded . . . Some of our wounded, says this witness, were left lying upon the battlefield (for two or three days). When brought in, their wounds were completely alive with larvae deposited there by the flies, having lain out through all the rainstorm of Monday, and the hot, sultry sunshine of Tuesday.

"The dead lay upon the field unburied for five days . . . ten or twelve days after the battle, he (the witness) saw some of the Union soldiers unburied on the field, and completely naked. Walking around were a great many women, gloating over the horrid sight."

Even more revolting was the reported desecration of the bodies. One man, searching for his dead brother, reported: "We found no head in the grave, and no bones of any kind — nothing but the clothes and portions of the flesh . . ." "The witness also states that Mrs. Pierce Butler, who lives near the place, said that she had seen the rebels boiling portions of the bodies of our dead in order to obtain their bones as relics. They could not wait for them to decay. She said that she had seen drumsticks made of 'Yankee shinbones,' as they called them.

"Mrs. Butler also stated that she had seen a skull that one of the New Orleans artillery had, which, he said, he was going to send home and have mounted, and that he intended to drink a brandy-punch out of it the day he was married!"

Is it any wonder, then, that Burgess, after saying a number of soldiers undoubtedly died at Stone House, adds, "it has every right to be haunted."

The Park Service brochure says, "very few contemporary accounts remain of what actually occurred inside the house . . . Perhaps soldier and surgeon preferred to forget their experiences rather than recall the terrible suffering in letters and diaries sent home. However, two soldiers from the 5th New York Volunteer Infantry did leave behind their own tangible marks. Privates Eugene P. Geer and Charles E. Brehm were wounded on August 30 (1862) in a futile attempt to halt Longstreet's counterattack.

Duryee Zouaves of the 5th New York Volunteer Infantry are attacked by General John B. Hood's Texans, August 30, 1862, during the Second Battle of Manassas, from a painting by Anthony Ranfone.

Somehow the two men found their way to one of the small upstairs rooms at the Stone House. There, carved in the floorboards in the late summer of 1862 and still visible today are the initials 'E. P. Ge' and 'Brehm Aug 30.'

Brehm recovered from his wounds and survived the war. Geer died a month later. He was 17.

Burgess relates that the haunting aura about the Stone House was first documented in the book, *Four Brothers in Blue*, by Robert Goldthwaite Carter. A chapter of this book is devoted to the author's visit to the battlefield in the early 1900s. During his visit he stayed at the Stone House as a guest of the owner, Henry Ayres.

Carter wrote, "We remained at the 'Stone House' all night. This house is frequently referred to in "The Surreys of Eagle Nest" by John Esten Cook, as 'The Old Stone House of Manassas' and again as 'The Haunted House' . . . Mr. Starbuck lived in 'Stone House' since the war, and Mr. Pridmore after him. Mr. Ayres' daughter stated that Starbuck put a curse on the house and on Pridmore's family. Certain it is that out of the Pridmore family six or more died in quick succession, and she thinks the house rightfully bears the name of the 'Haunted House.'"

Burgess admits that several curious incidents in recent times lend support to Miss Ayres' claims. One incident was reported in the late 1970s: "A park ranger and a volunteer were closing up the house one day," recounts Burgess. "It was after 5 p.m., late in the season and it was getting dark. The normal procedure is to bolt the doors from the inside, set the alarm, and then go out by way of the basement. This they did, but as they were about to exit, they both heard distinct footsteps in the room above. The steps went from the big tavern room, into the hallway and then into a smaller room. Thinking they somehow must have missed a lingering visitor, they both went back upstairs to look. Now, there are virtually no places to hide in the house. There are no closets, for example. They looked everywhere but found no one. At that point they got very nervous and left the place abruptly."

More recently a seasonal park ranger was on duty, alone in the house, on a slow, summer afternoon, according to Burgess. This employee began to nod off to sleep while reading a book as he sat just inside the front door. Suddenly, "someone or something" knocked his glasses off and he was jarred wide awake. He checked all around the house but soon discovered he was still alone.

A few years ago, when the Stone House had period furnishings, Park Service administrative officer Jane Becker, a "camera bug," went to take some photos of the interior rooms. She used a 35mm camera. When the color photos were developed, all came out well except for one picture which totally puzzled her. On this single print was a large, "fuzzy white blotch" which ran across the center of the photo from top to bottom. Part of the blotch was thick, like a dense cloud, obliterating the furniture beyond it. Yet part of the wispy "material" was partially transparent. A security rope could be seen in the midst of the strange white swirl. Jane looked at her negatives. All were fine, except the one.

She consulted with photographic experts. She sent the print and negative to Kodak, and also to the Federal Bureau of Investigation. No one could explain the phenomenon. There was, everyone agreed, no rational cause for the apparitional appearance. Jane keeps a copy of the photo on her desk. She has labeled it, "The Stone House Ghost!"

Burgess relates another humorous story that was told to him by a former landlord who in turn got it from old Mrs. Wheeler whose

Stone House "Ghost" photographed by Jane Becker, administrative officer, Manassas National Battlefield Park.

family, the Swarts, lived at "Hazel Plain," otherwise known as the Chinn House, sometime after the war. This house stood until the early 1950s and, like the Stone House, had witnessed the horrors of war as a temporary field hospital. The Chinn House had been abandoned for a number of years before the Swarts purchased the property. In its dilapidated condition, the house had a rather forbidding appearance and a reputation for being haunted.

The Swarts hired a team of workmen to repair and paint the house before moving in. Late one afternoon three men were busy trying to finish painting an upstairs room when the paint supply ran out. The foreman told one of his men to go downstairs and get another can of paint from the wagon outside. The house did not have any electricity and it was getting dark especially in the hallway where the workman had to go.

Having heard the stories about the house, the designated workman declared he wouldn't go by himself. His co-worker then volunteered to accompany him. As the two painters started down the stairs, the foreman came running after them, exclaiming, "You're not going to leave me up here alone!" All three had to fetch one can of paint.

Burgess says that while there have been few happenings in recent years which could be associated with spectral phenomena, one curious incident did occur in November 1994. "It was a pleasant Sunday morning with little or no breeze," he says. "The sun was beginning to dissipate the morning chill. A ranger was conducting a tour of the Henry Hill area for a group of about 15 people. At about 10:45 a.m., as the ranger stood just beyond the edge of a grove of oak trees explaining the capture of the Union battery position beyond, he was interrupted by a disturbance behind him. He turned to look half expecting to find a small child that might have strayed from the group, but saw only leaves swirling up a short distance behind him.

"He didn't think much about it and continued on with his interpretation of the battle. Later, when the tour was over, some members of the group approached him and asked if he believed in ghosts. When he asked them why, they said they not only saw the leaves being kicked up to his rear but it also appeared that the grass was being depressed as if some unseen presence was walking swiftly across the field between the opposing artillery positions," Burgess says. "Considering the lack of any wind that day, a supernatural explanation seemed to be the only other possibility."

CHAPTER 9

A Sampling of
Spectral Vignettes

THE SKELETON IN THE WALL
(Orange County)

(Author's note: Sometimes even though the major details are missing, the story is so interesting it deserves to be retold. Such was the case in October 1994 when I drove to Charlottesville to do a Halloween book signing at the Barnes and Noble super book store in the Barracks Road shopping center. There, a charming woman came up to me and related the following:)

can't remember the name of the house or exactly where it is located, but it is in Orange, Virginia," she began. "It happened during the Civil War. A minister and his wife lived in the house, and the Yankees were on the march through the area. There had been considerable fighting.

"One day the minister told his wife he was going out to visit wounded Confederate soldiers. He asked her to hide the family silver, because the house might be overrun by invading troops. He was killed by an errant bullet, and his wife and the silver were never seen again. She just disappeared.

"In time, the house acquired the reputation of being haunted. Over the years residents there said that an apparitional woman mysteriously appeared each October 14th at around 4 p.m. She would be seen for only a few seconds and then she would vanish. This went on for some time.

"One year two young men who had heard about the legend came to the house to investigate. They were kind of like amateur ghost detectives. They were not disappointed. She appeared before them and then was gone. They tried to follow her but could not. They began tapping on the walls in the room where she had last been seen. One spot was hollow and they tore into the wall. There, they found the crumbling bones of a female skeleton . . . and the family's silver.

"It was believed that the wife of the minister had somehow concealed herself inside the walls and then, for some inexplicable reason, had been unable to get out. She died there. Once her remains had been found and were given a proper burial, the ghost never again appeared in that house."

GRANT WON'T HANG HERE!
(Nokesville, south of Manassas)

*C*an a ghost perform physical acts? Connie Minnick whose family lives at an old house at Broadlands Farm in Nokesville is convinced they can. In fact, she credits the ghost of a young woman with saving her house from burning to the ground, not once, but twice!

Minnick says the previous owner of the house once hinted that it might be haunted. The lady said she often smelled a strong scent of lavender, but never could determine its source. Minnick says she first encountered the spirit when she was still a child. She heard "a skirt rustling on the stairs," and is not sure if it was caused by an unseen being or by her own imagination.

She believes it might be the lingering spirit of a young girl who lived in the house during the Civil War when it served as a hospital. The girl was allegedly shot. The Minnicks call her "Ruth." This belief is partially tied to the fact that the family could never keep a picture of Union General Ulysses S. Grant hung on the wall. "It kept crashing down," Minnick says. Yet, curiously, after the portrait was taken down, and a mirror weighing twice as much as Grant's picture was hung at the same spot, it has stayed on the wall.

Over the years there have been other manifestations, but the events that convinced the Minnicks that "Ruth" was a benevolent

Abingdon Church

spirit who had the power to act in a physical manner occurred on two separate occasions. Once, a burning log from the fireplace rolled out onto the floor when no one was home. For unexplained reasons, nothing caught fire.

Another time, a fire started in the attic. "It didn't burn nearly as much as it should have," Minnick says, "but just stopped when it got to the second floor. We expected the whole house to go up in flames." Minnick believes the lady ghost is there to protect the home she lived in 130 years ago.

THE APPARITION AT ABINGDON CHURCH
(Gloucester)

It is worth the trip just to see the splendid old church and to casually stroll through the adjacent cemetery which contains a number of tombstones with coats of arms carved upon them. Abingdon Church is said to have been planned by Sir Christopher Wren, the famous architect. It was built in 1755, in the form of a Greek cross, and replaced an earlier church that had stood since the mid-17th century. Abingdon is notable for an elaborate reredos representing in bas-relief the facade of a Greek temple.

For generations, many rich and aristocratic families worshipped here. Peculiarly, the building had no heat, and in the winter servants placed hot bricks at the pew owners' feet for warmth, while the less-endowed members of the congregation shivered. The silver service, still in use, was presented by Major Lewis Burwell of Carter's Creek in 1703. Some of the old box pews were used by the British as box stalls for horses during the Revolutionary War.

But the single ghostly tale about Abingdon, eloquently described by Caroline Baytop Sinclair in her interesting book "Stories of Old Gloucester," pertains to the Civil War. It occurred, as Ms. Sinclair wrote, on "a stormy, wet night in 1863." A lone, young Federal cavalryman was returning to his station at Gloucester Point late that night, tired, cold, wet and "disgruntled." He had become separated from his party and he and his horse had stumbled through grapevines, poison ivy and briar patches in their efforts to evade the Confederate enemy.

Near midnight, the storm intensified, and the soldier sought shelter. He came upon Abingdon Church and led his horse through the large doors and onto the stone floors. The building had recently been occupied by troops, and by the flashes of lightning, he could see it was in "desolate disorder;" pews and paneling were broken and charred wood and ashes were scattered on the floor.

But he sensed something else, too. In the intermittent light of the storm he perceived something moving in the north gallery. As his eyes adjusted, it appeared to be tall, white and descending the stairway. When another bolt pierced the sky revealing the filmy apparition of a human-like form, the soldier had seen enough. He mounted up and his horse clattered through the arched door and across the churchyard. Too late! As Sinclair told it, "the flashing streaks in the sky revealed two riders upon the horse's back."

* * * * * * * * * *

THE DOMESTIC WHO FORESAW DEATH
(Bath)

As the Civil War waged on it took an increasingly heavy toll of Virginians. This was true not only of the men who were killed in their prime or grievously wounded. It also affected the families left behind. Plantation fields once rife with crops went to seed as the masters and overseers left for battle and slaves fled to seek their freedom.

A case in point was the Johnson Orrick family of what was then Bath, Virginia. Captain Orrick was off to Winchester in the cause of the Confederacy. He left his wife and three small children, and one faithful maid, named Millie. They lived in a cottage and did their best to manage during a time of rationing and shortages.

As told by Margaret DuPont Lee, in her book, "Virginia Ghosts," Mrs. Orrick, after putting her children to bed one moonlit night, happened to glance out of her upstairs bedroom. She was surprised to see Millie walking up and down the porch outside. She had on her blue checked dress and her little brown shawl was pinned around her shoulders. Mrs. Orrick was surprised, because there was no physical way Millie could be there!

Millie slept in a downstairs room that had no door to the porch. The only entrance was through Mrs. Orrick's bedroom. Curious, Mrs. Orrick spoke to her maid but received no response. Millie seemed entranced, staring toward a distant mountain range. Mrs. Orrick then assumed Millie may have heard some sound in the distance, possibly the roar of a cannon. She then stepped out onto the porch, only to find that the vision she had seen had vanished! Yet there was no place for Millie, if it was Millie, to go. She would have had to enter through Mrs. Orrick's bedroom. The mistress of the house, now thoroughly mystified, went to Millie's room downstairs, and found her, in her bedclothes, sound asleep!

When she asked Millie about the encounter the next morning, the maid seemed to know nothing about it.

Two days later, Mrs. Orrick went to meet her husband, who had obtained a furlough and was to see her beyond the enemy lines. Her carriage was hailed by Confederate soldiers who told her her husband had been shot. They took her to a house where he had been carried. He looked up, smiled, and then died.

Several months later, Millie again appeared to Mrs. Orrick, this time walking in the front yard. Mrs. Orrick checked downstairs and there was Millie, sound asleep. When Mrs. Orrick looked outside again, the vision had disappeared.

Less than 48 hours later, Mrs. Orrick's father was stricken with paralysis and passed away.

Years later, long after the Civil War, Mrs. Orrick had moved to Baltimore and lost contact with her former servant. Millie, it was believed, was still somewhere in Virginia. One night, as Mrs. Orrick lay on her bed in her Maryland house, the apparition of Millie materialized in her room, still wearing the same blue checked dress. Mrs. Orrick sat bolt upright.

The next night her mother was stricken with apoplexy and died!

Later, Mrs. Orrick learned that other members of her family had reported seeing Millie on occasion when she was known to be miles away. They said each time she appeared, it was just prior to a death or grave illness of someone close.

Mrs. Lee noted in her book, "The travelling of the astral is a well known phenomenon."

MIKE HARDY MENDS HIS WAY
(Portsmouth)

One of the more colorful, yet least substantiated stories told during the annual Ghost Walk each Halloween in Olde Towne Portsmouth pertains to a local resident who fought for the Confederates in the Civil War. His name was Mike Hardy, and he was a swaggering braggart who often boasted about how many Yankees he had killed during the fighting. He did admit, however, that one of those who had died at his hands did occasionally gnaw at his conscience. It was a young drummer boy he had shot in the back.

After the war Hardy returned to Portsmouth and lived, as one reporter later phrased it, "a life full of carousing and lechery." Some years later, as the tale goes, the crusty ex-Reb was passing by St. Paul's Church when he suddenly felt a strong compulsion to ask forgiveness for his past sins. As he knelt in the unfamiliar position of prayer, he was startled to hear a voice behind him say, "I have long forgiven you for what you did to me."

Hardy turned and came face to face with the ghost of the drummer boy. The lad told him, "Change your ways Mike Hardy, or you won't be able to go where I am now!" Then he vaporized.

Appropriately awed by this omen, Hardy became an "upstanding citizen." And long after, as he lay dying on his bed, his doctor asked him why he had no fear of death. Hardy only smiled, because it is said he saw the Yankee drummer boy in the corner of the room, waiting to take him away.

MILLING SOLDIERS AT MANNSFIELD
(Near Fredericksburg)

annsfield was built in 1749 by Mann Page, a member of the House of Burgesses, in Spotsylvania County a short distance from town at site that is now part of the Fredericksburg Country Club. It was a large two-story stone mansion which overlooked the Rappahannock River, and was known for its avenue and grove of "magnificent chestnut trees."

During the Civil War, the house was occupied by both Union and Confederate troops — at different times — and also served as a hospital and headquarters for both sides. According to most sources, Mannsfield was burned to the ground by Union forces at the close of the war, although one account states that some Confederate soldiers from Louisiana, in trying to light a campfire on the marbleized wood floor, accidently gutted the structure in 1863.

In the years after the Civil War, stories of sightings of ghostly figures in military uniforms milling around the grove of trees near the ruins of the house became so prevalent that many people refused to go near the place after dark. Mannsfield's century-old reputation as being haunted is largely attributable to a woman who moved near the burned out mansion probably sometime in the early 1890s. She was described as being "clear seeing," which today is interpreted as being a clairvoyant.

According to old timers in the area, she saw mostly Confederate soldiers walking about, sitting or lying in the shade of the trees. At times she viewed doctors ministering to the wounded, and orderlies holding horses. Reportedly, she often became quite frustrated when others couldn't see what she saw, although in later years some residents did tell of witnessing the movements of the apparitional troops among the estate's large trees. Mannsfield was such a pleasant setting that perhaps the soldier spirits wished to linger there in restful repose long after the heat of the battle had abated.

A PSYCHIC PROPHECY OR INTUITIVE GENIUS?
(Near Fredericksburg)

Did Robert E. Lee have a psychic premonition after the battle of the Wilderness in May 1864, or was he just intuitively gifted in military matters? The following was told by General John B. Gordon after the second day of fighting at the Wilderness: " . . . While riding over the field covered with the dead, General Lee indicated by the peculiar orders he gave me, his high estimate of General Grant's genius for war. He ordered me to move that night to Spotsylvania Courthouse.

"I asked if scouts had not reported that General Grant had suffered heavy losses and was preparing to retreat. Lee's laconic answer revealed his appreciation . . . of the character and ability of his great antagonist. 'Yes,' he replied, ' my scouts have brought me such reports; but General Grant will not retreat, sir; he will move to Spotsylvania Courthouse. That is his best manoeuvre and he will do what is best.' General Lee then added, 'I am so sure of it that I have had a short road cut to that point and you will move by that route.'

"This was Lee's prophecy. Its notable fulfillment was the arrival of Grant's troops at Spotsylvania almost simultaneously with the head of the Confederate column and the beginning of the great battle of Spotsylvania."

RESTLESS SOULS AT WAKE HILL
(Spotsylvania Court House)

That Lee got to Spotsylvania Court House first was critical. Historian Bruce Catton has written that the outcome of the war might depend on which army got there first. Catton called the site a "sleepy village . . . the whole place was as insignificant and as unknown to the world at large as Chickamauga and Antietam creeks had been a year or so earlier. Now the village was to take on a sinister and enduring fame . . . "

Of the fierce battle that was pitched here, in May 1864, Robert Stiles has written that at a specific location later known as the "Bloody Angle," "for an hour or so along the sides and base of that angle the musketry fire is said to have been heavier than it ever was at any other place in all the world, or for any other hour in all the tide of time. But for frequency and pertinacity of attack and repetition and constancy of repulse, I question if the left of General Lee's line on the 10th of May 1864, has ever been surpassed. I cannot pretend to identify the separate attacks or to distinguish between them, but should think there must have been at least a dozen of them. One marked feature was that while fresh troops poured to almost every charge, the same muskets in the hands of the same men met the first attack in the morning and the last at night; and so it was that the men, who in the early morning were so full of fight and fun that they leaped upon the breastworks and shouted to the retiring Federals to come a little closer the next time, as they did not care to go so far after the clothes and shoes and muskets, were so weary and worn and heavy at night that they could scarcely be roused to meet the charging enemy."

Despite the tremendous onslaught, the Confederates held. Grant's attack failed. Of the carnage in mangled bodies suffered here, one surgeon exclaimed, "It is a scene of horror such as I never saw. God forbid that I should ever see another."

Of the thousands of casualties, a few were buried, probably hastily, in a small cemetery in the rear of a house known as Wake Hill. The house itself was used as a makeshift hospital. There are no names on many of the tombstones, only initials and numbers.

Louise and Dave Lamond of Fredericksburg lived in Wake Hill a few years ago and experienced various forms of psychic activity which they believe was caused by the Civil War soldiers who fell nearby and were buried, virtually, in their backyard.

"It was a very scary house," Louise says. "Cabinets would open and shut of their own accord, and one room was always icy cold even in the heat of summer. Our dogs would growl at things we couldn't see." Heather Lamond was only about eight years old at the time, and she heard heavy footsteps, like boots, walking on the floor above her bedroom "almost every night."

The strangest occurrence of all, however, centered on the Lamond's cat, "BB Feet." Says Louise: "He went into a closet when we first moved into the house, and he wouldn't come out for anything. He stayed in the closet the whole time we lived there." The Lamonds lived at Wake Hill for two years!

ESCAPE FROM THE GRAVE
(Gaine's Mill, near Richmond)

he following is not a ghost-related incident, but it is a true account that rings of Edgar Allan Poe's most macabre tales. It is told by an anonymous soldier following fierce fighting at Gaine's Mill in June 1862.

"Though I was suffering fearfully from my wounds, for one bullet had gone through my shoulder and another passed in through my jaw, coming out through my neck, still I was fully conscious, but could not speak.

"There were plenty of dead around me, both Union and Rebel, and one stalwart Rebel rolled right across me in his death-agonies. I was powerless to throw him off. Soon the Rebel line advanced over us and formed just in front. This revived my spirits, for now, I thought, some humane person will see me. Strange how strong the desire of life, even in such moments!

"Darkness soon set in, the men stacked their arms and commenced to light fires and cook their suppers. In removing the dead bodies out of their way, they piled a number of them on top of us. I thought to cry out; but no, I couldn't, my tongue was swollen and my mouth was full of blood. I heard ambulances moving around, and the sound of spades as they interred their dead. Now, thought I, they will come to bury those around, and will assuredly see me.

I lay there, I don't know how long, and must have fainted, for the next thing I recollect was, feeling myself being dragged out of an ambulance, and the subject of the following conversation:

"'By _____, Simon, this fellow has a splendid pair of boots. I guess he won't grudge them to a fellow: he'll be warm enough without them.'

"So off go my boots. Simon then took a fancy to my coat, which was a new one, and fell at tugging it off.

"I was all this time like a man in a nightmare, striving to waken from some fearful danger, but couldn't. The writhing pain, caused by twisting my shattered arm, broke the spell, and I groaned.

"'By _____, the fellow is not dead yet; what will we do with him?' exclaimed the ruffian who had taken off my boots.

"'Well, you see,' said the other Rebel, who had finished with my coat, and let me fall back heavily, 'if he ain't dead, he soon will (be); so shove him in.'

"I turned around, tried to rise up, and held out my good hand towards him.

"'No, Simon, no; I'm damned if I bury any poor devil alive; let him have his chance; we'll leave him here.'

"'Well, as you choose; it would be only putting him out of pain to cover him in, or give him a crack in the sconce.'

"They soon covered up the pit and left me, forgetting to return the boots or coat. I lay there in the most fearful agony under the scorching sun all the following day; towards evening, fortunately, a kind doctor, going over the field, stood to examine my wounds, and then sent me to the hospital. It took me some time to come around, but you see I did; and with the exception of this hollow in my jaw and the loss of some teeth, I am not much the worse for being twice shot and nearly buried alive!"

A GHOSTLY PRACTICAL JOKE?

Chuck Ferebee of Yorktown wrote the author and said he had been at several Civil War reenactments around the state where participants had told him they felt strange presences on some battlefields.

Chuck also told of a practical joke gone awry at one reenactment two or three years ago. "One of the guys laid down on the ground and was buried in a pile of leaves at a small cemetery." Chuck remembers. "The idea was that when someone walked by, he was going to rise up out of the leaves and scare them. But before anything could happen the guy that was 'buried' started screaming himself, leaped up, and ran toward us. He was three shades of white and obviously terrified.

"He said while he was laying under the leaves, something 'cold' reached up and touched his face!"

* * * * * * * * * *

A BLOODY IMAGE IN THE CHURCH
(Sharpsburg, Maryland)

he bloodiest single day's fighting in the entire Civil War took place on September 17, 1862, at an unlikely site near the Potomac River known as Antietam, next to Sharpsburg, Maryland. Here, the Union army under General George McClellan lost more than 12,000 men in killed and wounded, and General Robert E. Lee's Confederates lost nearly as many. Historian Bruce Catton said of the intense battle, "Never before or after in all the war were so many men shot on one day."

Civil War reenactor Gene Priory, of Poquoson, Virginia, visited the site with his unit, the 6th Virginia, a few years ago to take part in a recreation of the fighting. On the day that they arrived at the site — a warm, sunny day — Gene walked off by himself at one point, near Dunker Church. "As I was walking," he remembers, "I suddenly stepped into a frigid cold spot. I was still in the sun, but it suddenly became icy cold. I got a chill up my spine. I walked on a few feet and apparently stepped out of the cold spot. Then I turned around and walked back into it."

Gene called some of his buddies over and asked them to walk where he had been. Then he asked them if they felt anything out of the ordinary. None did. When he told them what he had experienced, they laughed. But then they found a marker designating the exact location where the 32nd Virginia unit had marched on that fateful day in 1862. "As I stood there, I had the strangest sensation that I was standing exactly where some Confederate soldier had been killed," Gene says. "I had never had a feeling like that before."

Late that same day, Gene walked up to the old Dunker Church, around which some of the fiercest fighting had taken place. Some of his friends were already in the building. "The darndest thing happened as I went up to the front door," he adds. "It's kind of hard to put into words, but I got the strongest feeling that I wasn't supposed to go inside the church. I can't explain it, but it was almost like a force or something was trying to hold me back."

Gene said the feeling reminded him of a time when he was a child visiting his grandmother's farm. He said his grandmother had gone out to a well in the yard, looked down, and said she saw a doll burning in the bottom of the well. She said that she knew then her sister was dead. Soon after, they learned that his grandmother's sister had, in fact, died in a fire.

Gene walked into Dunker Church that day and immediately got a chilling cold feeling deep in his stomach. One of his friends, Billy Smith, was sitting in a chair over against a wall. When Gene looked at him, he began to tremble. "I looked over at Billy, and it appeared that blood was gushing out of the side of his head. He was covered with gore, as if he had just been shot in a battle. He was just sitting there staring at me. I was very shaken. I then got out of the church as quickly as I could. I guess Billy had seen me and he came out after me and asked me what was wrong. Of course, there was no blood on him whatsoever."

Gene did some research later and learned that the 32nd Virginia unit had fought in the vicinity of Dunker Church and had suffered 45 percent casualties. One officer commented on the bloodbath this way: "As the afternoon wore away . . . the fires of death were rekindled along the whole line." To this account, Major Rufus R. Dawes, of the 6th Wisconsin, added: "A long and steady line of Rebel gray . . . comes sweeping down through the woods around the church. They raise the yell and fire. It is like a scythe running through our line."

That same evening, Gene Priory went back to the place where he had experienced the cold spot, and he felt it again. This time he noticed that this was the only patch of ground around that was covered with green flowing moss which reflected light at night.

"I'm convinced someone must have been killed right there," he says, "and his spirit must still be there!"

* * * * * * * * * *

THE SENTRY WITH NO FEET
(Fort Harrison, near Richmond)

Bill Jackson of Richmond is an active Civil War reenactor with the 23rd Virginia. During the 130th reenactment of the Battle of Sailor's Creek, on April 8, 1995, (for the record, the actual battle took place on April 6, 1865) Bill told the author the following account:

"A few years ago I was at a campout at Fort Harrison (a few miles east of Richmond near Varina). It was at dusk, and another fellow and I were out walking over the ground. It was on the anniversary of a battle that had taken place there in 1864. Anyway, there was an eerie ground fog, and both of us, suddenly, smelled a very distinct acrid odor. The closest I can describe it would be like the smell of rotten eggs.

"Then we looked up, and there, on the parapet above, was a florescent figure; the whitish outline of a soldier. It was hazy, but it as a definite human form. And then we both noticed that the image faded below the knees. It had no feet! We figured it was a sentry walking his post. But he didn't seem to be walking. It was more like he was *floating*!

"We watched him for a few seconds, and then one of us stepped on a twig, making a snapping sound. With that, the apparitional sentry vanished from sight. I never much thought about ghosts, but when that happened, I became a believer very quickly!"

CHAPTER 10

A Psychic Premonition in the Parlor

(Somewhere in the Shenandoah Valley)

(Author's note: Though the details of the following supernatural account have been lost in time, the legend has been faithfully passed down by members of the Donnely family, whose ancestors farmed in the valley during the 19th century. This experience was recorded by Elizabeth Proctor Biggs in her 1978 book, "Beyond the Limit of Our Sight," and in subsequent newspaper reports, and is hereby recounted.)

Bridget Donnely and Gabriel Shenk had known each other since their childhood in the 1850s. They were married in 1863, but were soon separated by the war. A Confederate soldier, Gabriel was wounded in battle and sent to a military hospital near Staunton. It was there that he learned his young bride was pregnant. He was soon after returned to duty, was subsequently captured and taken to that most dreaded of Federal prisons, Fort Delaware. There, already in a weakened state from his previous wounds, he contracted small pox and lay "gravely ill."

All this was unbeknownst to Bridget and the Donnelys at the farm in Virginia. There, as she awaited the birth of her child, Bridget one day in June 1864, stood transfixed before the locked entrance to the parlor, a room that had been shut off and was unused during the war years. For some inexplicable reason, she felt compelled to enter the parlor where she and Gabriel had exchanged their vows. She got the key from her mother and entered. Once inside, she began crying, "her eyes shut tight against some yet unrevealed sorrow."

When she opened her eyes, they seemed drawn to an old marble-topped table which had served as the altar for her wedding. She perceived a faint glow coming from the table. She walked closer, and there she stared, unbelieving, at a pointed taper "fixed lightly on an exquisite saucer she had never before seen." The tiny flame burned steadily, *but no wax melted or ran down the taper*! (The family, for some unexpressed reason, always used the term taper, and never candle.) Bridget stared at the light perplexed. How could a taper be lighted in a room that no one had entered for some time? Who had put it there, and why? Why was the wax not melting? Where had the strange saucer come from? Bridget could not answer any of these questions, but she later said the atmosphere in the parlor felt "seemingly vibrant with a presence she could not see."

Trembling with emotion, she backed out of the room, told her mother of what she had seen, and they both reentered the parlor. Bridget's mother saw the burning taper, too, and felt "an unearthliness about her but nothing ominous; rather, the sense of 'smiling' somehow accompanied the rosy, slender flame." Again, the questions arose. No one else had access to the room. Together, the two women felt an instinctive chill as they left the parlor.

That afternoon, Bridget reentered the room. As author Biggs described it, "She opened the door upon a musty darkness no longer penetrated by the mystical glow of an uncannily burning taper in a fragile saucer. It was as if an invisible hand had removed all evidence of the scene, restoring the musty scent of total enclosure, every speck of finest dust, and the hollowness of solitude to the room." According to Donnely descendents, Bridget then whispered, "Goodbye. Goodbye," and left.

Ten days later word came from some Virginia prisoners recently released from Fort Delaware, that Gabriel had died of disease and neglect — on the exact day and time that Bridget had entered the parlor and witnessed the burning taper!

Upon hearing the news, Bridget was said to have shrieked from pent-up anxiety. She lifted her hands to her head and pressed her fingers into her scalp in utter anguish. That night she gave birth to a baby girl. Upon its scalp on each side, through the dark, silky hair, were the clear imprints of ten perfectly formed finger marks!

* * * * * * * * * *

The child who was born that night in June 1864, grew up to be Mrs. Rebecca Kirkpatrick, a woman who 80 years later demonstrated "psychic qualities" similar to those which surrounded her birth. She was then, in the 1940s, spending the summer with her daughter, Hannah, at Hannah's home in the valley. Mrs. Kirkpatrick always read herself to sleep at night; the light in her bedroom stayed on until well past midnight. One evening, however, when Hannah and her husband came home at about 9:30 p.m., her mother's bedroom was dark.

Hannah went up to check. Her mother said she had been "distracted," and had not been able to concentrate. She then asked about Hannah's sister, Anna, who lived in Baltimore. Hannah said that as far as she know, Anna was fine. She had talked to her by phone recently.

Early the next morning, word came by telephone that Anna had died in her sleep the previous night. When Hannah approached her mother to tell her, Mrs. Kirkpatrick said, "I know something has happened." She then told Hannah of an ethereal experience she had had the previous evening. She said she had been reading, when, at half past nine, she felt a distinct chill. She looked up and saw an apparition of Anna. She was standing at the foot of Mrs. Kirkpatrick's bed. She smiled, but said nothing. She was wearing, a gray dress with ruffles at the neck and wrists. "I know it sounds strange, but she held a deep red American Beauty rose, in her right hand," Mrs. Kirkpatrick said. "I started to call her name and she just vanished."

Hannah then went on to tell her mother than Anna had died in the night.

At the funeral service, Mrs. Kirkpatrick viewed her deceased daughter in the casket. She was enshrouded in a *gray dress with ruffles at the neck and at the wrists*! Her right arm lay across the body, and cupped in her hand was *a deep red American Beauty rose*! Anna had died, the medical examiner estimated, at *9:30 the previous evening*!

CHAPTER 11

The Ghost With Stonewall Jackson's Arm

(Richmond)

Curious Item Number 1

Quote from a Confederate officer who served with Thomas J. "Stonewall" Jackson: "Crowds were continually hanging round his headquarters, and peeping through the windows, as if anxious to catch him at his 'incantations.' Others, again, actually thought that he was continually praying, and imagined that angelic spirits were his companions and counsellors . . . and many began to think (of) him (as) supernatural."

Curious Item Number 2

Quote from Civil War author E. A. Pollard: ". . . When he (Jackson) made his terrible wintry march in 1861-62, from Winchester to Bath and Romney . . . it was actually reported that he was insane. A colonel came to Richmond with the report that Jackson had gone mad; that his mania was that a *familiar spirit* had taken possession of a portion of his body; and that he was in the habit of walking by himself and holding audible conversations with *a mysterious being*!"

With the exception of the final surrender at Appomattox, it probably was the saddest day in the history of the "Lost Cause." It was Sunday May 10, 1863 — the day General Thomas J. Stonewall Jackson died. The entire

Stonewall Jackson statue at the Manassas National Battlefield Park.

South mourned, and it is arguable that the hopes of a Confederate victory died with him. For without him, Robert E. Lee marched northward two months later to Gettysburg, and the tide of the war turned. There are those who contend that had Lee had Jackson in Pennsylvania, things might have been   different.

Jackson was mortally wounded during the battle of Chancellorsville — by his own men! On the evening of May 2, Jackson and members of his staff rode out past the Rebel lines on a reconnaissance mission to assess the location and strength of the enemy. Sometime after 9 p.m. on the moonlit night, the party rode back towards the southern position, but they were mistaken for Yankee cavalry and fired upon. Two officers were killed, and Jackson was struck by three balls: one broke two fingers on his right hand; one went through his left forearm; and the third shattered his left arm near the shoulder.

As Jackson lay in shock, the enemy began shelling the area with artillery fire. Captain James Power Smith was one of the first to reach the wounded general. He described the attack thusly: "Great broadsides thundered over the woods; hissing shells searched the dark thickets through, and shrapnel swept the road along which we moved. . . over us swept the rapid fire of shot and shell — grape-shot striking fire upon the flinty rock of the road all around us, and sweeping from their feet horses and men of the artillery just moved to the front. Twice, as men tried to rush Jackson to safety, litter bearers were felled by the raking fire, and Jackson was thrown to the ground with a groan of deep pain. Greatly alarmed, I sprang to his head, and, lifting his head as a stray beam of moonlight came through clouds and leaves, he opened his eyes and wearily said: 'Never mind me, captain, never mind me'." He then gave his last command on the battlefield, telling Brigadier General Pender, "you must hold your ground, sir."

Biographer R. L. Dabney, who served on his staff, and wrote about the life and campaigns of Jackson in 1866, added: "While General Jackson lay bleeding upon the ground, he displayed several traits very characteristic of his nature. Amidst all his sufferings, he was absolutely uncomplaining; save when his agonizing fall wrung a groan from his breast. It was only in answer to the questions of his friends, that he said, 'I believe my arm is broken,' and, 'It gives me severe pain;' but this was uttered in a tone perfectly calm and self possessed. . . When he was asked whether his right hand should not also be bound up, he replied: 'No, never mind; it is a trifle.' Yet two of the bones were broken and the palm was almost perforated by the bullet!"

Jackson immediately asked for his surgeon of the corps, and by now his close friend, Dr. Hunter McGuire, a native of Winchester, and a much gifted medical practitioner then in his mid-twenties, who had spurned offers of promotion to remain with "his" general. McGuire and his associates were convinced, after examining the whole extent of Jackson's injuries, that his left arm should be removed as soon as possible. They explained this to the general. "Dr. McGuire," he answered, "do for me what you think best; I am resigned to whatever is necessary."

It was then that, as biographer Dabney, of the Union Theological Seminary in Richmond, wrote: "Dr. McGuire, with a steady and deliberate hand, severed the mangled limb from the shoulder. . . The general seemed insensitive to pain."

Sometime shortly after the operation chaplain Tucker Lacy went to the tent where Jackson lay, saw the stump where the left arm had been, and remarked, "Oh, general, what a calamity." Jackson then lectured Lacy. "You see me severely wounded," he said, "but not depressed; not unhappy. I believe that it has been done according to God's holy will, and I will acquiesce entirely in

AN EVIL OMEN

There is an interesting footnote to the wounding and death of Stonewall Jackson. It was offered, 24 years later, by A. L. Long, who served as military secretary to Robert E. Lee, and afterwards as a brigadier general with the 2nd Corps. Long was with Jackson at Chancellorsville on the morning of May 2, 1863, the day of the fateful wounding. Here is what Long wrote, in 1887:

" . . . Jackson was the first to rise from the bivouac . . . and observing a staff officer (General W. N. Pendleton) without cover, he spread over him his own overcoat. The morning being chilly, he drew near a small fire that had been kindled by a courier, and the writer (Long), who soon after sought the same place, found him seated on a cracker-box. He complained of the cold, and as the cooks were preparing breakfast, I managed to procure him a cup of hot coffee, which by good fortune our cook was able to provide.

"While we were still talking, the general's sword, which was leaning against a tree, without *apparent* cause, fell with a clank to the ground. I picked it up and handed it to him. He thanked me and buckled it on. It was now about dawn; the troops were on the march and our bivouac was all astir. After a few words with General Lee, he mounted his horse and rode off. This was the last meeting of Lee and Jackson.

"I have spoken of the falling of Jackson's sword, because it strongly impressed me at the time as an omen of evil — an indefinable superstition such as sometimes affects persons on the falling of a picture or a mirror. This feeling haunted me the whole day, and when the tidings of Jackson's wound reached my ears it was without surprise that I heard this unfortunate confirmation of the superstitious fears with which I had been so oppressed."

it. You may think it strange; but you never saw me more perfectly contented than I am today." He added that he didn't look upon his loss as a calamity, and, although it would be a great inconvenience, Jackson said he would be happy to wait until God revealed to him the reason for the event.

As Lacy was leaving the tent, he saw the amputated arm wrapped up. Because it was feared that ghoulish souvenir hunters might be on the prowl, (Southerners treated objects associated with the wounding and death of Jackson as "sacred relics"), Lacy took the arm to the family burying ground of Major J. H. Lacy's home site at Ellwood, near Jackson's last battlefield.

When Robert E. Lee heard of Jackson's wounds, he immediately fired off a dispatch: "General: I have received your note, informing me that you are wounded. I cannot express my regret at the occurrence. Could I have directed events, I should have chosen, for the good of the country, to have been disabled in your stead." When Captain Smith read the message to Jackson, he replied: General Lee is very kind, but he should give the praise to God."

Lee also said, "He has lost his left arm; but I have lost my right arm."

Jackson appeared to have survived the amputation and his other wounds in reasonably good shape, and he was taken in a field ambulance about 25 miles to the Thomas C. Chandler house near Guinea Station to convalesce. Dr. McGuire accompanied him. When the main house was found to be full of refugees and wounded soldiers, the general was placed in the Chandler's adjacent small office building.

While Jackson lay in bed, apparently on the road to recovery, he had what may have been an ethereal revelation. At one point he said, speaking of his amputation, "I have always thought it wrong to administer chloroform, in cases where there is a probability of immediate death." (He had been given chloroform during his operation.) "But it was, I think, the most delightful physical sensation I ever enjoyed. I had enough consciousness to know what was doing; and at one time I heard the most delightful music that ever greeted my ears. I believe it was the sawing of the bone.

"But I should dislike above all things, to enter eternity in such a condition." This statement is subject to more than one interpretation. It could have meant, as Dabney wrote, "that he would not wish to be ushered into that spiritual existence, from the midst of sensations so thoroughly physical and illusory." However, it is possible he was saying, in a way, that if he died and "went on," he wished he could do so with his severed arm intact.

It is known that as Dr. McGuire was dressing his wounds one day, Jackson asked a curious question. Biographer Lenoir Chambers wrote: "He turned upon the doctor with a question as to whether people whose bodily afflictions had been healed by Jesus would ever suffer again from the same affliction. . . The general felt strongly that once such a person was healed, he would never again suffer in the same way."

Despite the careful and constant attention of the medical team — Dr. McGuire himself got practically no sleep for three straight days and nights — Jackson, who at first appeared to have survived his wounds in good condition, slowly began to deteriorate. Apparently, when he had been flung to the ground in the litter basket, it had caused fatal damage which at first was not obvious. Dr.

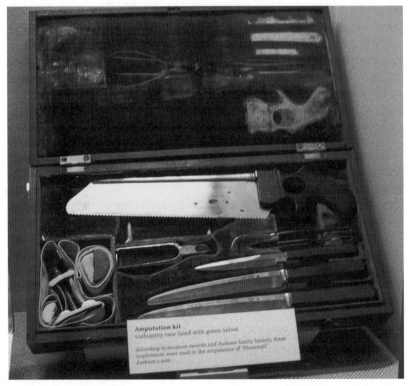

Saw and equipment used by Dr. Hunter McGuire to amputate left arm of Stonewall Jackson, in display case at the Museum of the Confederacy in Richmond. (Photo taken with permission of the museum.)

McGuire, in his report, wrote: "Contusion of the lung, with extrava-sation of blood in his chest, was probably produced by the fall referred to, and shock and loss of blood, prevented any ill effects until reaction had been well established, and then inflammation ensued."

As the days passed, Jackson's wife, Anna, was sent for. On see-ing him, she noted, "His condition had changed rapidly and was now approaching crisis." He was developing pneumonia. Even as his strength weakened, the general believed he would pull through. He felt strongly that his mission on earth had not been completed. "I am sure," he said, "that my Heavenly Father designs this afflic-tion for my good. I am perfectly satisfied, that either in this life, or in that which is to come, I will discover that what is now regarded as a calamity, is a blessing. . . I can wait, until God, in his own time, shall make known to me the object he has in thus afflicting me."

Even under the most darkened circumstances, Jackson's rock-hard faith sustained him. He at first thought he might die of his wounds on the battlefield, and at that time said he had given him-self up into the hands of his Heavenly Father without a fear. As Dabney reported: "He declared that he was in possession of a per-fect peace, while thus expecting immediate death. 'It has been' Jackson said, 'a precious experience to me, that I was brought face to face with death, and found all was well'."

Despite his iron resolve, however, Jackson continued to slip. Yet even as he approached death's door, he said, "I am not afraid to die; I am willing to abide by the will of my Heavenly Father. But I do not believe that I shall die at this time; I am persuaded the Almighty has yet a work for me to perform."

It was not to be. As Captain Smith later recorded: . . . "At 3:15 p.m. on the quiet of the Sabbath afternoon, May 10th, 1863, he raised himself from his bed, saying, 'No, no, let us pass over the river, and rest under the shade of the trees;' and, falling again to his pillow, he passed away, 'over the river, where, in a land where warfare is not known or feared, he rests forever, under the trees'."

Of Jackson's final words, Dabney asked: "Was his soul wander-ing back in dreams to the river of his beloved valley, the Shenandoah, (the 'river of sparkling waters,') whose verdant meads and groves he had redeemed from the invader, and across whose floods he had so often won his passage through the toils of battle? Or was he reaching forward across the River of Death, to the gold-en streets of the Celestial City, and the trees whose leaves are for the healing of the nations? It was to these that God was bringing him, through his last battle and victory; and under their shade he walks with the blessed company of the redeemed."

Dabney eloquently wrote of the aftershock of Jackson's death. "In a few hours the electric telegraph had conveyed the news to all the Confederate States; and to every heart it came as a chilling shock. All over the land, hundreds of miles away from the regions which he had illustrated by his prowess, the people who had never seen his face, grieved for him as men grieve for their nearest kindred. Other countries and ages may have witnessed such a national sorrow; but the men of this generation never saw so profound and universal grief as that which throbbed in the heart of the Confederate people at the death of Jackson."

Jackson's body was taken to Richmond, where it lay in state in the hall of the lower house of congress in the Capitol building, and where, as one historian put it, "No such homage was ever paid to an American. Businesses in the city were closed for the day and thousands of citizens filed past his casket to pay their last respects.

At the end of the day, as the doors were closing, Dabney tells of a compelling and poignant incident which reflected the deep feelings of all: "Just then, a mutilated veteran from Jackson's old division, was seen anxiously pressing through the crowd, to take his last look at the face of his beloved leader. They told him that he was too late, that they were already closing up the coffin for the last time, and that the order had been given to clear the hall. He still struggled forward, refusing to take a denial, until one of the Marshalls of the day was about to exercise his authority to force him back. Upon this, the old soldier lifted the stump of his right arm toward the heavens, and with tears running down his bearded face, exclaimed: "By this arm, which I lost for my country, I demand the privilege of seeing my General once more.' Such an appeal as this was irresistible; and at the instance of the Governor of the Commonwealth, the pomp was arrested until this humble comrade had also dropped his tear upon the face of his dead leader."

Jackson was then taken to his home at Lexington, where, "with full military honors," he was committed, minus his left arm, to a grave on the smooth crests of a hill that commanded "a full view of all the smiling landscape, and of the grand ramparts of mountains in which it is encircled."

In a Virginia Cavalcade article written a few years ago, it was said that "Two years later (1865) the Federal invaders would come to Lexington. They would desolate the Valley, burn the Institute (the Virginia Military Institute), and seize the mountain ramparts.

But they would show a proper respect for a fallen foe. They would leave the grave of 'Stonewall' Jackson unmolested."

There is no record, documentation, report of a sighting, or even a legend of Jackson's ghost returning — at Chancellorsville, Guinea Station, Lexington, or anywhere else. He was, as evidenced, completely at peace with his Maker. There are, however, a number of separate accounts of the spectral return of the man who amputated his arm — Dr. Hunter McGuire — and in at least one reported vision, he has been seen carrying the severed arm!

Dr. McGuire, tall at six feet three inches, and exceedingly handsome, went on to consummate a long and distinguished career. He was a pioneer in the use of chloroform and a promoter of antiseptic surgery. He helped found the Retreat for the Sick, a charity hospital, and after the Civil War taught surgery at the Medical College of Virginia without pay for more than 15 years. He was so well respected that today one can view a seated bronze statue of Dr. McGuire in the Capitol Square in Richmond.

Early in the year 1900, he was taken ill and rushed back to the house he lived in for many years, on the grounds of the Union Theological Seminary. There he diagnosed his own affliction. He could not speak, but, as doctors assembled, he tapped the left side of his head with his finger. He was telling them, in his own way, that he had an embolism of the brain which had paralyzed his right arm and leg. He died six months later at age 65.

His spirit, however, seems to have remained, as there have been "numerous soundings of McGuire's ghost" in an around the house. According to an article written by W. Sibley Towner, Professor of Biblical Interpretation, "One UTS (Seminary) alumnus reports that as a student resident of Westwood House (where McGuire lived) back in the late 1940s, he and his toy shepherd encountered the ghost while they were walking on the grounds. The dog put up quite a fuss. Our friend heard a sword clanking and assumed the ghost was dressed in full Confederate uniform, but there was no sighting. Nor have the current neighbors sighted the ghost, even though they see the chairs rocking on the front porch of Westwood House and hear creaks in the walls at night.

"But dogs see it. That's right, friends! We've got a ghost visible only to dogs. German shepherds, toy shepherds, labradors, mutts — it makes no difference. They all see him and by all reports, they whine and whimper and their hair stands on end."

The student who heard the sounds of the phantom at the McGuire House, was James Luthur Mays, a former faculty member

House of Dr. Hunter McGuire, on the grounds of the Union Theological Seminary, Richmond.

at the Seminary. He and his wife, Mary, were residents at the house in the mid-1940s. "At that time," he recalls, "the surroundings here were still very rural. There were lots of trees, and the house was actually kind of isolated.

"When we first moved in, we were told stories about the appearance of an apparition which would materialize at the head of the stairs. We never saw or experienced this, however. But I can tell you that we did experience something very strange in front of the house. We had a little toy shepherd. We would let him out to run in the evening. Sometime, I guess it was in 1946, or 1947, the dog would go out and then come racing back to the front door with its hackles up. It obviously had been frightened by something.

"Mary and I would go out to look, but we never saw anything. But on two or three different occasions we did *hear* something. It was the sound of someone on a horse, slowly walking on a gravel road by the house. We heard the creaking of a saddle and the clinking of something, like maybe a sword.

"When this happened, the curious thing was our dog. As the sound moved, the shepherd would move its head around following it, as if the dog could *see* the rider. It would growl and bark. The great puzzle to us was that we could clearly hear the sounds, but we couldn't see anything. Apparently, Dr. McGuire must have had

Statue of Dr. Hunter McGuire, Capitol Park, Richmond.

a favorite horse he liked to ride around the grounds."

There is one account, too, according to Seminary librarian John Trotty, that a painter once experienced a haunting presence at the house. The painter claimed he was pushed off his ladder one day by unseen hands, although Trotty is not sure of the reliability of this episode. Perhaps Dr. McGuire didn't like the color of paint being applied to his residence.

The best documented ghostly encounter was reported in a 1942 article in The Reader's Digest by Archibald Rutledge. The source was a lady in Illinois who wrote the following: "My mother went with my sister to live in Richmond, Virginia, while my brother was studying there for the ministry. They rented a large, rambling old house. During the two years of her residence in this house there frequently appeared before my mother an officer of the Confederate army whose left sleeve had a band of crepe on it.

"She told my brother and sister of seeing this figure, but they teased her about it. Later she told me, because I was a more sympathetic listener. She said that one day, tiring of his repeated appearance, she remarked to him as if he were human, 'Oh why do you bother me so? I wish you would go away and leave me alone.' He looked up at her, sadly shook his head, vanished out the dining-room door, and never returned.

"Several months later, in some museum or art gallery, my sister was looking over the catalogue. Suddenly she said to my mother, 'Here is a picture of your ghost.' My mother's description of the apparition had been so accurate that my sister had recognized it immediately; and there, too, on the left sleeve was the band of crepe. The catalogue said that the soldier in the picture was Dr. Hunter Holmes McGuire.

"Later in the day they told the whole story to their hostess at a luncheon, and this lady said, 'Why, don't you know who Dr. McGuire was?' Mother declared that she had never before seen his picture or heard of him.

"'Well,' said her hostess, 'he was a surgeon in the Civil War. He attended Stonewall Jackson when the latter was mortally wounded. The crepe band covers a spot of Jackson's blood. Dr. McGuire remarked that since an officer must have a spotless uniform, he covered his beloved general's blood. The house you are living in was built and lived in by Dr. McGuire'!"

And, finally, there are still persistent rumors that the ghost of Dr. McGuire has been seen, allegedly by several witnesses, *carrying the arm of Stonewall Jackson*! Towner, in his article, disclaims such sightings, saying, "We all know that it was buried at Ellwood, near Guinea Station, by the Presbyterian preacher Beverly Tucker Lacy."

But one may wonder. One may refer back to a possible interpretation of the remarks that Jackson made upon his death bed about wanting to enter the beyond as a whole person, and that if one had been once afflicted with a certain injury, wasn't it probable that he would never again suffer a like injury. Was he somehow referring to his desire to be reunited with his severed arm? And if so, is his loyal servant, Dr. Hunter McGuire trying, in spirit form, to accomplish this last mission for his fallen leader?

* * * * * * * * * *

METHOD IN JACKSON'S MADNESS
(Malvern Hill, Charles City County)

he Battle of Malvern Hill, which took place on July 1, 1862, was one of the bloodiest in the entire Civil War. Thousands of Confederate soldiers, charging up the hill against a solid row of artillery, and a well-armed and protected Union infantry, were cut to pieces during the ill-advised assault. While, strangely, there are no ghosts heard haunting the sacred grounds where the men fell, there is an interesting anecdote that gives a good read into the brilliant military psyche of General Thomas "Stonewall" Jackson.

It is said that after this battle it took several hours to remove the wounded and collect the slain Southerners. Jackson, generally absorbed in planning and strategy, took an inordinate amount of time to personally help clear the fields. This was considered unusual. It aroused the curiosity of Lt. Colonel W. W. Blackford, CSA, who later wrote about the incident. The account was published in a book a half century ago.

"He (Jackson) had the bodies laid side by side in rows, numbering from a dozen to 40 or 50, according to convenience to the places they occupied, and he then had their blankets and oil-cloths spread over the rows, concealing their faces and figures completely. After this was done he had their muskets and accoutrements collected and laid in piles in gullies so as to be out of sight; then, not satisfied with this, he made the men pick up every scrap of clothing and caps, and every piece of human flesh scattered around, such as legs and arms, etc.

"I had heard that 'Old Stonewall' was eccentric, and indeed at that time some who disliked him said he was unsound in his mind; and I thought this attention to cleaning up the battlefield was an evidence of it. Still, he evidently had a motive and to him an urgent one. There was nothing idle or objectless in the way he acted, but on the contrary, the intense vigor and sharpness of his commands, as he trotted incessantly about in every direction among the working parties, so hurried them that the men omitted even to rifle the pockets of the slain, venting their feelings at this loss of opportunity in suppressed curses . . .

"My curiosity was aroused, and I determined to watch for an opportunity to ask him his reasons. Stonewall Jackson was very pleasant and agreeable when he chose to be so and when his mind was at ease, but he was not the man to talk to when he was busy, by any manner of means . . . After a while even he could find nothing more to pick up, and the field certainly did look very differently, the dark bloodstains, soaking the ground, alone marked the numbers who had fallen. The number of the dead now appeared very much less. There did not appear to be one in ten since they were collected together. Jackson had swept his dust into piles, like a good housewife, and the floor looked clean though the piles were still there.

"When at last he became quiet and disposed to talk, I asked him why he was having the field cleaned in that way. 'Why,' said he, 'I am going to attack here presently, as soon as the fog rises, and it won't do to march the troops over their own dead, you know; that's what I am doing it for.'

"Then, I thought to myself, it you are crazy there is surely 'method in your madness,' for it would have been a most demoralizing preparation for battle for men to have marched over the field as I first saw it that morning."

A MOST CURIOUS COINCIDENCE!

Who shot Stonewall Jackson? That question has endured for more than a century and a quarter. No one is sure, although experts believe the fatal firing may have come from Company E of the 18th North Carolina. A young lieutenant gave the order to fire as Jackson and his party were returning to the Confederate lines after a reconnaissance excursion. This lieutenant believed it was his men, following his order, that led to Jackson's death. He suffered anguish over this belief for the rest of his life.

His name was George W. *Corbett*.

As you read on, in chapter 33, there is a reference to the man who allegedly shot and killed John Wilkes Booth, Lincoln's assassin, in a barn in Caroline County.

His name was Boston *Corbett*!

CHAPTER 12

The Guest Ghost in Room 403

(Abingdon)

t the southern end of western Virginia's chain of valleys, bordering the Tennessee line, Washington County was formed in 1776, and it is the first locality in the United States known to have been named for George Washington. The county seat is Abingdon, a few miles northeast of Bristol. The town's rich historic district extends along Main Street, and, says the Virginia Landmarks Register, Abingdon "is unusual for its large quantity of federal and antebellum buildings of brick, which serve to give the district an air of permanence and prosperity lacking in similar settlements containing mostly wooden buildings." Confederate General Joseph E. Johnston, and no less than three Virginia governors lived in Abingdon.

General Francis Preston built one of the largest houses in the Commonwealth here in the 1830s. This was later converted to Martha Washington College for girls, and is now the famous Martha Washington Inn. It is a four-star, four-diamond hotel adorned with antiques and period furniture that serves, in addition to champagne brunches, complimentary tea and crumpets on the scenic veranda. The dining room features such traditional dishes as Virginia country ham and hot spoonbread.

This venerable old inn, steeped in southern custom and old fashioned, pamper-the-guest service, also is host to a variety of spectral activity. In fact, it may well be one of Virginia's most haunted edifices. If not, it certainly is one of the most discussed and written about. Most of the active psychic phenomena here swirls around incidents which occurred during the Civil War.

There is, for example, an alleged apparitional horse which sometimes roams the grounds on moonless nights, seeking its rider, a Union officer who was shot down in front of the college in 1864. There, too, is the touching saga of a young Confederate soldier who raced into the Martha Washington Inn one day to warn of approaching Federal troops. He ran up the spiral stairway just as his pursuers broke down the front door. From the top of the stairs, it is said that he felled seven men before he was mortally wounded and bled to death in the arms of one of the student nurses outside the door of the governor's suite.

The legend is his bloodstains could never be washed away, and still can be seen under the carpeting. "It's a strange thing about that spot in the carpet," says Pete Sheffey, a bellhop who has worked at the hotel for more than 30 years. Every time new carpet was put down, it seemed like a hole would somehow appear where the young Confederate soldier had fallen. "I can remember my grandfather talking about it back in the 1930s," Pete says. "He saw the blood stains then, and he said every time they covered it up, a hole would show through at that spot. I think they have replaced the carpet there six or seven times since 1937. No one could ever explain why that happened."

Pete says many hotel workers have experienced various forms of otherworldly manifestations over the years. "There were old slave quarters here on the grounds, and I've been told that some of the slaves were buried under the hotel and even in the walls of the old quarters. I don't know if that means anything, but I can tell you a lot of peculiar things have happened here." Steffey's grandfather said he once encountered the spirit of a Confederate soldier while walking down a long, darkened corridor one night more than 50 years ago. "He said the man had on a gray uniform and that part of one leg had been shot off."

A number of employees have reported seeing wispy figures "floating around." Maids have entered certain rooms and walked into inexplicable icy cold spots, even in the middle of summer. Others have seen door knobs turning when no one was outside the door. A housekeeper said she once encountered a "smoky-like object" at 6:30 in the morning as she sat in the lounge. Stunned into silence, she watched as it drifted across the room and then headed toward the door and vanished. Desk clerks have seen a similar figure appear and then disappear in the lobby during the pre-dawn

Martha Washington Inn

hours. Others have seen apparitions ascending and descending the stairs, and one woman screamed one night when she said she woke up and "something" was hovering over her in bed.

It is an old building, Pete Sheffey points out. "There are a lot of long hallways and high ceilings and creaking stairs and the such. But too many things have happened here to dismiss them all as being the settling sounds of an old hotel," he says. "I've seen what I could call 'flashes' myself, like someone or something was passing by you and you just caught a sidelong glimpse of it. But when you turned around, there was nothing there."

Of all the episodes at the Martha Washington Inn, however, perhaps none is more intriguing, or more romantic for that matter, than the periodic appearance of a lovely young lady named Beth, who infrequently returns to room 403 to care for the handsome young man who died there more than 130 years ago! She was a student at the college in early 1863 — a time when part of the school had been turned into a hospital to tend grievously wounded soldiers.

One of these was John Stoves. He had been brought in one day, half shot full of musket balls, and placed in what is now room 403.

Beth changed his bandages and comforted him as best she could. When Stoves learned that she could play the violin, he asked her to do so. She happily obliged, and although he was suffering from severe pain, her playing seemed to put him at ease. He would fall asleep listening to her. As the young officer slipped ever closer to the "other side," Beth, it is said, fell in love with him.

One day she was summoned to come to the room quickly. Lying near death, he smiled and asked her to play her violin for him. As she did, he closed his eyes and passed on. She grabbed his hand and cried. She never got over the shock and within a few weeks she, too, was dead. Some said of complications from typhoid fever. Other said of a broken heart.

Ever since that time there has been a haunting presence that has kind of enveloped room 403. A security guard at the inn recalls one night when making his rounds, he passed a milky-like figure with long flowing hair on the stairway. He asked if he could help her. She did not reply. She instead seemed to glide up the stairs and then she went *through* the door to that room! Maids have told of seeing the wraith of a slim young girl sitting in a chair by the bed. Others say that in the late hours of the night they have sometimes heard the soft wafting refrains of a violin being played.

* * * * * * * * * *

In the past year some additional spectral activity has occurred at the Inn. The account surfaced in a recent newspaper article in which Pete Sheffey was interviewed. Here is what he said: "About two months ago I had to go in the Virginia Suite to get a TV remote control for another room . . . and when I put my key in the door to open it, it felt like something was holding the door shut. I'm a big strong man, and it felt like something was pushing against the door. When I stepped in the room, something touched me on the face, sort of like a light slap, you know. I thought it must be somebody behind me, but when I turned around there was nobody there. It really scared me. I started out toward the hall and it felt like something was following me, and I thought it was Beth (the ghost of the Civil War), and I said, 'Beth — God loves you! God loves you, Beth!' And it felt like I was pushed out the door!"

Sheffey also tells of another incident. "There was a security guard on patrol down near the First Lady's Table (the dining room) last February (1994)," he said. "He was walking down the hallway about 4 a.m., and passed a woman dressed in a bonnet, long apron dress, and high-button shoes, and she streaked past him. He turned and said, 'Ma'am, may I help you?' She kept walking, and he said it again, but then she just turned into a swirl of some sort and took off toward the staircase." Sheffey said the guard followed 'her' up the steps and saw a 'whitish vapor' go through the door of a room.

It was room 403!

CHAPTER 13

The Winged Harbinger of Doom

(Chesterfield County)

On the morning of April 3, 1865, shortly before the final meeting at Appomattox, General Robert E. Lee, along with General Longstreet and their staffs, were at Summit, a small village about 20 miles from Richmond and adjacent to Clover Hill in Chesterfield County — the ancestral home of the Cox family. Hearing of Lee's proximity, Judge James H. Cox dispatched a messenger to invite the Confederate leaders to a noon-day meal.

Upon Lee's arrival, Judge Cox's daughter, saying "the uppermost thing in her mind," told the general, "We shall gain the cause. You will join General Johnston and together you will be victorious." Whereupon Lee smiled and commented, "Whatever happens, know this, that no men ever fought better than those who have stood by me."

Kate Virginia Cox remembered, too, that Lee drank ice water while the others indulged in mint juleps, and that after an "abundant dinner (for the best of everything that was left was brought out in honor of the general"), Lee put cream in his coffee. When Kate asked him about this he smiled again and replied, "I have not taken coffee for so long that I would not dare to take it in its original strength." Kate mentioned this later to one of Lee's staff, and he told her, "You know the general sends all his coffee to the hospital." Soon after, the general mounted Traveler and was on his way, having eaten his last meal under anyone's roof until after the surrender.

Such marvelous anecdotes seem to abound at Clover Hill, which has been described in a Virginia Historic Landmarks Commission report as "one of the most historically significant plantations in Chesterfield County." Some of the legends, passed down through the years by slaves and others who have lived there, involve bizarre tragedies, and with them are associated some classic ghost stories. These include tales of a bird swooping through a window at the approach of death; an eerie rapping on a certain side door when an adult member of the family is about to die; phantoms and banshees flitting through the skeletal branches of the once-stately Lombardy poplars; mysterious deaths, including a disembodiment at an old spring; and the often-repeated story of "Cox's Snow."

But first it is appropriate to set the scene with some background on the house and property. The Landmarks Commission report states simply that "this house has a complex history." Further, it says, "While the dwelling is said to have been built in 1787, there is no architectural evidence for so early a date. Two distinct segments of the house date from the early 19th century, the large two-story section was built shortly after the Civil War, and since then various one-story additions have been put on."

In contrast, Cox family records indicate, "the older wing of the house dates to the 18th century." Regardless, it is believed that James H. Cox moved to the farm known as "Winterpock," (from an old Indian name for a neighboring creek), in 1835, and sometime after that his wife changed the name to Clover Hill. Cox was the eldest son of Major Henry Cox, Sr., who served in the War of 1812.

The James Henry Cox who came to Clover Hill in 1835 had graduated from Hampden-Sydney College six years earlier; had "read law" in the office of his cousin, John Winston Jones, Speaker of the U.S. House of Representatives; and, in 1832, had gone to the Territory of Florida as headmaster of Tallahassee Academy, then the largest school in Florida.

All of this is recorded in a Cox family history which is prefaced with this colorful note: "Grandmother's knee is a wonderful place to learn about the Bible, ghosts, and even Santa Claus, but a mighty poor place to learn history."

It is established that a rich vein of coal was discovered on the property by a slave in 1837. The productive Clover Hill Coal Mines were worked extensively during the 1800s, as were the Bright Hope and Coalboro coal pits, which became the Bright Hope Coal Company. The coal was carried to the James River on the Clover Hill Railroad.

Of all the stories swirling about Clover Hill certainly the most famous concerns the great blizzard of 1857, which has become known in Chesterfield County lore as "Cox's Snow." The date was January 17, and Dr. Joseph Edwin Cox, a cousin of Henry, was called from his home in Petersburg to visit a patient in Chesterfield. According to one account of the incident, published in 1937, "It was snowing furiously, and his horse sloshed through the muck hour after hour. Finally, completely exhausted and chilled to the bone, the doctor and horse reached the gate of Clover Hill in the night. The snow was piled high about the fence posts and the wind whipped around in icy flurries . . . Ask any oldster in the county, and he will tell you that such a storm has not been seen since.

"Dr. Cox edged his numb body out of the buggy and plodded through the drifts to unlatch the gate. It was icy, frozen, immovable. He called through the black murk of falling snow. He called again and again, until his voice was a faint whisper."

Here, the story is picked up by Mrs. Jennie Patterson, a former slave at Clover Hill born about 1846, who was interviewed when she was 91 years old. She was about 11 years old at the time. "I was up yonder in de big house, settin' knittin' socks fer my master. Dr. Cox . . . had been drinkin' heavy dat day when he came from Petersburg. When he got most to de house, we heard him callin' but thought t'was some of de t'other folks 'round dar. His daughter (Mrs. Grimes), wouldn't git up to open de do' 'cause we all was gittin' ready to go to bed."

The next morning slaves found Dr. Cox near the gate frozen to death. As Jennie Patterson recalled it: "I seed him dar when dey all went out. Fus' seed his horse an' buggy comin' to de house dout (without) nobody in hit. All got scared an' went a-searchin' an' callin' him. An' lo' an' behold, dar was Marse Cox stiff in de snow. Chile, I'se been feard to tell all I know 'bout dis here thing. Dar's bin all kinds of tales de white folks bin all kiverin' hit over. Marse Cox liked his liquors so he was drunk an' couldn' make hit, not bein' of his self. I bet you ain' heard dat. Yes, yes, dar was a big botheration at de big house. Naw, I ain't said nothin' 'tall 'bout dem ghost."

What the ex-slave wouldn't refer to, was what has happened at Clover Hill ever since. "Sperrits," some of the former servants called them. The phenomenon involves a specific upstairs bedroom. Something, or someone — the most commonly offered explanation is that it is the ghost of frozen Dr. Cox — "keep watch over the bedroom in a most discomfiting (sic) manner." He will not let the sleeper keep any bedcover on himself after midnight, especially if he is the only person in the place.

There apparently is some credibility to this because it is told that once a certain "minister of the gospel (whose word, naturally, goes unquestioned) spent the night there and was "so harried by this persistent ghost that he grabbed a blanket and spent the night out of doors."

There are a host of other hauntings at Clover Hill, some fanciful, some more difficult to explain away by rational means. For example, cedars now line the old carriage drive, where once tall Lombardy poplars stood. In pre-Civil War days slaves believed "Haidless ho'semen" rose at night among them. Looking at the shimmering branches on dark nights, the slaves said they saw "folks made out o'bones wid wings, an' hants flappin' roun'! They made such a hue and cry that Judge Cox had the trees cut down.

Then there are the gruesome stories of the spring from which fresh water was drawn for the house. Ex-slave Jennie Patterson:

"Dar was a slave amongst us who 'cided to run away an' a 'oman slave heard him doin' his plan. She ups an' tells his mistress, an' mistress sends dis man to de spring to fetch water. Down dat spring dar was dem overseers. De man stayed so long fo' he brought de water up to de house (that) another slave went to look for him an' do you know dat man was found all cut up in de water bucket. Yes, dem buckets was big buckets; no setch buckets like you see now."

In all probability, Jennie's tale has been considerably embellished in the retelling, and the land owners probably did nothing to discourage it because fear was one of the best resources in keeping slaves from running away. Still, there was something mysterious about the spring because there is a much better documented account of what happened there to another slave, Aunt Jensie. She was dispatched one day to the spring for water and when she failed to come back they found her head and upper torso in the water, "dead as a doornail." So profound was the terror among the servants after that, that none would go to the spring again for water, even under the threat of a whipping. Subsequently, the spring was bricked up and never used again.

Several members of the Cox family have died suddenly at Clover Hill, and each time, servants say, it was preceded by a harbinger of death. This took the form of a "sharp rapping" on a particular side door of the house. While there is little to substantiate this legend, there is a fairly detailed remembrance of the "swooping bird" who made a sign of death.

It was during the early days of the War between the States. One evening in early October, Judge James H. Cox was "taking his ease in the double parlors." His three sons had recently left to join the Confederate Army, and he was alone in the room. He heard "a fluttering of wings, 'tis said, and instantly a small dark bird circled about his head, then flew out the window."

In a few days the judge and his wife and daughter left for Norfolk, where Edwin, the favorite son, was stationed. The servants said they made the trip, "cause de bird had done gib de sign." They found the boy "thin and rosy-cheeked with the flush of ill health." The family brought him back to Clover Hill, where his health became worse. He died the day after Christmas, and was laid out in the parlor where the bird had appeared.

The Coxes called the death, after the appearance of the bird, a coincidence. The servants had another name for it. It was "hants," they said.

CHAPTER 14

A Release Ceremony at Selma

(Staunton)

hen the magnificent, 20-room, white columned mansion known as Selma was built in 1856, it stood isolated in the center of a 790-acre estate well outside the confines of the town of Staunton. In the nearly century and a half since, the city has grown to more or less "enclose" the three-story Greek Revival home. Yet still it maintains its splendor. Inside are no less than 13 fireplaces, one of which curiously has no opening into a chimney. Handcarved mantels are different in each room, with the most intricate, featuring a Grecian design of Bacchus, God of Wine, in the dining room. The parlor ceiling is vividly painted with cherubs holding garlands, circled by plaster bas-relief flowers, leaves and garlands.

Despite the pleasant surroundings, however, Selma was the scene, during the Civil War, of a dark tragedy which, until 1982, cast an unhappy pall over the environs. It seems that in the last stages of the war a young Confederate soldier was chased into the house by a Union trooper and was killed at the dining room mantel, where his blood stained the floor, allegedly for years. For the next 120 years, the slain Reb's spirit remained in the house, confused and perhaps angered, roaming about in the attic, on the stairs and elsewhere. One well published account of his presence was said to have taken place in 1872 when the property was then owned by the Williams family of South Carolina.

Several members of the family as well as the servants told others that they often saw the ghost about in the house. On this particular occasion, a visitor at Selma arose from a tea table downstairs to go upstairs, and when she returned she asked her hosts, "Who was the gentleman entering the room as I went out?" She was told that no one had come in. She then insisted that a "soldier in uniform" had passed her as she went out. The lady had no prior knowledge of what had happened at the mansion. Later, when the H. Arthur Lamb family occupied Selma, the same manifestation appeared. The Confederate would be seen on the stairs, entering the dining room, or standing quietly by the blood-stained hearth "as if he were a member of the family circle!" Once, a new servant asked if she should lay a place at the table for the "gentleman." When she was asked what gentleman, she replied, "Why, the soldier gentleman."

Although ownership of the mansion passed through several hands over the years, the apparitional soldier stayed on. In the early 1900s, when Colonel William Beard of Tallahassee, Florida, bought the place, he had great difficulty getting servants "on account of the ghost." Members of the Beard family said they distinctly heard steps of a "ghostly patrol," night after night, passing and repassing across the rustic bridge on the grounds, but because they wanted to sell the estate they were reluctant to talk about it.

In the mid-1960s, Richard and Claudette Obenschain, the current owners, told of the bizarre incident which happened to a woman overnight guest. She was sleeping in the same room that the soldier's mother apparently once occupied, and in the middle of the night she was unceremoniously shoved out of the bed onto the floor. No one could convince her that it wasn't the spectral soldier who had pushed her.

It wasn't that the young man was mean. Quite the contrary. One writer described him as "polite, attentive, as though listening to the conversation of the family, but not taking part." His image was described as "so clear and distinct that he was often mistaken for a living man, his manner was so calm and casual, his presence so convincing, that residents often accepted him . . ." With the lone exception of the lady who was nudged from her bed, no one really had fear of the soldier.

Everything remained relatively calm at Selma until 1982, when a Blue Ridge Community College parapsychology class visited the house as part of a field trip. One of the 30 members of the class was

Selma

Phyllis Atwater of Charlottesville, a woman who said she was "very sensitive" to psychic phenomena. She has had past encounters with haunted houses. Once, for example, in Boise, Idaho, she went with a newspaper reporter to a house said to be haunted by a young boy. Manifestations supposedly included doors and windows opening and closing by themselves, and a rocking chair that would float in the air unassisted. During the search, the boy appeared to Mrs. Atwater on a staircase, straddling the family cat. The reporter wrote an article on the experience and on the day the story was published the house burned to the ground!

Another time, beside a fresh grave site in a cemetery outside Roanoke, she saw "what appeared to be a small boy standing downcast and lonely." She conversed with him, asking him why he hadn't gone to the "light," a reference to the intense light claimed to have been seen by many who have been declared clinically dead and were then returned to life. The boy said he had seen the light, but hadn't followed it because his mother told him never to go anywhere without her permission. At Selma, Mrs. Atwater said the landlady told the group they could go anywhere in the house with the exception of the attic. "She was adamant that no one should go up there." As soon as no one was looking, Mrs. Atwater went straight to the attic. "I had to," she said. "The feelings were very strong from that portion of the house. Once her eyes adjusted to the dim light there, she saw a spirit which "had no earthly form, but rather presented a hodgepodge of blotches hanging in mid air. I'd never seen anything like it," she recalled. "I was shocked, but I knew better than to show fear or react emotionally."

The entity then spoke to her, demanding that she go away immediately. She told it she was not there to do harm, merely to help it. "Something was happening I didn't think was possible," she said. "This was a soul that literally was dissipating. All the other energy forms I'd dealt with stayed true to their own coherent structures. This one was breaking up."

She then went downstairs, and on the way out of the attic met a man and his wife who was blind, headed for the attic. The blind woman said, "You saw it, didn't you?" Mrs. Atwater acknowledged that she had, and then she told the group instructor, David McKnight, that a "release ceremony" must be conducted at once if the spirit of the Confederate was to be saved. At a discussion held by the group, the blind lady, too, said she had felt the presence of the ghost and found it to be "very foreboding and confrontational." After Mrs. Atwater stressed to the landlady the importance of releasing the soldier from an unhappy existence, the release ceremony was set up for that evening. Its purpose, she said, was to contact the spirit and let it know what was happening.

In a subsequent article in the Waynesboro News Virginian by staff writer Charles Culbertson, Mrs. Atwater told of how she conducted the ceremony. "I counseled it," she stated. I said I understood the circumstances of its death, of the terrible era it had come from, and I told it forcefully that it needed help. I said it must go to the light before it was destroyed. She added that the soldier resisted all the way, and then she had to force it "by dint of will" to leave the house. She said the spirit finally "sighed with resignation" and moved on to the after life it had avoided for 118 years.

At that precise moment, the clock struck midnight.

"The soul is an extension of God, and after death it normally progresses on," Mrs. Atwater said. "But here we had a young man who died traumatically. He was imprisoned in Selma by his own emotions and by the selfishness of others." She noted that she believed the spirit of the soldier was dissipating because "the energy of other people sapped his vital force over the years. "We did the right thing and freed him."

The landlady wasn't so sure. "I liked my ghost," she said. "He made a wonderful conversation piece."

CHAPTER 15

The Ghost Train at Cohoke Crossing

(Near West Point)

ost forms of psychic phenomena are quite limited in scope. Generally, whatever the manifestation, be it the sighting of a milky apparition, the sound of muffled footsteps in the attic, or a blood stain that cannot be scrubbed clean — the particular characteristic is experienced only by a relatively few people. In some cases, only one person, usually psychically sensitive, is involved. In old ancestral homes, often just the immediate family members encounter the extraordinary. Only in a few instances are the occurrences seen, heard, smelled, felt or tasted by appreciable numbers of people.

That is why the mysterious light at West Point is such a rare example. Over the past 100 years or so literally thousands of Tidewater residents swear they have witnessed the light that seemingly appears and disappears before their eyes. In fact, this sensation is so well known and so reliable in its recurrences, that, for decades area teenagers considered it a "cool" thing to drive to the site late at night and wait for it to show up. As often as not they were not disappointed. It is a story that has been retold from generation to generation with many common threads, but with conflicting accounts as to what the actual source is.

Skeptics scoff that what is seen is marsh gas, which is common in the area near West Point at a crossroads called Cohoke. Others say that many of those who come looking for the light are well fortified with "liquid courage" and are likely to see anything. But the

majority of those who have been there don't buy these explanations.

"There is definitely a light there," counters Mac Germain, a mechanic in Hopewell. "I've seen it and I wasn't drunk and it wasn't swamp gas. If it was swamp gas then why would people have seen the light at all times of the year?" he asks.

"I've seen it and it's real," adds Mrs. Thomas Whitmore of West Point. "It was so bright. When it got close to us we got off the railroad tracks real fast, but nothing came by."

Ed Jenkins, a native of Gloucester says, "We used to go up there (Cohoke) when we were teenagers. It was the thing to do. I saw it. It would come closer and closer and would almost get to you, then it would vanish. Was I scared? Absolutely! One time I shot at it with a shotgun and it disappeared. But it always came back."

I've seen it a hundred times," says John Waggoner, who grew up in Newport News and is now retired at Hilton Head, South Carolina. "It was just a big old light and it came straight down the tracks, but when it got to you there was nothing there. It used to scare the hell out of the girls I took there. That's what I liked about it."

One person who firmly rules out a spectral source is Lon Dill, the late local historian who has written extensively of the area, and is the author of "York River Yesterdays." "Oh, there is something there," he once said. "There is a light. I've never seen it, but a friend of mine has and I believe him. But it is some form of luminescence, which can be caused in several ways. Your eyes can fool you at times, especially at night. The best way to see the light is to be young and take your girl friend and a six-pack to the site," Dill claimed.

Another person who has tried, with some success, to play down the supernatural aspects of the light at West Point is King William County sheriff W. W. Healy. He recalls that in the 1960s and '70s, "It was almost like a state fair down there. People would come by the carload to see it. It got to the point where the road was blocked." Healy has done his best to discourage curiosity seekers. He even dissuaded NBC Television's "Unsolved Mysteries" crew from coming to film the phenomenon. "For the past few years we haven't had too many problems because there has been nothing written about it," he says. "Personally, I'd be scared to go down there at night. I've known people to go down there with shotguns and shoot at anything resembling the light!"

Maggie Wolfe, a former reporter for the Virginia Gazette in Williamsburg, tells of the time she and her husband were driving from Richmond to Williamsburg late at night. "We were taking some back roads just to do something different, and when we got near West Point I got the strangest feeling that is hard to describe. It was overpowering, as if we were in the midst of a super strong presence. We were paralleling the railroad tracks and when we looked over, there was this light. It seemed to be following us. And then it was gone. There was no train, no noise, or anything. I'll never forget it. We didn't know the story of the light until we told friends about it later.

Bruce Johnson is a local farmer who grew up in the Cohoke area and still lives there. His father's farm is within a stone's throw of where the light is most often seen. "A lot of people have gone to see it," Bruce says. "I've seen license plates from all over the country. It seems like it's most often sighted on cloudy or rainy, dismal nights. I only saw it once. It was back when I was in high school, and I was driving home alone one night after a football game. I stopped at the tracks and I definitely saw some type of light. It looked to me like some sort of welder's arc. It had a gaseous type glow. It was kind of scary actually. I didn't stay long." Bruce's wife, Kay, saw it once, too. She described it as a "big bright round ball of light."

Most everyone who has seen the light (or lights) is pretty much in agreement as to its method of appearance. It first shows up far off, maybe several hundred yards down the tracks, then noiselessly, it approaches, glaring ever brighter as it nears, until its frightening closeness scares off viewers. Its relentless journey can only be impeded by the foolhardy actions of those who either try to run it down or shoot at it. This causes its instant disappearance. Also, although many have tried, including a national magazine film crew, no one has successfully photographed the light.

The source of the light, however, remains a mystery, and, to this day, stirs heated arguments. Many who have seen it contend it is a large lantern, carried by a conductor or brakeman, who allegedly lost his head, (literally), in an unspeakable accident and returns to search for it. One might reasonably ask, why does he look only at night? Others who believe the decapitation story say the light is too large and too bright to be a lantern; that it definitely is a train headlight.

But just as many people believe in the "lost train" theory. They have heard that after the battle of Cold Harbor during the Civil War, in 1864, a train in Richmond was loaded with wounded Confederate soldiers and dispatched to West Point, where they could recuperate or be sent by ship farther south for recovery and regrouping. The train left Richmond amid a soft chorus of moans but never reached its destination.

One person who has tried to trace the origins of the legend is Bill Travers of Hopewell. He has concluded that there might be two lights involved. "Many people I've talked to say they have seen a bust, that is the head and shoulders of a Confederate soldier, but without distinct features," Travers says. "He is carrying a lantern about 10 feet off the ground. And, beyond the soldier, maybe 300 yards or so, is the large headlight of a train."

The train theory was given some support by the experience of Tom Gulbranson of Oceanview and members of his family one night in 1967. Tom is an amateur psychic sleuth who, over the past 20 years or so, has investigated dozens of haunted houses and sites.

He had visited the Cohoke location several times and had seen the light on a few of them. This time he was with his mother, father, brother and a friend.

As they drove up and parked at a strategic point, they noticed another car a few hundred feet away, only about three feet off the tracks, parallel to them. Tom got out his camera equipment and set it up and they waited. It was a bitterly cold night and, after a couple of hours of nothing but silence and darkness, they decided to leave. Just as they were packing up, the light appeared.

"This time it was brighter than I had ever seen it," Tom recalls. "It was an intense light and it came closer and closer. As it neared the other parked car, its startled occupants flicked on their headlights, and when that happened, we all *clearly saw the outline of a train!*"

Apparently, whatever mission the ghost train is on, it hasn't yet been fulfilled, because accounts of the eerie light persist to this day.

CHAPTER 16

The Disaster of Dahlgren's Raid
(Richmond)

here was a time, early in 1864, when a siege of the city appeared imminent. Richmonders feared not only that their town would be sacked and burned, but there had been vicious rumors circulating that the hated Yankees intended to publicly execute Jefferson Davis and his entire cabinet. As fear swept through the town, talk of violent retaliation increased. One idea fostered by Southern zealots was to hang the Union prisoners at Belle Isle — all 15,000 of them. Such thoughts were quickly quelled by cooler heads.

Still, for a time Richmond was in some danger, and had a rather ingenious plan hatched by Brigadier General Judson Kilpatrick worked, the Capital of the Confederacy could have fallen. As it was, Kilpatrick's idea led to a colorful sidebar to the war that came to be known as Dahlgren's Raid. Therein lies a strange and absorbing story complete with the unfortunate hanging of a poor young Black, the mutilation of the body of the Raid's leader, and the haunting recurrence — to this day — of the ghosts of a Federal officer, and a tortured slave.

Kilpatrick reasoned that with Lee's Army of Northern Virginia off fighting in the Wilderness, Richmond was vulnerable to a bold surprise attack. He sold his superiors on a plot where he would lead a detachment of 4,000 troops through the thin Southern lines and openly confront what defenses the city still maintained. The key would be while he drew the major fire, a smaller force of 500 men would sneak in behind the home guard, ford the James River, and free the 15,000 Union prisoners. This, Kilpatrick believed, would break the Confederate spirit, and the city would surrender. Admittedly, it was a gamble, but one daring enough to have the possibility of succeeding.

To lead the smaller raiding party, Kilpatrick, who was only in his mid-twenties, chose a man named Ulric Dahlgren. At 21, he was said to be the youngest colonel in the Northern army. Earlier in the war, the tall and dashing Dahlgren had been severely wounded in the cavalry skirmish at Boonsboro, Maryland, and his right leg had to be amputated. After months of convalescence and fitted with a wooden leg, Dahlgren and his 500 men started out.

It was an innovative plan, but one destined to disaster by the elements of reality. Confusion, foul weather and the unerring accuracy of persistent Confederate snipers along the route all took their toll. Dahlgren lost contact with Kilpatrick's larger force and attempts to reestablish communications proved futile. The ultimate irony occurred when a young Black, who had told the youthful colonel he knew the best place to cross the river, led the troops to a point where the James, swollen by storms, was both deep and treacherous. Dahlgren thought the Black had betrayed him and, probably impetuously, ordered his hanging.

Realizing the mission was lost, Dahlgren ordered his soldiers to retreat. They got separated in the darkness of the woods. About 300 eventually made it back to the Union lines. Dahlgren and the other 200, however, were missing, and it was days before their fate was learned. He had struck off for the northeast and made reasonably good progress, at one point making a spectacular crossing of the Mattaponi River. But by now, word of the invasion had spread, and snipers seemed to loom behind every barn and tree.

In the middle of the night a force of Virginia cavalry, reinforced with home guards and rifle-carrying farmers, positioned themselves for an ambush in the forest. Dahlgren, leading his men, pistol in hand, heard men moving in the woods and shouted: "Surrender, you damned Rebels, or I'll shoot you!" His challenge was met with a heavy volley of fire, and he fell dead from his horse, his body riddled with bullets. Chaos reigned and most of his men were either killed or captured. Little mercy was shown since the raiders had set fire to barns, flour mills, railroad buildings and freight cars along the way. They had ravaged farms and stolen what little food they could find.

Some of the hatred was vented on Dahlgren's body. One man

cut off his finger to get a ring. Another took his artificial leg as a souvenir, and he was stripped of his watch, other valuables and his clothing. Ingloriously, his body was carted to Richmond in a lidless pine box where it was displayed in a railroad station.

Later, as Dahlgren's rude coffin was being lowered into a grave, orders came to send the body to Richmond for internment at Oakwood Cemetery. Sometime later the remains were again dug up and moved to the neighborhood of Laurel, at the request of Union sympathizers. After the war his body was exhumed once more by his family for final disposition. The poor man was thus buried four times, causing one to wonder that if his spirit was ever to surface, where might it appear?

At one point a letter was found on Dahlgren's body. It had an incendiary effect on Richmonders. In it, Dahlgren had written: "We hope to release the prisoners from Belle Island first, and having seen them fairly started, we will cross the James River into Richmond, destroying the bridges after us, and exhorting the released prisoners to *destroy and burn the hateful city, and do not allow the rebel leader Davis, and his traitorous crew to escape."* When the letter's content was exposed the press, saying that the thousands of Union prisoners were to have been let loose on the city, it conjured up wild visions of rape, plunder and murder. The Richmond *Examiner*, for example, said: " . . . turning loose some thousands of ruffian prisoners, brutalized to the deepest degree by acquaintance with every horror of war, who have been confined on an island for a year, far from all means of indulging their strong sensual appetites — inviting this pandemonium to work their will on the unarmed citizens, on the women, gentle and simple, of Richmond, and on all their property."

Northern journalists, in turn, decried the mutilation of Dahlgren's body, the hanging of the young Black man, and the hunting down of Union soldiers with packs of bloodhounds. The furor rose to such heights that Lee sent General Meade a message asking for an answer to charges of intended barbarity. Meade replied that no one had ordered any cities burned or civilians harmed.

And thus ended Dahlgren's Raid, and, for a time, the threat to Richmond. The two ghostly sidelights to this historic vignette linger on, however. One, which was mentioned in the Sunday magazine section of a Richmond newspaper nearly half a century ago, concerns an "old house on Three Chopt Road owned by Ben Green." It was there that some of Dahlgren's men tried to learn the location of the household silver, which was "known to be extensive," and thought to be buried nearby. When a "faithful" old slave named Burwell refused to disclose the hiding site he was strung up by his thumbs. This house, according to the article, "is known to be haunted." Some believe it is the spirit of Burwell who remained, seeking some form of retribution for the brutal pain he suffered so long ago.

The other legend centers around one of Dahlgren's young officers. He rode his horse into a dense patch of honeysuckle thicket surrounded by trees somewhere on Cary Street Road in an area where an old ice house once stood. He immediately fell, mortally wounded by a sniper's bullet. It has been reported that on calm nights "are frequently heard moans from the luckless victim."

CHAPTER 17

Nonpaying Guests at the Wayside Inn

(Middletown)

(Author's note: Middletown is on Route 11, just off Highway 81 a few miles south of Winchester and west of Front Royal. As early as 1766, the village was recognized as a clock making center, and its reputation increased as wooden-wheeled timepieces gave way to those of brass, which bowed in turn to elaborately patterned eight-day clocks. The same artisans fashioned watches and surveyors implements. One of them, Jacob Danner, constructed compasses of such mathematical precision that their reputation endures to this day. Middletown's streets today are lined with antique stores and other shops which sell Civil War relics. Down the road a short piece is Strasburg, the self-proclaimed "Antique Capital of Virginia." And, within a short distance (15 or 20 miles) is the famous and haunted Cedar Creek Battlefield, and the magnificent, and haunted, Belle Grove Plantation.)

O n occasion, they serve pheasant at the old Wayside Inn in Middletown. When pheasant isn't on the menu, one can order everything from Virginia country ham to fresh caught trout and catfish with such side dishes as old fashioned spoon bread. The waitresses serve you in 18th century costumes, carrying on a tradition of feeding and housing tired travellers that dates back to 1797. In those days it was known as Wilkinson's Tavern, and when the valley pike was cut through

The Wayside Inn

some years later, the tavern became a popular stagecoach stop, a relay station on "the old Black Bear Trail, where fresh horses were ready, and where "bounce-weary passengers could rest and refresh themselves."

According to an Inn brochure, "In coaching days, a servant boy would be sent to the nearby hill to sight an expected stagecoach. When a cloud of dust appeared over the horizon, the servant waited anxiously, straining to sight the outline of the stagecoach, and then hurried back to the Inn to report its approach. By the time the passengers arrived, delicious hot food would be waiting and they would dine and drink in comfort while the team of horses was being changed."

During the Civil War, soldiers from both the North and South marched and fought back and forth through Middletown so many times it confused townspeople as to just who was in command on any given day. The Inn survived those treacherous times by "offering comfort to all who came." The name changed to Larrick's Hotel after the Civil War, and then again, later, to the Wayside Inn. Today there are 22 guest rooms and suites, "uniquely decorated with rare antiques, fine art, objets d'art, and an interesting potpourri of memorabilia." There are also four poster beds with canopies and cannonball and acorn carved details.

It was here, on May 24, 1862, that, according to a state highway historical marker in front of the Inn, "Stonewall Jackson attacked Banks retreating from Strasburg and forced him to divide his army." For a time during this period, the Inn was used as a hospital. Although there are no records of exactly how many men lost limbs or their lives in the vicinity, a number of Confederate and Union troops fell here, including one colonel whose stone marker sits just off the Inn's front porch.

That undoubtedly is why witnesses — guests and hotel workers alike — have reported seeing the ghostly images of Civil War veterans "milling around" in the lobby on occasion. "Oh yes, that's what people tell me," says amiable Molly Clough who has worked at the Inn for the past eight years. "Some have said they have seen the figure outlines of soldiers dressed in Civil War uniforms; others have said they just felt something, you know, like a presence here.

"There are sounds, too," Molly adds. "Of course, you have to remember this is a drafty old house. It has been an inn since 1797, but the earliest part of the house, the old slave quarters, dates back to the 1740s. Old houses have a lot of creaks and groans. But I have to admit, I have heard footsteps right outside the front door when there was no one there. I never could explain that. Then you have to remember that this place was a hospital during the Civil War. A lot of young boys never left here alive. They weren't ready for that."

Molly is not the only employee to experience such manifestations. A co-worker who prefers not to be identified said she had seen "shadows pass by the front windows at night." She was told it was just the reflections from car lights going by, but she didn't believe this. "There weren't any cars going by," she exclaimed. "And there were no people outside either. It was pretty eerie."

The night auditor has had the most dramatic encounters. "She swears there's a ghost who talks to her when she works late at night here," Molly says. The auditor told one co-worker at the Inn that she felt someone breathing on the back of her neck as she walked through the ancient slave quarter section of the building one evening. She was reportedly "pretty spooked" by it all. Molly adds that sometimes at night, she would be waiting for the night auditor to show up. "It was then that I heard the footsteps. At first I assumed it was the auditor, but when I got up to check, there was no one around. The odd part was that it was always at precisely 11:15 p.m. when I heard the footsteps."

Molly and others say that several guests have reported to them that they "felt something" in rooms 22 and 23. "They never said they saw anything, just that they felt a presence, like someone else was there. "There's nothing harmful about any of our ghosts," says Molly. "I think it kind of gives the place an added charm."

* * * * * *

(Author's note: I had called and talked to Molly prior to visiting the Wayside Inn in February 1994. When I arrived there and walked into the lobby, she immediately asked if I felt anything. I had to admit I didn't, but I told her I was not sensitive to such things, as other people are, so she shouldn't be disappointed. Subsequently, I spent the night in room 22. Again, I sensed no spirits. Perhaps I was too tired from the journey from Williamsburg. It had been a long day. I can, however, vouch for the hospitality and the atmosphere at Wayside. It is delightful. And, too, the pheasant was delicious.")

CHAPTER 18

The Battlefield Ghosts of Cedar Creek

(Near Strasburg)

or Confederate General Jubal Early, it was a time of hard decision. He had about 15,000 tattered and hungry soldiers under his command in October 1864 at a site in the burned out Shenandoah Valley a few miles from the town of Strasburg. Early and his men had been beaten back twice in the past few weeks by the superior-in-strength forces of General Philip Sheridan. In the process, the Union soldiers had torched the Shenandoah to the point where one Reb officer wrote about the "great columns of smoke which almost shut out the sun by day, and in the red glare of bonfires which, all across the Valley, poured out flames and sparks heavenward and crackled mockingly in the night air, and I saw mothers and maidens tearing their hair and shrieking to Heaven in their fright and despair, and little children, voiceless and tearless in their pitiable terror."

Early really had no choice. He could launch an all-out surprise attack on Sheridan's army, encamped comfortably at a site known as Cedar Creek, which flowed from the northwest to join the north fork of the Shenandoah River. Or he could retreat, and cede the Valley to the Yankees. Early, who historian Bruce Catton described as being "as pugnacious a man as ever wore Rebel gray," chose, not surprisingly, to fight.

The historic battle commenced early on the "shivery, misty dawn of October 19, with fog hanging in the low places and the darkness lying thick in the graveyard hour between moonset and dawn." The Confederates rose up out of the gorge and came in yelling and shooting on the "drowsy flank" of Sheridan's army. They caught the Union forces completely off guard.

Amidst the barrage of gunfire and total confusion, one Northern soldier recalled, "We see nothing but that enormous disk (the sun), rising out of the fog, while they could see every man in our line and could take good aim." Another terrified trooper described the attack like this: "Men seemed more like demons that human beings as they struck fiercely at each other with clubbed muskets and bayonets."

The result, for Sheridan's men, was disastrous. There was no orderly retreat. There was a rout. It was, as one witness wrote: "a disorganized, routed, demoralized, terrified mob of fugitives . . . crowds of officers and men, some shod and some barefoot, many of them coatless and hatless, with and without their rifles, but all rushing wildly to the rear, oaths and blows alike powerless to halt them . . ."

As the Federals raced as fast as they could scamper northward, towards Winchester, a curious thing happened. Many of the Southern troops, instead of chasing and capturing them, stopped instead at the Yankee encampment near Cedar Creek to forage food, clothing, weapons, and anything else left behind in the rush.

And then another remarkable happening occurred. Philip Sheridan, the Northern commander, had been 20 or so miles north in Winchester when Early's attack began. He was on his way to Washington for a conference, but when he heard the artillery shelling, he immediately turned back and rode hard to Cedar Creek. And in so doing, he achieved immortality as a charismatic military leader. Almost singlehandedly, he rallied his forces from chaotic retreat, turned his men around, and led a devastating counter charge against Early's tiring troops. As historian Catton phrased it: "The effect was electric." Riding at "furious speed," General Sheridan projected a picture to his men of which legends are made. They followed him with an enthusiasm and a sense of mission almost beyond their physical capabilities.

The result, within hours, was a complete reversal of the morning's rout. The courageous but spent Southerners were driven back almost as fast as they could run, and a resounding Union victory was snatched from the jaws of defeat. For all intents and purposes, the great Valley campaign of 1864 was over. But it was not without an awful cost. As one chronicler wrote, simply, "The victory was dearly bought."

Thousands, on both sides, lay dead or grievously wounded, and the bitter physical and emotional effects would endure long after the last gun fired. In fact, said many of the area's residents, the ghosts of the Blue and the Gray continued to fight shadowy battles along the gentle streams of Cedar Creek and over the-blood-soaked ground for years afterward.

Witnesses reported that many of the wounded later died in a nearby Episcopal Church, which had served as a hospital during the battle. Countless bodies were hastily buried in the churchyard. A short time later, many of these men were dug up and placed in pine box coffins, which were then stacked high against the back wall of the church. They stayed there for a month or more. Curiosity seekers pried some of the coffins open. Said one person who was there at the time, "Some of the dead men was very natural and others wasn't fit to look at. One man with a blanket wrapped around him was petrified, and his appearance hadn't changed any since he was buried, only his hair had grown way down and his beard had grown long."

It was while these massed coffins lay stacked against the wall, that ghostly manifestations began to take place. Some of them were recorded in detail during interviews of survivors of the scene by author Clifton Johnson for a book published in 1915 called "Battlefield Adventures." Some said they had seen a strange light come out of the church and dance around the coffins at night, "as if someone was searching around with a candle," although there was no one there. Others saw an unworldly calf-size animal at the site.

Following are selected excerpts from an interview Johnson did with an aged servant who lived near the church in the 1860s: "The boxes was taken away presently, but the ghosts stayed at the church, or came there often at night, and we'd hear them walking, groaning, and carrying on." Several people recalled hearing an army band playing in the church. The servant said everyone around was called out of their houses one night to listen to the mysterious music, and all swore they heard it clearly. It was described this way: "The music sounded way off, but we could hear the lead horn start and the drums tap. The kettle drum would rattle it off and the bass drum would go bum, bum, bum!

"Right after the war we used to hear the soldiers' ghosts shooting here all around the battlefield, and we'd hear horses in the back lane coming klopity, klopity, klopity. The horses would ride right up to you, but you couldn't see a thing. I know one man who lived out on a farm and he come in to the town one night to a prayer meeting. As he was going home, about ten o'clock, he heard the bugle and the rap of the kettle drum. While he was listening, he seen an officer walking ahead of a squad of soldiers. The officer hollered 'halt!' to them and they stopped. But the bugle kept blowing, and pretty soon they marched off."

The interviewee told of another man who came into town often during this time while he was courting. "Some of the nights was tolerable dark. Many a night he'd hear horses coming across the fields, and canteens and swords hitting the sides of saddles, blangity, blangity, blangity!"

He also told of a ghost in a barn near Cedar Creek. "The ghost is supposed to be a soldier that was killed thereabouts. He has Yankee clothes on and wears cavalry boots that come way up to his knees. Some say he has no head, and others say he has a head and wears a plug hat. People see him at night, just about dusk, and he only comes at that time of evening." Apparently, many residents and others saw this apparition, because the old man said the railroad ran excursion trains to the area so people could come and see the ghost. "I went there to see him once, but I was afraid to go in the barn."

One man who had first hand experience with this military apparition was Holt Hottel, who rented the farm. He first saw him one evening as he was in the barn feeding his horses. "It was just after sundown," the old servant remembers, "and (Holt) was going to throw some hay down the hold to the feeding room when he noticed the ghost. But he thought it was a tramp, and he told him to get out of there. The ghost didn't say anything and just stood there. Holt got mad then and tried to gouge the ghost with his pitchfork, and the fork went right through the ghost into the weather-board-ing. Holt's horses didn't get no hay that night! There's people who have tried all sorts of ways to see that ghost and never could, and there's plenty of others who have seen it. I know this — that Holt Hottel was a reliable a man as there was in the state. His word was as good as his bond.

"Around here it was only a few years back that we'd see plenty of strange sights and hear plenty of strange noises. We don't see and hear them things so much now because the battlefield has been so stirred up by plowing and raising crops. That's driving nearly all the battlefield ghosts away, but there's some left yet. Yes sir, there's still ghosts. I can take you out with me tonight, and if you'll look across my left shoulder I'll show you something!"

And so it seems, for some poor lost souls, the fighting never ceases; apparitional warriors continue to wield spectral weapons across the hallowed grounds of historic Cedar Creek.

CHAPTER 19

The Searching Spirit of the Shenandoah

(Shenandoah Valley)

e was, in his time, a legitimate legend; a wily military genius revered by his men, respected by his enemies and as courageous and unafraid of looking death squarely in the face as a Kamikaze pilot. "Adventures are to the adventurous," he liked to say, and there seemed to be no challenge or dare he would not accept, no matter the odds, in his bold, audacious raids against Union army troops during the Civil War.

In time, he gained a well-earned reputation as a wizard; a guerrilla commander who drove Northern generals to drink or worse with his daring, swift-as-lightning attacks and his equally-quick disappearances, almost before the eyes of his pursuers. Once, as 3,000 Yankees chased his band of but 20 men, after they had captured and burned a Union supply train, he later wrote: "We vanished like the children of the mist." There were even those who considered him a ghost, or myth, so will-o-the-wisp were his forays.

His name was John S. Mosby, Colonel, C.S.A. For years, with only a handful of crack-shot calvarymen, he ruled like a military Robin Hood in the northern end of the Shenandoah Valley. But while Mosby and his bands fought as guerrillas, they nevertheless also fought with honor. Other groups at the time, calling themselves guerrillas, were actually no more than a step above being common outlaws, ravaging, pillaging, plundering and terrorizing any local citizens who got in their paths. They also indiscriminately killed any Yankee soldiers straggling away from their units.

117

Such bushwhacking tactics not only sickened General Robert E. Lee and his officers, who abhorred such maneuvers, but also infuriated the Northern forces. This was one of the reasons the Valley was so devastated during the war, with many farms burned and crops destroyed, until, as historian Bruce Catton phrased it, "Even a crow could not support himself."

It got so bad, that by 1864, whenever the Confederate guerrilla got caught — whether he was a member of Mosby's raiders, or just a common thief-murderer on his own — Union soldiers were determined to punish him on the spot. This generally meant a hasty firing squad or a hanging, whichever was more convenient.

Unfortunately, sometimes the innocent became victims of such wanton revenge. Such was the case of a blameless youth who lived in the Front Royal-Riverton area. He was suspected of being a member of Mosby's raiders, though he wasn't, and he was pummelled by Federal soldiers in "murderous violence." It was said that after the troops were finished with him, his battered body was thrown into a field where cattle stampeded over him.

It was this undefiled youth, many area oldtimers believe, who returned to the Valley in spirit form at varying times for more than 50 years seeking an answer to why he had been so cruelly treated by fate. His nightmarish appearances, spanning a period from the 1870s until at least 1925, stirred stark fear in the few residents who actually saw him; a fear that spread with the telling and retelling of his sightings, throughout entire communities.

It was commonly thought that the apparitional figure reemerged about once every six or seven years, and while there are numerous accounts of his manifestations over the last third of the 19th century, and the early years of the 20th, it was in 1912 that a detailed description of the phenomenon was first preserved through the eyes of a person who can be described as an unimpeachable witness: Judge Sanford Johnson.

The judge was outside feeding his dogs on a freezing wintry day that year on his spacious estate near the village of Riverton, when a sudden movement down near the bank of the creek, which ran across his property, caught his eye. As Johnson looked up he saw the "form" of a young man dressed in a Confederate uniform with a visored cap pulled down low over his eyes, shading his face. Stunned into silence at the unexpected sight, the judge watched open-mouthed as the figure "jerked and stumbled" out of the creek.

The judge's first impulse was to go forward and offer aid to the soaking stranger, but there was something about this whole vision that wasn't right; something that caused Johnson to, instead, race in panic back to his house and bolt the door. He peered out the back window but saw nothing. Then he moved to another window and saw the strange form, again moving rapidly and jerkily, wend its way down the long road past the front of the house. It was at this point that the conservative and practical judge observed something that chilled him to the bone: although there was fresh snow several inches deep on the ground, the form of the soldier *left no tracks*!

In relating his eerie experience to a close friend, the judge's normally logical mind seemed a total blank to explain what he had seen. Where, for example, had this "creature" come from? Had he arisen out of the middle of the half-frozen creek? Secondly, Johnson said not even a bird in direct flight could have moved as rapidly from the river bank to the point down the road where he next appeared in the time it took the judge to go from just outside his back door to the window. And, lastly, how could anything mortal move through the snow without leaving a trace?

The next "major" return of the mystery figure took place at a nearby farmhouse 13 years later, in 1925. The timing of the year and the particular circumstances varied somewhat from those Judge Johnson experienced, including a frightening eruption of psychic activity. But when everything was over, there was no doubt, among four eye witnesses this time, that the young Confederate soldier had reappeared. This visitation took place at the home of the Brad Cook family.

It was late on an autumn afternoon. There was a "friendly stillness" in the air, when, without warning, what has been described as a violent burst of wind shrieked and thrashed through the tall trees down by the river in back of the Cook farmhouse. As two of the Cook women looked on in surprise, the disturbance stopped as abruptly as it had begun, and a stealth-like quiet followed.

Next came plodding, heavy footsteps up the path toward the fence gate, and then the gate itself creaked under some burden invisible to Mrs. Cook and one of her daughters who stood in the center of the kitchen looking out, trembling. Gusting winds again whipped up, fearfully shaking the trees. And then, as the shadows seemed to darken along the river banks, the women saw, suspended over the gate, an "odd, ovally massed, silver-greenish light that quavered in a shimmering motion."

In her fine book, "Beyond the Limit of Our Sight," chronicling supernatural stories of the Shenandoah Valley, author Elizabeth Proctor Biggs wrote of what happened next: "Peering uneasily at the strange spectacle, the two women watched in disbelief as the splay of subtly shifting luminescence stirred and began to shape itself. Gradually there appeared the form of a man wearing plain gray trousers and jacket. A visored cap shaded his face. He leaned, arms folded, against the gate and appeared to be intently watching the house . . . the shimmering countenance commanding the frightened attention of the two women. The form maintained continually the weird wavering motion — never completely stilled."

The two other Cook daughters were called down from upstairs to view the incredible figure. It next moved, in a wink of the eye, from the front to the back gate of the fence, yet maintaining his mesmerizing stare fixed on the women in the house. One daughter then ran back to the front of the house to lock the door, and nearly fainted at the glowing form, which had seemed to follow her back to the front gate. Amidst a whirling wind, the strange apparition stilled itself, its light disintegrated, and it vanished!

Mrs. Cook later was to say there was no humanly way possible for anyone *living* to move that quickly around the yard and up a hill from the front gate to the back and then to the front gate again. Also, an examination of the grounds revealed that although there had been much rain in the area recently, there was not a single footprint or other sign of mortal movement around the house.

Curiously, there have been no reports of the mysterious visitor since 1925. If indeed it was the youth who had been suspected of being a Mosby raider and consequently was mauled and stampeded to death in 1864, had he at last somehow found peace? The definitive answer will likely never be known. But it may be fair to surmise that Mosby himself might well have welcomed such a fleeting young man into his guerrilla troop; one who could dart about quick as a whip without even leaving the faintest trace of his surrealistic movements!

CHAPTER 20

The Legendary Lady of Luray

(Page County)

uray, Virginia, lies at the crossroads of highways 211 and 340, roughly halfway between Winchester and Harrisonburg, in the heart of the Shenandoah Valley. It is in Page County, formed in 1831 from Rockingham and Shenandoah Counties, and named for John Page, the governor of the Commonwealth from 1802 to 1805. The Blue Ridge Mountains, and the Skyline Drive, are just east of Luray, and Massanutten Mountain is to the west.

Of this abundantly scenic area, Henry Howe, author of "Historical Collections of Virginia," written in 1845, said: "These mountains ever present a beautiful and picturesque appearance, whether viewed robed in the snow, ice and clouds of winter, the refreshing green of summer, or the gorgeous hues of autumn. The soil of Page is generally of the best quality of limestone valley land; a very considerable portion is bottom, lying on the Shenandoah River, and Hawksbill, and other creeks."

For decades, Luray was a sleepy little town largely unknown to anyone living outside its immediate area. All this dramatically was changed one day in August 1878 by a startling discovery. It was then that Andrew Campbell and Benton Stebbins were lowered into the mouth of a cave on the end of a rope. Once inside the earth, they followed a series of winding passageways from one gigantic room to the next. They stood in awe at their spectacular finding. The soaring cavern walls reflected every color of the rainbow. The light from their candles danced over the surface of crystal-clear pools. And every way they turned, there were formations more breathtaking than the last.

Campbell and Stebbins had discovered the Luray Caverns — the largest cave in Virginia. Among the subterranean rooms are the "Cathedral," in which there is a remarkable organ-like formation of stone, "Giants Hall," the "Throne Room," and the "Ball Room," in addition to two bodies of water — "Dream Lake," and the "Silver Sea." The Smithsonian Institute has said of the caverns: "It is safe to say that there is probably no cave in the world more completely and profusely decorated with stalactitic and stalagmitic formations than Luray."

The town has never been the same since. Millions of visitors from all over the world have descended on Luray over the past 100-plus years to view this underground wonderland.

Both Northern and Southern forces marched back and forth through this area during the Civil War, and major battles were fought all up and down the valley — at Winchester (three times!), Kernstown (twice), Front Royal, Cedar Creek, and Cross Keys and Port Republic. The closest heavy fighting got to Luray was a few miles west of the town, at the historic Battle of New Market, on May 15, 1864.

It was there that Confederate General John C. Breckinridge's forces, outnumbered, drove the Union army, under General Franz Sigel, north to Mount Jackson and beyond. This was the site where 247 teenaged cadets from the Virginia Military Institute fought with uncommon valor and courage, causing Sigel to call them "little devils."

Although no great battle was waged directly in Luray, there was a lot of movement through Page County during the war, and there is one long-standing legend of ghostly lore in the area associated with that period. It was graphically recorded decades ago by the artist-author James Reynolds in his book, "Ghosts in American Houses."

It began in the very early 1800s when a farmer of some considerable means named Winston Pardue came east and settled in the county. He apparently had made his money in the whiskey distillery business, and he and his wife, the beautiful former Della Courtland, built a handsome house in the mountain foothills bordering a forest. They brought two slaves with them — a woman known as Mammy Duro, and a man called Domeny.

But soon after the couple had moved in, Pardue died suddenly, of an enlarged spleen. It wasn't long after this that the widow Della was besieged with male suitors, all of whom had heard about the supposed fortune she had inherited at her husband's death. One was a strapping young man named Ham Corry, who was described by Reynolds as a "ne'er-do-well" from Newmarket. Nevertheless, the shifty Corry persuaded Della to marry him, and, in time, they had a daughter who was named Henrietta, but everyone called her Hetty.

There was something different about her from early childhood. She seemed to have a flair for wildness, isolation, and independence. As the Civil War clouds were darkening, Hetty evolved as a striking teenager, tall, with long-flowing taffy colored hair. At this age she had become a true free spirit, and would spend her days mysteriously away from her home. Astride her favorite steed, she would be occasionally seen in Newmarket, Luray or Staunton, but no one really knew where she went or what she did.

One day, while exploring in her beloved woods, Hetty came upon a huge old rusted iron pot. It had probably been long abandoned by trappers or loggers in the area. As author Reynolds noted, "From that day on, Hetty had a mission in life. She made wild-grape jelly, masses of it. For all around in these woods and in the river bottoms over toward Charlottesville, the trees and snake fences were hung with thick garlands of wild-grape vines."

According to the legend, which has been passed down through the years, Hetty by theft or otherwise, gathered as many glass jars and jugs as she could find from that time on. Then, deep in hillside forests, she would stir her bubbling grape juice for hours in the old iron pot, sweetening the concoction with wild honey. She would repay those she had confiscated glassware from by leaving jars of her fresh jelly on their doorsteps. She saved her best for her mother, who by then was in frail health. Della Corry died when Hetty was just 19, and she died worrying about what was going to become of her daughter; a girl who spent every agreeable day in the woods making grape jelly.

But at least Hetty seemed happy. Reynolds described her as "like a virgin priestess, she chanted songs learned from Domeny and Mammy Duro, while she stirred." In the winter, when the cold mountain snows blanketed the ground, Hetty was forced inside, and became a virtual recluse. She stayed in her room mostly, and taught herself to read.

Then her father died when he was struck in the head with a horseshoe. But Hetty never seemed close to him, and as soon as

spring thawed the snows, she would set out again for the woods. As the Civil War was about to break out, Hetty was visited by her cousin, Thaddeus Corry, from "the Blue Ridge country." They felt an immediate affection for each other, and "Thaddy" promised to take her to see their grandmother in the mountains. But before he could make good, he was conscripted into the Confederate Army and she never saw him again.

In 1862, after General Stonewall Jackson had fought in the Battle of the Banks near Winchester, and there was a constant threat of a Yankee invasion, things began to get "real strange" at the Corry house. For some unexplained reason, Hetty sent her two faithful servants, Mammy Duro and Domeny away, to a small farm she had bought for them on the Mary-Ann Creek.

Always thought to be on the eccentric side by townspeople, Hetty now began to gain the reputation of a hermit. Her house was shuttered tight, the front door was nailed shut, and not even the flicker of a light could be seen inside. No one came to visit. Still, the young lady continued her jelly making.

And, occasionally, she would take a load of jelly, and some chickens into Luray or Newmarket to sell, apparently out of need. Her infrequent appearances always stirred rumors and gossip. As Reynolds told, "she dressed like a man. Her once golden hair, though still worn in a thick braid, was streaked with gray, and an old butternut-felt hat was pulled down over her ears. A long ulster, made of homespun of her own weaving, and baggy breeches stuffed into high boots comprised her costume, no matter what the weather or season."

Hetty aroused further curiosity with her purchases. She bought large supplies of laudanum pills and liniments. No one could figure out why. As far as they knew, she was as healthy as a horse and had never known a sick day.

The mystery deepened one day in late summer, when a young boy, out trapping otters along Mary-Ann Creek, "was terrified to hear the bloodcurdling, choking screams of a person in mortal agony." A man then came crashing through the underbrush. His face was flush purple and he clawed at his mouth and eyes. As the boy stood transfixed, Hetty charged out of the woods, "wild-eyed . . . and waving a shotgun." The lad, in stark fear, ran down the creekbed as fast as he could. He later told the sheriff that a shot rang out as he ran, and whizzed by his ear.

That evening the sheriff went out to Hetty's house, and when no one answered the door, he forced his way in. In an attic bedroom he found a box of bloodstained bandages and dozens of empty bottles of liniment. Hetty apparently had nursed someone there; someone severely hurt and wounded. In every other room in the house the sheriff found scores of crocks, jars, bowls and basins of wild grape jelly. And then, in Hetty's bedroom, the law officer discovered the "ragged and bloodstained" uniform of a rifleman of the Northern Army.

The search for Hetty continued, and three days later the sheriff and a posse came upon the cabin Hetty had given to her servants. Mammy Duro had died, but Domeny, then aged and feeble, met the men at the door. He told them that "Miss Hetty" was there, but that she was near death.

The sheriff was then led into a small room, and there was Hetty Corry, laying on a pile of cornhusk sacks. She had taken poison. But before she died, she helped clear up the mystery. She said she had found a young Union soldier in the woods near her home. He had escaped from a Confederate prison and he was badly wounded. He was from Pennsylvania. She had taken him to her house, hidden him (explaining the boarded up seclusion), and nursed him. In the process, she had fallen in love with the man.

But he had betrayed her. After regaining his health he had snuck up on her as she was boiling wild grapes, and, with a rifle, had intended to rob her and leave her. She had doused him with the scalding grape juice, and that is what caused the scene the young boy-hunter had witnessed three days earlier. Reynolds did not specify what had happened to the soldier.

After relaying this, Hetty died, and the legend was born.

She began reappearing to the people who had moved into her house. They would hear her "rattling jars and crockery" late at night, and the next morning they would find purple stains on the floor and shelves. They would see the apparition of a young woman, wearing a long ulster-like coat and high boots, walk up the stairs to the attic, carrying a tray of medical supplies. They would hear the soft sobs of what sounded like a man in pain, and they smelled the distinct odor of carbolic acid in the hall.

One Page County resident said one night years later, he was out in a swampy river meadow gigging for frogs, when he noticed the light from a fire glowing deep in the woods. He went to investigate. He said he saw "the outline of a tall, slender woman, with a wreath of grape leaves in her hair, bending over an iron pot." He added that the scent of wild grapes filled the night air. The man said he then walked away, but later decided to go back. He went to the same spot, but there was nothing there, not even ashes from a fire.

And one evening at dusk a young man and his girl friend were walking down a country lane near Luray in the 1880s when they were suddenly confronted with a frightening vision. They said the figure of a tall woman, wearing a Civil War soldier's forage cap, and carrying an army rifle, "stepped out of the tree shadows" in front of them, and approached "in a threatening manner." The couple fled.

And the legend of Hetty Corry grew.

CHAPTER 21

Weird Wanderings at Willow Grove

(Orange County, near Gordonsville)

(Author's note: I am indebted to Clifford Elow of Fairfax for the following chapter. Mr. Elow, an avid reader of past books in this series on the ghosts of Virginia, wrote me in December 1994, as follows: "This is a brief recollection of my one and only experience of seeing an apparition or 'ghost.' Several years ago I had spent a few days at a bed and breakfast in Orange, Virginia. The inn where I stayed is called Willow Grove . . . It is a magnificent antebellum mansion redolent of stately Virginia plantation life in the mid-19th century. The grounds of this inn are so evocative of the tragic history of the 'Lost Cause' that, as I understand it, the grounds have been used for Civil War reenactments and the filming of at least one movie. I believe it was 'North and South,' which was shown on television.

On Sunday morning, the last day I was staying there, about 11 a.m., I was staring out of the Dolley Madison dining room window when suddenly I felt a frisson (a brief moment of emotional excitement), and actual chill. It was my perception that the entire room became cold.

"Immediately, I saw outside, no more than 20 or 30 feet from me, a very tall Black woman wearing a turban and dressed in clothing that was definitely not modern. She wore some sort of homespun frock and what appeared to be an apron. Her complexion was more coffee colored than black. The image lasted mere seconds, yet it is indelibly etched in my mind.

"Shortly after witnessing this apparition, I asked the owners if

127

there were any Black workers on the premises. At this time of day there were very few people on the grounds and the owners said there were no Blacks around. When I told the owners what I had seen, they explained that other people have seen the same apparition. I was told that this Black woman had been a slave at the Willow Grove plantation. Perhaps the present owners can give you some more information concerning the strange occurrence."

Needless to say, I called.)

W illow Grove, it turns out, is listed on the National Register of Historic Places, and has been designated a Virginia Historic Landmark. Located about 10 miles from Gordonsville, it was built about 1778 for or by Joseph Clark. The original building was a modest frame structure featuring woodworking done by the same artisans who crafted Montpelier, the Orange County mansion of President James Madison.

Sometime in the first half of the 18th century, William Clark, Joseph's son, substantially enlarged the house by adding a brick wing and a unifying Tuscan portico. The brick portion was constructed to Thomas Jefferson's design by the workmen who had recently finished work on the University of Virginia in Charlottesville. According to the Virginia Landmarks Register, the resulting structure "stands as an example of the influence of Jefferson's classical revival style on the country homes of Piedmont Virginia. The portico is accented by the distinctly Jeffersonian touch of Chinese lattice railings. The house is enhanced by its pastoral setting and collection of out buildings." Among these, still standing, are an old school house, a weaver's cottage, a milk house, a spring house, a tenant farmer's house, an 18th century bank barn, and a pre-Civil War barn.

Nestled on 37 acres, the 19th century has been carefully preserved at Willow Grove. The manor house is impeccably decorated with fine American and English antiques dating predominantly from the 18th and 19th centuries. Formal gardens and sloping lawns feature original English boxwood, stately magnolias, and the willows for which the plantation was named.

Today, it is a thriving bed and breakfast owned by Angela Malloy and her husband, Richard Brown. There are seven guest rooms and an elegant restaurant with three separate dining areas, ranging from the casual Clark's Tavern, to the more formal Dolley Madison room. "Our specialty is what I call upscale Southern," says Angela. The menu includes such entrees as: local trout crusted with cornmeal and a black walnut and country ham sauce; tenderloin of beef with Jack Daniels sauce; chicken Napoleon with smoked forest mushrooms; and a spice-crusted swordfish with shallot sauce. A house favorite is the sweet potato hash.

There may be several spirits active at Willow Grove in addition to the Black woman Clifford Elow saw. "A lot of strange things have happened here," admits Angela. "I personally have never seen a ghost, but a lot of guests tell me they have. And I can tell you there have been plenty of happenings that I can't explain."

Angela first noticed it back about 1987 or 1988 after they had just bought the house. "They were still working on it, when Richard and I decided to spend the night here one evening," she says. "We stayed in one of the upstairs bedrooms which was still unfinished at the time. I hadn't brought any bed clothes, so I took off my clothes and carefully laid them on a chair in the bedroom. I wore one of Richard's tee shirts to bed. When we woke up the next morning, my clothes were gone. They had just vanished. We couldn't find them anywhere. We know the door had been closed all night and no one had entered the room. Well, two weeks later the clothes suddenly turned up, washed, folded and put away. How do you explain that?"

On another occasion, about a year later, Angela says there was a guest in the bar downstairs who was flirting with one of the waitresses and making kind of a pest out of himself. "We have an old elevator in the house, and it stays on the top floor," she says. "It is disconnected and hadn't been in service for years. All of a sudden that elevator started, and it came right down to the floor where the bar is. We were shocked. My sister said it shouldn't move, and as she did, the elevator started up again and returned to the upper floor." The objectionable gentleman abruptly left the premises.

Angela believes a lot of the mysterious activity at Willow Grove is linked to the Civil War era. "I did some research on the house, and the family that lived here during that time had to flee the house in 1862, when Union soldiers came through the area. When the family moved back a year later, the Confederates were occupying the house."

Angela also discovered a secret passage which leads from a little hidden door under the attic floor to a space beneath the porch. She says there is an opening in the passage large enough to conceal a six-foot-tall man. "I read where William Clark was a suspected Union sympathizer, and one might wonder if he harbored a Northern soldier there. Or maybe it was used to help slaves escape. Anyway, we know there was a lot of activity, skirmishes and such, during the war years, but the house appears not to have been damaged, other than we dug out a cannonball in the roof."

Angela says a number of guests have reported apparitional sightings at Willow Grove. "We have a little sitting room outside of our best bedroom upstairs," she notes. "Once, a guest woke up and said he saw a young man dressed in a Confederate uniform courting a maiden as they sat on a couch in the sitting room. On another occasion, we had a wedding at the house, and one guest reported seeing a young lady, part of the wedding party, go down the stairs. The guest said he saw the ghostly image of a young Civil War soldier beside her as she descended the stairs."

One lady, who was apparently a psychic, told Angela that she had some "wonderful ghosts" in the house who were protective of her. "I have a collection of teddy bears in an upstairs room," Angela says, "and the lady said she picked one of them up and put it in her arms and started to walk out of the room. She told me a 'force' blocked her way. She couldn't get through the doorway, yet she couldn't see anything. It was a very unnerving experience. The lady said when she put the teddy bear back, the force was gone."

But what of the mysterious Black lady? "Oh, we've had a number of people here who said they have seen her and a few said they've even talked to her," Angela says. She is reluctant to discuss what they have told her, but there is a persistent legend that has circulated in the area for generations, and is consistent with what those who have communicated with the spirit have reported.

She allegedly was a maid servant in the house working for a previous owner of Willow Grove in the days prior to the Civil War. Her main duty was caring for the owner's children. She is described as being tall, attractive, and light-skinned. According to the legend, she had two children by the owner, and he killed the woman and both the children. It also has been rumored that she is buried somewhere on the property, as is the past owner, although no gravestones have ever been found. And so it apparently is the grieving apparition of this unfortunate slave who so often reappears in the house, still vainly searching for her children, so cruelly taken from her so long ago.

CHAPTER 22

Visions of the
Seaford Psychic

(Seaford)

The instant Clara Gysbers set foot for the first time into the house she and her late husband, Willis, were buying in 1961, on Back Creek Road in Seaford, Virginia, she knew she had seen it before — even though she had never been there before. "I walked right into a wall," she says. "I turned around and told my husband there's supposed to be a door here. He just looked at me kind of funny. "I walked over to another wall and told him there's supposed to be a chimney here. He said there's no chimney there. I said, well, there used to be one. Upstairs there was a chimney, and I said this one is not supposed to be here. Willis just looked at me like I was crazy."

When Clara was washing dishes the first night she was in the house, she automatically reached out her left hand. Willis asked her why. She said there was supposed to be a pump handle there. "I envisioned an old pump handle, but Willis said there was no well in the yard. I said there used to be. I also clearly saw where there had been a wash basin on an antique wash stand on the porch. Willis asked me where the bathroom was, and I pointed out in the backyard. I said over there under that old maple tree. He just shook his head, yet I was convinced I was right.

"And then I remembered where I had seen the house before. I had drawn this exact house in 1931, when I was five years old! I had shown it to my grandmother and told her I wanted to live in a house just like this. This was my house!"

Clara said Willis went down to the records office one day and looked up the records when the house was built. He came home mystified. "He said everything I said had been exactly right. There *was* a chimney where I said it had been. It had been walled over. And the chimney I said shouldn't be there had been added on to the house at a later date. And there had been a door where I had walked into the wall, and there had been an old pump by the kitchen sink. A well on the property had been filled in. I had been right on every count. And I nearly fell over, when Willis told me when the house had been built — in February 1926 — the exact month and year that I was born!"

If you haven't guessed by now, Clara is psychic.

"I was born psychic," she says. "If I am around people, I can pick up on their thoughts. Sometimes when I go in a grocery store it's like listening at the Tower of Babel. It gets so strong, I have to turn it off. I can read people's past lives. It got so that I got calls all hours of the day or night from people asking for readings. I had to cut it off. It was too much."

Clara says her "gift" has enabled her to see and sense things other people can't. "One time a relative of mine died. No one had told me about it. When I was called about it, before they could say anything, I said she just died. They asked me how I knew, and I said because she was just here standing beside me! It gets scary sometimes even for me."

Clara also knew when her grandmother and her husband were going to die, and she had visitations from her long-dead grandfather. "When grandma was ailing, I took care of her for awhile," she says. "My grandfather had been dead for sometime, but when he was alive he had a pronounced limp. When he walked across a floor, you knew it was him. You couldn't mistake his walk. When grandma was sick in an upstairs bedroom, I used to hear him limp-walk across the floor up there all the time. One time when some of my relatives were here, we all heard it. We went upstairs to see grandma, and when she asked what was the matter, we told her we had heard footsteps in the room. She said, oh that's just grandpa. He's standing right over there. Maybe she was psychic, too."

Clara also has a ghost in her house.

"Well, he manifests both here and in the house next door," she says. She believes he is a Civil War Confederate officer, because she saw him once wearing a gray uniform. "Willis never believed in ghosts, but he couldn't explain what used to happen here. One time I was sick in bed for three days, and all the doors in the house kept opening and closing by themselves. Willis accused me of doing it. I said how can I be doing it when I'm lying down in bed. He said he didn't know, but he still thought I was somehow responsible.

"Just as he said this, every door in the house, even the door to the attic, opened and slammed shut, and Willis threw up his hands and said 'I believe!' Even after Willis died, I still found locked doors unlocked and opened in the house. And one time, when the next door neighbors were remodeling, I saw the ghost standing by their mailbox. He looked at me as if to ask, 'what's going on,' so I told him that they were renovating the house and that he would like the changes they were making. Then he disappeared."

Clara says there have been various other manifestations in her house over the years. "I first saw him about 1970. Or rather, I felt him. I was hanging curtains and when I bent over to pick up a hammer, something patted me on the behind. I thought it was my mother who was staying with me, but she was no where around. Another time, he threw a wadded up piece of paper at me. Again, I thought it was mother, but she was in another room. When he patted me on the hiney once more, I told him I didn't appreciate that, and he materialized right before me. He was there only for a second and then he vanished."

Clara says she often hears him walking about the house. "He wears boots, and when he walks, you can hear his spurs jingling," she notes. "I hear him often, and my neighbor hears him jingling next door, too."

Intrigued, Clara did some digging into the history of the house and the area. She couldn't understand why a Confederate soldier would return to her house because it wasn't built until 1926. Then she discovered that there had been a Southern encampment near there, and, she reasoned, probably some skirmishes during the Civil War.

Things seemed to come together one day when she was visiting a friend and was handed a bullet from the War between the States, which had been found in the area. Clara says a lot of relics are uncovered in Seaford. "They told me that when they built these houses years ago, the carpenters would ruin their saws when they cut down trees, because they would cut into so many minie-balls and small cannonballs that had been embedded in them."

When Clara held the bullet her friend had found, suddenly a clear vision came to her. She saw a very tall young Confederate officer, leading his troops in a charge. All of a sudden, he fell from a bullet wound to the head. He had been killed instantly. Clara says her friend later had the bullet analyzed, and there were skull and brain fragments still on it.

Perhaps it is the young officer she envisioned who periodically returns to the neighborhood, clanking his spurs and opening and closing doors as he walks through the house. Perhaps it was he who playfully tapped her on the fanny.

"Can you think of a better explanation?" she asks.

CHAPTER 23

The Sad Specter at Black Walnut

(Halifax County)

t one time, in the period between the Revolutionary and Civil Wars, Black Walnut, complete with manor house, nearly a dozen out buildings, and more than 2,000 acres of land in Halifax County at the bottom middle of the Commonwealth, was a lively, thriving plantation. There are conflicting reports as to when the first part of this clapboard house was built, the dates vary between 1765 and 1776. A large addition was made about 1850.

In its heyday, Black Walnut featured a huge silver tea service, so large that the sugar dish held five pounds of sugar. It is said that one of the owners of the plantation brought $500 in Mexican silver dollars from the Mexican War and had these melted down and made into the service by a Philadelphia silversmith.

Today, Dr. William Wadkins owns the estate, which still includes about 400 to 500 acres, several of the original outbuildings, and an old family cemetery. He uses it as a summer home. In recent years, Black Walnut has been listed on both the Virginia and National Registries of Historic Places.

It was on part of the plantation property, on June 25, 1864, that the Battle of Staunton River Bridge was fought. This was the only fight of any consequence in Halifax County, and although historians have largely passed it over, it was of significance because, had the Union won the bridge and destroyed the railroad beyond it, a key supply line to General Robert E. Lee would have been cut off.

The battle also was of more than usual interest because of the *ages* of the combatants. To set the scene, by 1864, the county was suffering severely from the draining effects of the war. All the young men of age had long since left their homes to fight for the Southern cause. Consequently, once-thriving plantations and large farms, once lush with healthy crops, were barren and neglected. Even the horses had been drafted; thoroughbreds had been sent to General J. E. B. Stuart's cavalry forces, and workhorses were used to haul supplies and artillery.

When word came that Federal troops were heading toward the Staunton River Bridge, the Confederates had only about 250 reserves ready to defend. A call was made for volunteers. Most of them came from the Halifax County "home guard." They included middle teenage students from a boys' academy, and a batch of grizzled men in their 60s and 70s. They formed the now legendary "Old men and Young Boys" brigade, and marched off to the bridge, carrying whatever leftover weapons were available.

Two companies of regular troops were positioned at the right of the bridge, and the old timers and young boys occupied the left entrenchment. They dug into position and waited. On the afternoon of the 25th, the attack began. Four times that day, the Union soldiers charged across the fields trying to take the bridge, and four times the heavily outnumbered home guard repulsed them. The North lost 300 men, killed or wounded, that afternoon; the South suffered but 35 casualties, and held the bridge. One officer later remarked, "Each man (and boy) was actuated by a feeling of his own responsibility for the successful termination of the fight, and no army that ever trod the earth had produced a braver band than the 300 who saved the day at Staunton River."

John Thrift, III, grandson of the present owners of Black Walnut writes of the resident ghost there: "It was a regular plantation, it being like most in its day. It raised tobacco and other crops that would bring quick as well as easy money for the owner. Money was even of greater importance to the owner during the mid-1800s being that he saw war approaching. He had to do everything possible to ensure the future of his family. That meant to him working hard and avoiding all issues of the war.

"When his young, determined daughter fell deeply in love with a Confederate officer, he was very distressed and forbid her to see her lover anymore. It practically broke her heart. Nevertheless, she met the officer still, in secret places, keeping the romance alive, and still hoping that one day her father would 'come around.' During one of these visits, the officer told her of a battle that was to take place on plantation land at the Staunton River Bridge the next day. He seemed very excited as he rode off after their meeting. It was the last time she saw him.

"He died in the fighting. This sent the young woman into a dark depression. She became ill, and with little will to live, died within a year." Since that time, Thrift says, the spirit of the saddened young woman has never left the plantation grounds. She roams the house at night, her softened footsteps and rustling skirt, have been heard by many over the years. She also has been heard wandering about the lawns and gardens outside, crying, and calling out the name of her fallen hero. Thrift says, too, that visitors to the house "are always thoroughly checked out in their sleep by the ghost. She seems determined," he concludes, "to find her lost love."

CHAPTER 24

A Reunion at Hollywood Cemetery

(Richmond)

hen Dr. John Brockenbrough had his magnificent columned home built at 1201 East Clay Street in Richmond in 1818, neither he, or anyone else for that matter had the slightest inkling that one day his home would become a national historic landmark and a revered shrine to the Southern Cause, open to tens of thousands of visitors annually.

Typical of city houses of that era, it was designed by Charleston architect Robert Mills, who trained under Thomas Jefferson, and featured its portico on the garden side. The house was remodeled in the 1840s and received a third story in 1857. It gained international acclaim in 1861, when it was chosen to be the White House of the Confederacy during the Civil War, and served as the home and headquarters for Jefferson Davis, the first and only President of the Confederate States of America, and his family.

The house was thus held in reverant pride and respect by Richmonders from 1861 till April 1865, a distinction that it bears to this day.

Located at the southeast corner of 12th and East Clay Streets, it is a white-stuccoed brick structure in the Roman-Doric style with a small cupola which, as one historian put it, "stands rather incongruously in the center of the roof."

When the Civil War broke out in 1861, and the capital of the Confederacy was moved from Montgomery, Alabama, to Richmond, the city bought the house and offered it as a residence for Confederate President Jefferson Davis. Typical of the man, he declined to accept it under those conditions, so it was then rented to Davis and his family.

They lived there until the first week of April 1865, when Richmond was evacuated and the Davises left for Danville. It then served as a Union army headquarters until 1870, and afterwards became a public school. In 1893, the house was acquired by the Confederate Memorial Literary Society, and was made into a museum of Confederate memorabilia.

The museum was opened to the public in 1896. Prized among its collections were: General Robert E. Lee's coat and the sword he wore when he surrendered at Appomattox; the original great seal and provisional constitution of the Confederacy; General Stonewall Jackson's sword and cap; and the military equipment of Generals Joseph E. Johnston, J. E. B. Stuart, John Hunt Morgan, A. P. Hill, and John Bell Hood, as well as a splendid accumulation of paraphernalia belonging to rank and file soldiers of the Civil War. Also on display is a rich selection of historic books, manuscripts, documents and imprints, including many of Jefferson Davis' personal papers.

In 1976, all of this material was moved to a new building adjacent to the White House of the Confederacy, and the house was then completely renovated with great care taken to preserve the cornices, woodwork, mantels and other trim, so that the rooms would appear as President Davis and his wife, Varina, knew them. This restoration has returned to the principal rooms the "elegant mid-Victorian character that they had during the war years," according to the Virginia Landmarks Register. Original marble mantels, rococo gas chandeliers, the classical entrance portico, and the monumental veranda facing the garden are distinctive features. Today, both the White House and the museum are open to the public for a modest admission fee.

All indications are that Jefferson Davis, Varina, and their children were comfortable and happy in Brockenbrough house, at least during the early years of the Civil War. As time went on, however, the enormous pressures and tensions of the bloody conflict wore heavily on Davis. His health slipped steadily, and became a constant source of worry among his friends and associates. By early 1864, the toll had become obvious and friends warned him, "your nervous system is at present outraged by labor and anxiety." They told him the long hours of working through the night must stop, and that he should "devolve all the smaller matters upon some

White House of the Confederacy

of your accomplished aides and give your own care to only the great matters of vital moment." They begged him to take rest and exercise.

Biographer William C. Davis said the President's "only release at times was his family. In the children especially he took solace, for they robbed his mind of its cares for a few minutes each day. As a result, he indulged them constantly. Many an important meeting with Lee or a cabinet official came to a temporary halt when little Joe burst into the room or the children raced around the house in play."

Joe, who turned five-years-old in April 1864, was Davis' special favorite, according to his biographers, including Mary Chesnut, author of the popular "Mary Chesnut's Civil War." As William Davis wrote: "The President delighted in hearing the little boy say evening prayers at his knee. Davis might be in a meeting, entertaining guests, or about to leave on a long evening ride to see Lee. No matter, when bedtime arrived, Joseph came padding down the stairs to the entrance foyer in his nightgown, walked to his father wherever he sat or stood and kneeled to say his prayer. Jefferson Davis rested his hand on the boy's head, bent down, and whispered the prayer with him. The child was Mr. Davis' hope and greatest joy in life.

On April 30, 1864, Varina Davis left her children playing downstairs while she prepared lunch for her husband. At about 1 p.m., little Joe, and his older brother, Jeff, wandered out of the house onto the balcony in the back. Apparently, Joe began climbing on the railing. He lost his footing and fell 15 feet to the brick pavement below. The fall fractured his skull. Jeff ran to him, but he was unconscious. An Irish nursemaid named Catharine dashed upstairs to tell the President and his wife. Although Joe was still breathing when they reached him, he died shortly afterwards.

Varina became hysterical. As biographer Davis said, "Throughout the afternoon and into the evening passersby could hear her shrieking inside the house." Jefferson Davis sat with Varina for more than three hours, saying again and again, "Not mine, oh, Lord, but thine." Then a courier arrived with an important message from General Lee. Davis, it is said, obviously disoriented, cast it aside, and in heartbreak, said, "I must have this day with my little child."

He then went upstairs, and for the rest of the day and through the night, no one saw him. He paced the floor all night long. Mary Chesnut wrote: "As I sat in the drawing room, I could hear the tramp of Mr. Davis' step as he walked up and down the room above — not another sound. The whole house was as silent as death. . . Before I left the house I saw him (Joe) lying there, white and beautiful as an angel — covered with flowers.

"Catharine, his nurse, lying flat on the floor by his side, weeping and wailing as only an Irish woman can." Curiously, the nurse abruptly packed her bags and left the house. Some believe she was consumed with guilt, having not been with little Joe when he fell.

In another historic coincidence, President Abraham Lincoln sent the Davis' a message of condolence. Jefferson Davis, too, sent Lincoln a similar message upon the death of Lincoln's son, Willie. Both children had died while their fathers were sitting Presidents.

The officials at Richmond's Hollywood Cemetery offered a free plot for the burial. Mary Chesnut wrote: "Immense crowd at the funeral. Sympathetic but shoving and pushing rudely. Thousands of children. Each child had a green bough or a bunch of flowers to throw on little Joe's grave, which was already a mass of white flowers, crosses, etc." Richmond children collected 40 dollars and bought a monument for their former playmate's grave.

Jefferson Davis' last year in the Southern White House was one of extreme sadness, torment and grief. He had the balcony from which little Joe fell torn down. The only respite from this agonizing pain was the birth, on June 27, 1864, of Winnie Davis, who was called "The Daughter of the Confederacy."

On Sunday April 2, 1865, on receipt of dispatches from General Lee that the Army of Northern Virginia was about to evacuate the Petersburg and Richmond lines, and as the Union forces neared the city, Davis assembled his cabinet and directed the removal of the public archives, treasury, and other property to Danville.

A vivid description of what Richmond was like on that fateful day, when news of the evacuation swept through the city, was recorded by E. A. Pollard, author of "The Lost Cause: " " . . . The news fell upon them (the people) like a thunder-clap from clear skies and smote the ear of the community as a knell of death.

" . . . One could see the quiet streets stretching away, unmolested by one single sign of war; across the James the landscape glistened in the sun; everything which met the eye spoke of peace, and made it impossible to picture in imagination the scene which was to ensue. There were but few people in the streets; no vehicles disturbed the quiet of the Sabbath; the sound of the church-going bells rose into the cloudless sky, and floated on the blue tide of the beautiful day. How was it possible to imagine that in the next 24 hours, war, with its train of horrours, was to enter the scene; that this peaceful city, a secure possession for four years, was at last to succumb; that it was to be a prey to a great conflagration, and that all the hopes of the Southern Confederacy were to be consumed in one day, as a scroll in the fire!

"As the day wore on, clatter and bustle in the streets denoted the progress of the evacuation, and convinced those who had been incredulous of its reality. The disorder increased each hour. The streets were thronged with fugitives making their way to the railroad depots; pale women and little shoeless children struggled in the crowd; oaths and blasphemous shouts smote the ear. Wagons were being hastily loaded at the Departments with boxes, trunks, etc, and driven to the Danville depot. In the afternoon a special train carried from Richmond President Davis and some of his cabinet.

" . . . Outside the mass of hurrying fugitives, there were collected here and there mean-visaged crowds, generally around the commissary depots; they had already scented prey; they were of that brutal and riotous element that revenges itself on all communities in a time of great public misfortune."

Abraham Lincoln arrived in Richmond two days later and walked to the White House of the Confederacy. The housekeeper directed him to Davis' office. He seated himself and remarked, "This must have been President Davis' chair." He then looked far

Tombstone of Joe Davis, foreground, and tomb and statue of Jefferson Davis, Hollywood Cemetery, Richmond.

off "with a serious, dreamy expression," possibly thinking of all the suffering both he and Davis had endured, both personally and as heads of their countries.

There are at least three ghostly legends associated with Jefferson Davis and his family. In the journal she kept, Varina Davis made several references to changing things in the garden at the White House of the Confederacy. She kept writing, "I hope the 'lady in blue' approves of them. Staffers at the Museum of the Confederacy think she may have been referring to the spirit of one of John Brockenbrough's daughters, who took extreme pride in tending the garden when she lived in the house.

Secondly, there have been, over the years, persistent reports of Varina's apparition appearing at a house at Fort Monroe, Virginia, where her husband was taken after being captured in May 1865. (See chapter 34.)

And, finally, there is the spectral return of little Joe Davis. For nearly 30 years after Jefferson Davis moved out of the White House in April 1865, numerous witnesses reported seeing the apparition of a small boy, about five years of age and resembling the appearance of Joe Davis, wandering about aimlessly on East Clay Street in Richmond, and mumbling, "He's gone! He's gone!" Says one worker at the Museum of the Confederacy, "There must be something to this since the legend has survived so long."

Jefferson Davis lived on for 24 years after the end of the Civil War. He traveled extensively, wrote, and pondered about the "Lost Cause" and its consequences. When he died in 1889, he was buried in the Metairie Cemetery in New Orleans, near the Louisiana division of the Army of Northern Virginia.

But Varina Davis was not content. She wished to move her husband's remains to Beauvoir, the family home in Mississippi, but the estate was situated on a narrow peninsula on the Gulf of Mexico, and she feared that flooding and erosion might ultimately destroy the site.

At this time, large numbers of Confederate veterans wrote her asking her to choose Richmond for the late President's final resting place. They pointed out that Davis was loved and honored in Richmond during the most eventful and trying years of his life; that, in Hollywood Cemetery, he would rest among the dead of all the states who fell for the South.

She agreed, and in the spring of 1893 a special train carrying Davis' body left New Orleans. The trip took several days because the train stopped many times along the way so people could view the coffin of the only President of the Confederate States. On the train were 300 family members and guests. They arrived in Richmond on the morning of May 30, 1893, and the body was taken to the rotunda of the Capitol building where it lay in state for a day.

On the afternoon of May 31, a caisson covered with black netting and drawn by six white horses bore the coffin to Hollywood. A band played Dixie as the cortege moved from the Capitol to the cemetery. The whole city was draped in mourning for the fallen chieftain.

Little Joe's body was moved next to his father's. After this was done, the apparition of the lost child crying "He's gone!" on East Clay Street . . . was never seen again!

CHAPTER 25

The Ominous Cloud Over Cold Harbor

(Hanover County)

unny thing about Cold Harbor. It is not particularly cold, except for a few short months in the dead of winter. And there is no water within miles!

There is a colorful legend that a sailor of long ago came here to court the lady of his dreams. But when she gave him the brush off, he was said to have said, "Now that really was a cold harbor." But historians generally discount this.

A more likely possibility for the name is that in stagecoach days open shelters in remote areas were erected as passengers waited for their rides. They were known as cold harbors because they had no heat. Such shelters still exist in parts of the state where school children wait for their buses.

Cold Harbor, Virginia, though still a remote site east north east of the center of Richmond by a few miles, is today world famous, and is visited by thousands every year. It gained its fame instantly, within a few minutes, in fact, on June 3, 1864.

For it was here, on that infamous day, that one of the bloodiest and most one-sided battles of the entire Civil War was fought.

A Federal officer who participated in that battle, was one of many who wondered how Cold Harbor got its name. He reflected: "It was very much like a bake oven, and the roads were ankle-deep in powdery dust that hung in choking clouds whenever a marching column went by. And it seemed that no man in his senses would ever want to come here!"

Civil War Cemetery at Cold Harbor.

Bruce Catton, the renowned Civil War historian, wrote that: "Dust hung in the air like a gritty cloud bank." Such "clouds" that seem to linger over the battlefield have been reported for the past 130 years! Others have said it was more like a curious mist, or fog. In a Richmond Times-Dispatch article, staff writer Bill Lohmann mentioned a "haze" at the site. He quoted Charlottesville psychic and author Nannette Morrison, who was with him at the battle-field, as saying the haze was "like a mysterious old friend." She said, "Sometimes it's gray, sometimes it's blue. It's not a fog. It's not mist. It's constantly shifting." She described it as "a very thick energy that is stuck here." Her friend, Tim Fredrickson of Richmond, added that the cloud was "a portal in time." Lohmann referred to the phenomenon as "eerie."

According to many, the battle here was a dreadful and tragic mistake from the start. For example, Major General Martin T. McMahon of the Union forces, wrote: "In the opinion of a majority of the survivors, the battle of Cold Harbor never should have been fought. There was no military reason to justify it. It was the dreary, dismal, bloody, ineffective close of the Lt. General's (U. S. Grant) first campaign with the Army of the Potomac." (Grant himself later said in his memoirs, "I have always regretted that the last assault at Cold Harbor was ever made.")

The situation in June 1864, was like this: Grant, a man of action, had been placed in charge of the main Federal forces following a frustrating succession of futile generals who either lacked the heart or the ability, or both, of hammering hard against an enemy vastly inferior in numbers, weapons, equipment and food. In desperation, President Abraham Lincoln, seeking a tough fighter who would not be afraid to press the action, chose Grant to push Robert E. Lee's forces back, capture the Confederate capital at Richmond, and dismantle Lee's army.

Although Grant was still licking his wounds suffered recently at the Battle of the Wilderness near Fredericksburg, he was anxious to launch an all-out assault, come Hell or high water, to bring the war to a close. He chased Lee southward, and the two rivals dug in at Cold Harbor. At least the Confederates dug in. They built an intricate network of trenches, on ground they had chosen to defend, and awaited Grant's advance.

Many historians feel Grant committed a monumental blunder by ordering a no-holds-barred frontal assault on Lee at Cold Harbor. First, his troops were exhausted after the hard battles to the north and then the long march toward Richmond. They were described as being "dirt-caked and worn out." They had slogged through choking dust to get to Cold Harbor, and when they arrived they literally dropped in their tracks and fell into a drugged sort of sleep. The original attack has been set for June 2, but had to be delayed 24 hours — a delay which allowed the Confederates ample time to better position themselves. And they took advantage of every ravine, knoll and hillock, as well as every clump of trees, patch of brambles and bog.

Second, the Union officers did not know the land. Inexplicably, neither Grant nor General George Meade had ordered anyone to make a detailed survey of the ground. Thus when the charge came, their infantrymen ran into dense thickets, impassable briar patches, and swampy bogs which slowed to a crawl their advance and exposed them to enemy fire.

And third, as Catton put it: "The hard fact was that by 1864, good troops using rifles and standing in well-built trenches, and

Garthright House at Cold Harbor.

provided with suitable artillery support, simply could not be dislodged by any frontal assault whatever." He cited Pickett's ill-fated charge at Gettysburg as an example.

The battle that took place on June 3, 1864, was one of the most disastrous debacles of the entire war. For the Federals, it was doomed from the start. A gigantic clash of artillery broke the morning quiet. When the courageous but foolhardy Union troops got within range of the Rebel muskets, they were cut to pieces. One survivor later described the action by saying the Southern riflemen opened fire with one long, rolling volley — "A sheet of flame, sudden as lightning, red as blood, and so near, it seemed to singe the men's faces."

Catton wrote: "Rebel trenches were dotted with black slouch hats and thousands of musket barrels. Long sheets of flame ran from end to end of the trench lines. An immense cloud of smoke blotted out the sight of them, and the rocking volume of sound dazed men who had been in the war's worst battles. . . Rebel gunners were sending shell and solid shot plowing the length with murderous effect. There was an unbearable volume of musket fire. The men knew they were marching into a death trap."

Said a New Hampshire captain: "To those exposed to the full force and fury of that dreadful storm of lead and iron that met the charging column, it seemed more like a volcanic blast than a battle, and was just about as destructive." To this, a Union sergeant added: "The men involuntarily bent forward as they advanced as if they were walking into a driving hailstorm . . . They fell like rows of bricks pushed over by striking against one another."

Major General E. M. Law, C.S.A., summed it up this way: "I could see more plainly the terrible havoc made in the ranks of the assaulting column. I had seen the dreadful carnage in front of Marye's Hill in Fredericksburg, and on the 'old railroad cut' which (Stonewall) Jackson's men held at the second Manassas; but I had seen nothing to exceed this. *It was not war; it was murder'!"*

Catton said the battle of Cold Harbor was a wild chain of doomed charges, most of which were smashed in a few minutes. "In all the war," he wrote, "no attack had ever been broken up as quickly or as easily as this, nor had men ever before been killed so rapidly." It is estimated the 7,000 Union soldiers died in one half hour period, and more than 13,000 were lost overall, compared to 1,700 dead Confederates.

One historian said the smoke from the artillery and musketry fire, mingled with the dust, made the sun appear dull-red and enormous through the haze. Perhaps this helps explain why reporter Lohmann described a similar haze at Cold Harbor, 130 years later, as eerie.

There is also this chilling note. As the two armies moved out of Cold Harbor, they left a ghastly scene behind. Scattered in the trenches, across the open areas, and in the woods were hundreds of corpses. Some apparently laid there for *years* afterward! A traveler visiting the site in 1869 — five years after the battle — recalled seeing partially exposed skeletons "all over the field." The Cold Harbor National Cemetery contains nearly 2,000 graves, but as Blue and Gray Magazine recorded in a 1994 issue, "Clearly, some unprotected Civil War dead remain today on the battlefield . . ."

Ample justification for ghostly phenomena? Possibly.

Over the years there have been many reports of strange sounds and sights across this desolate battlefield. There have been Civil War reenactments here, and some of the reenactors have told of ethereal encounters . . . mysterious cold spots in the torrid heat of the summer . . . fleeting glimpses of phantom soldiers scurrying for cover . . . the sounds of moans and cries and weeping. . . and of cocking muskets.

In 1993, a young lady, Ann Bailey, living in Richmond wrote to the author and told of experiencing vivid psychic phenomena.

During a living history reenactment at Cold Harbor in 1992, she said, "My husband and I were in a tent on the battlefield." At about one a.m., she felt a pair of unseen hands running up her left leg. She immediately awakened and sat bolt upright, cursing the phantasmal intruder. Her husband saw nothing, but she said she looked directly into the apparitional face of a soldier wearing a Yankee uniform. She said he had a hairy face, and definitely was *not* one of the reenactors! She also told of hearing distant musket fire, military drum beats, and bodies being dragged across the ground.

Charlottesville author Morrison, a self-described psychic and holistic health practitioner, believes spirits of the dead soldiers are stuck at Cold Harbor, perhaps as a result of their sudden, traumatic and violent deaths, and are unable to move on to the afterlife.

While visiting the battlefield, Morrison felt "compelled" to take a photograph of a tree. She saw nothing out of the ordinary when she took the picture, but felt "psychically and mentally tuned to certain places." When the photo was developed an image of a man sitting against the tree appeared on the print. The tree had grown out of the earthwork in front of a Confederate trench. Morrison believes the "man" is wearing a Union uniform, and may have been killed at the spot where the figure materialized.

Frederikson, too, told Lohmann he had sensed spirits at the site. These have included: walking into pockets of cold, bone-chilling air; sharp pains in his right knee, which he described as feeling like bullet or shrapnel wounds — pains which disappear when he leaves the battlefield; and the sounds of the footsteps of "platoons" of men. His most frightening experience came one day when he said he saw the ghostly image of a Union soldier running toward him. He said the image "passed through his body as he stood stunned," and that it felt "like a wave of emotions washing over me." Fredrikson told Lohmann that he was thus certain he must have fought at Cold Harbor in a past life. He didn't care what other people think. "I know what's happened to me," he said.

Does all this explain the eerie haze that seems to persistently rise over the battlefield more than a century and a quarter after the fighting took place? Is the haze a reminding recurrence of a combination of the dust and the smoke and the blood which mixed here amid such violence and tragedy so long ago?

One wonders.

Leslie Winston of the National Park Service staff at Cold Harbor lived in the Garthright House on the site for six years. This house was used as a field hospital, as was the Watt House, during the battles. There have, for years, been rumors of unexplained noises and wispy sightings at both houses, but Winston has experienced none of them. "Oh, you hear some things from visitors from time to time," he acknowledges. "We have a candlelight walking tour on the anniversary of the second battle here each year, and people have told me of getting an 'eerie feeling' during these tours."

"I can't speak of anything specific," adds park superintendent Mike Andress, "but there is a kind of indescribable ambiance about such places as here and at Malvern Hill and Gaines Mill. You have to remember that two great battles were fought at Cold Harbor, and at Manassas, for example. They definitely are very powerful places."

Robin Reed, executive director of the Museum of the Confederacy in Richmond, and a Civil War reenactor himself, may have put it best when he said, "There's no question that you can go to certain battlefields and feel a sense of foreboding . . . There's something strange about this site."

CHAPTER 26

All is Not Quiet on the Petersburg Battlefield

(Petersburg)

fter the folly of the Battle of Cold Harbor, General U.S. Grant shifted his strategy. Instead of trying to use brute force to directly assault Richmond, a tactic that had cost the Union forces dearly up to this point, Grant, in June 1864, chose to withdraw from the immediate vicinity of the Confederate Capital and instead head south. His plan was to strike Petersburg, which he felt would deal a death knell to the Southern Cause because it was such an important site. It was a vital railroad center, linking Richmond to the south. If Grant could take the city the war, for all intents and purposes, would be virtually over.

Accordingly, he marched his army south from Cold Harbor and crossed the James River at Wilcox's Landing in Charles City County with more than 100,000 men. But any hopes he had of surprising the enemy and making a quick capture of Petersburg were repulsed by three primary factors. One was General Robert E. Lee anticipated Grant's move and reached the city ahead of him. Secondly, Lee was able to do this because Union generals under Grant botched the initial attack. They delayed the fighting long enough for Southern reinforcements to arrive. The third factor was the fierce tenacity with which the Confederate warriors fought to preserve Petersburg.

There is a sign today in the door of the Petersburg Visitor's Center. It reads, "The tornado did in 22 seconds what the Union army could not do in 10 months!" It refers to a terrible tornado which set down in the city a couple of years ago and did widespread damage to many of the town's historic buildings. It also refers to the fact that Grant, meeting unbelievably stiff opposition when he approached Petersburg, was forced to settle down for a siege which lasted for the better part of a year.

For months, he shelled the Confederate lines and the city relentlessly, but the Southern troops had dug their heels in deep, both figuratively and literally. Extensive and comprehensive entrenchments and earthworks lined the fields outside the town limits, running for miles in a semi-circle, and although the Rebels were heavily outnumbered in both manpower and weaponry, they refused to budge. On both sides, almost every hill and rise of ground was capped with a fort and artillery batteries, and in some places, the enemy lines were less than 400 feet apart.

Thousands were killed through the summer, fall and winter of 1864, and well into the spring of 1865. When the stalemate became apparent, Union Lieutenant Colonel Henry Pleasants, a mining engineer by profession, came up with an ingenious idea. He proposed using a unit of Pennsylvania coal miners, to dig a tunnel to a point just below the Confederate lines at Elliott's Salient, and set off a charge of four tons of gunpowder. With this, said one of Pleasants' men, "we could blow that damned fort out of existence . . ."

The mine was begun in late June 1864, and was completed about a month later. The charge was detonated early on the morning of July 30, and, in the words of one writer, "earth, timbers, guns and soldiers were hurled into the air in horrible confusion." Said a Union officer-witness: "It was a magnificent spectacle, and as the mass of earth went into the air, carrying with it men, guns, carriages and timbers, and spread out like an immense cloud as it reached its altitude, so close were the Union lines that the mass appeared as if it would descend immediately upon the troops waiting to make the charge." Added another witness, "Early in the morning of July 30, 1864, Petersburg was rocked as if by an earthquake."

The explosion tore a gaping hole 30 feet deep, 60 to 80 feet wide, and 170 feet long, which was, said one observer, "filled with dust, great blocks of clay, guns, broken carriages, projecting timbers, and men buried in various ways — some up to their necks, others to their waists and some with only their feet and legs protruding from the earth." The blast wounded, buried or killed 278 Confederate soldiers and completely destroyed two guns of the battery.

Crater memorial at Petersburg Battlefield.

In an old book, titled "Bravest Surrender," the author told of a Confederate soldier who had gone to historic Blandford Cemetery, adjacent to the site of the explosion to lay down to rest: "One of the stories that has come down to us is of a soldier who settled himself on a large, flat tombstone for a long night's sleep. It came near to being his last. In fact, he told his family afterward, he thought it *was* his last. . .

"He awakened to find he was buried, covered with mud and stones (from the blast). He mused on his fate, tentatively moved one foot — the other. Then came the glorious discovery — he was buried but not dead! He dug his way through the debris, pulled himself up on the tombstone, and stood erect — muddy but unbowed!"

A similar incident happened to a Petersburg soldier named Jim

Green. It was recounted in M. Clifford Harrison's book, "Home to the Cockade City," published in 1942. According to Harrison, Green was blown up in the explosion and buried under a pile of loose earth. "On his person he had a spoon, which proved to be of priceless value to him. With it he dug slowly, laboriously, up through the dirt, until he had a small air hole to the surface. Then, just as he was feeling a breath of air and a surge of hope, a Negro was shot and fell over the hole. Again, Mr. Green went to work with his spoon and dug himself another hole. Eventually he was rescued from his living tomb. For years after the war he kept that spoon as a relic."

A third interesting anecdote occurred to a Confederate soldier named Hugh Smith. Exhausted from the fighting, he fell into a deep sleep in the midst of several dead comrades. Sometime later he was rudely awakened and realized he was being dragged by his heels across a field by a Negro member of a burying squad. He immediately screamed, "hold on, uncle. You're not going to bury me!" With that, Smith later noted, the man dropped his feet as if they were hot bricks, and "like something propelled from a catapult, the corpse-gatherer went sprinting away as fast as he could go. He did not wait to have further words with a dead man!"

The whole idea of the massive explosion was not only to destroy a Confederate stronghold in one blow, but also to follow up with an all out assault, since the Union hierarchy felt the Southerners would be confused and unprepared to fight after such a disastrous occurrence. The problem was, the blast was so monumental, it also stunned the Yankees. Instead of immediately attacking, they ran from the blast and it took several precious minutes to reform them and go forward. By the time they did reach the site, the Confederates had regrouped and their intense firing drove the Northern soldiers into the very massive hole — called the Crater — that they had wrought. As one writer observed, the Rebels ran "straight to the brink of the Crater . . . After pouring volleys into the mass of Yankees crowded in the hole, they leaped into the pit with clubbed muskets and brained their enemies. What resulted was a catastrophic defeat of Grant's men. The Union suffered some 4,400 casualties in killed, wounded and missing, as opposed to about 1,500 for Lee's forces.

The siege of Petersburg then settled into a cruel waiting game. Grant was well supplied, while the men under Lee were cold, hungry, and wracked with disease. As historian Joseph Cullen wrote: "Grant gave the weary, half-starved Confederates no rest. . . the two armies settled into the awful monotony of living in the trenches through the cold winter. And as the long winter months of the siege dragged on, the Confederate soldiers began to know real despair for the first time."

Hopelessly outnumbered, Lee eventually was forced to abandon Petersburg and move west, in April 1865, in a last-ditch effort to evade his pursuers and head south to join the forces of General Joseph Johnston in North Carolina. This resulted in the final retreat to Appomattox.

Petersburg Battlefield

Of all the suffering from both sides, and of all the deaths and dreadful injuries during the 10 months, there is only one report of a ghostly encounter in and around the great battlefields of Petersburg. It is related by Will Hunt, who works for the Petersburg Tourism department. The site, says Will, is at an obscure place called Hatcher's Run, southwest of the city and near Five Forks in Dinwiddie County. It apparently was here, on the night of March 31, 1865, that units of the Union army, weary from constant skirmishes, saw a patrol of soldiers approaching. Fearing a counter attack from the Confederates, they fired into the mass, killing several men. To their dismay, however, they learned that they had shot their own soldiers — reinforcements who had come up to replace them.

Ever since, according to residents now living in that area, a spectral brigade of the slain Yankees can be seen on or near White Oak Road on the anniversary of that "friendly fire" tragedy. Every March 31st, the apparitional patrol is seen. Hunt says the ethereal entities strike such fear in that region that few who live there will venture out on that night. And those who do, drive very fast when they get to the site of the ghostly reenactment.

There also is one account of a Confederate soldier appearing at a historic house in Petersburg at 416 High Street. "This house dates to 1798, and was built by a Scottish immigrant named Robert Stewart who was in the tobacco business," says Suzanne Savory, who works in the city's Tourism Department. She adds that residents at this house have reported strange noises and unexplained footsteps on the staircase. Suzanne notes that the Stewart House is pointed out on the annual Petersburg ghost tour each Halloween. What is related is that people walking past the house have reported seeing the apparitional image of a Confederate soldier peering through one of the front windows. Perhaps he is still in fear of being captured by the Union forces which overran the city in early April 1865.

One wonders, however, why there are not more spirits roaming the battlefield. Why is the area of the Crater, where so many were killed so suddenly and traumatically, not haunted? And why are there no specters roaming along the hallowed grounds of old Blandford Cemetery, where 30,000 Confederate soldiers lie buried, all but 2,000 of them unknown? As Captain Carter Bishop, in his book, "The Cockade City of the Union," published in 1907, wrote of Blandford, "with the rows of Confederate dead, whose names will only be known at the Resurrection, in hope of which they now rest."

Marker at Blandford Cemetery, Petersburg.

During the long siege, a portion of the battlefield was adjacent to the cemetery, and during the action, shells riddled the area, causing some bodies to be temporarily buried elsewhere. A number of tombstones were destroyed or badly damaged. The remnants of the brick wall which surrounds the church clearly shows the storm of shot and shell which swept the area.

There are relatively few markers of these lost souls at the cemetery. A city employee said they were laid to rest in rows, "shoulder to shoulder," without benefit of coffins. Many are as far from their homes as Florida and Texas. Visitors daily walk over their grave sites without realizing the hallowed grounds upon which they tread.

In 1901, the Ladies Memorial Association of Petersburg was delegated the authority to convert old Blandford Church into a mortuary chapel and a Confederate Memorial. The women took as their objective the reburial of Southern soldiers who were left on the battlefields or just anywhere they fell.

Within a stone's throw of the church are the graves of "the gray haired sires and beardless youths" who rallied under CSA Colonel Fletcher Archer, and with only 129 men and boys, held off a Union attack of 1,500 cavalrymen, thus saving Petersburg from an early capitulation. Here are buried: a 16-year-old lieutenant; a 46-year-old father of five children, buried near his 21-year-old son, who had been killed in 1862; a 54-year-old deaf father, killed after the command to surrender, which he could not hear, who lies buried beside the grave, containing the remains of two of his sons who were lost a few months later; and a 56-year-old widower.

Yet, all seems to be quiet in the Confederate sectors of Blandford.

Still, there is one curious episode here that has yet to be satisfactorily explained. It involves the burial of a man known as "Major Jarvis." It is not known whether or not the major fought and possibly died in the Civil War. What is known is that when he died his widow did a strange thing. She left his grave unfilled! That is, she left his glass-topped coffin in the grave uncovered. The legend is that when she went to the cemetery to visit, she wanted to see her dead husband in repose.

Sometime later, she remarried, and no longer feeling the need to view the major, she enclosed the open tomb with a thick marble slab.

Apparently, the ghost of Major Jarvis took offense, for it is said that this heavy slab would not stay in place!

M. Clifford Harrison referred to this eerie phenomenon in his book: "At sunset, when the cemetery gates were closed, it (the slab) would appear to be in its proper position. The next morning the slab would be lying obliquely across a partially open grave. When workmen with crowbars would restore it to its right position and all would seem well, the ponderous slab would persist in slanting again during the ensuing night."

Harrison said he personally experienced unexplained activity at the site. "Once," he wrote, "when walking with a friend in Blandford Cemetery, I mentioned the legend of the hollow tomb. We walked to the Jarvis square and paused outside the iron fence. As we loitered there, we suddenly heard a metallic 'Clink!' down in the grave. We looked at each other with queer expressions on our faces. We felt that the story of the hollow grave was confirmed . . . "

GENERAL GRANT UPSTAGED

There is a humorous anecdote associated with Union commander General Grant during his time spent at Petersburg. He had issued orders that anyone within

Yankee lines not having an official pass was to be apprehended. One day such a person, an elderly Negro, was brought before him. Grant immediately recognized that the old man obviously was not a spy and offered no threat, yet he teased the fellow for awhile by questioning him.

As the Negro was about to leave he turned and said since the general had asked him so many questions, could he ask the general one. Grant smiled and said okay. The man then asked him where he was going after he left the place where he was now encamped.

Grant said he would be going to one of four places. "I'm going to Richmond, to Petersburg, to Heaven, or to Hell." The aged Negro thought for a moment and then replied: "You can't go to Richmond, because General Lee is there. You can't go to Petersburg, because General Beauregard is there. You sure can't go to Heaven, because General Stonewall Jackson is there. So I don't see but one place left for you to go, sir!

CHAPTER 27

The Gentle Spirit of Burnt Quarter

(Dinwiddie County)

urnt Quarter, a large, rambling frame house in Dinwiddie County, southwest of Petersburg, was built around 1750, and is one of the oldest continuously operated farms in the region. The main part of the 15-room mansion, a two-story building, is flanked on each side by one-and-a-half story wings, each having a gabled roof.

In addition to having its resident ghost, Burnt Quarter has survived the ravages of two great wars — The Revolutionary and the Civil War. In fact, the house got its name from an incident that occurred during America's fight for independence. Banastre Tarleton, the notorious British Colonel who nearly captured Thomas Jefferson in Charlottesville (see "The Ghosts of Virginia, Volume I, 1993), passed through Dinwiddie County enroute to Yorktown. He had the granary, and all the slave quarters and outbuildings on the plantation burned to the ground, but for some reason, inexplicable to this day, the main house was spared. From that time on, the estate has been known as Burnt Quarter.

For the next 80 or so years, the plantation experienced peace and prosperity, and was one of the ante-bellum social centers of the area. A young mistress of the household who got married there in 1854 is said to have descended the stairway in a dress that cost $1,000 with a $500 veil!

Such opulence ended abruptly during the War Between the States. It was largely on plantation grounds that one of the last and bloodiest battles of the war was fought, the Battle of Five Forks on April 1, 1865, just a few days before General Robert E. Lee surrendered at Appomattox. Lee and his soldiers had been entrenched in a last-ditch effort to protect Petersburg at all costs, since its fall would open the Union army's path to Richmond and the collapse of the Confederacy.

Realizing this, Federal General Ulysses S. Grant felt if Lee's railroad supply line could be severed at a place near Dinwiddie called Five Forks, where five roads converged, the end of the war would be near; Lee then would have to give up his defense of Petersburg. Historian Bruce Catton called Five Forks "a lonely country crossroads," and much of the battleground was on Burnt Quarter property.

BURIED
IN THIS YARD
SIX UNKNOWN
CONFEDERATE
SOLDIERS
KILLED IN BATTLE
OF FIVE FORKS
APRIL 1 1865

The two forces squared off on April Fool's Day: the overall Union army commanded by Philip Sheridan; the Confederates by Generals George Pickett and Fitzhugh Lee. Although eventually heavily outnumbered, the Southerners fought fiercely and the battle lines waged back and forth across Burnt Quarter's fields.

At one point Pickett told Fitzhugh Lee to warn the Gilliam family, which then owned the plantation, to vacate the house, as it was directly in the line of fire. With the 'Confederates in the peach orchard at the rear, and the Union forces in the front, Burnt Quarter was used for protection by both forces. Mrs. Gilliam, the owner's grandmother, sent her daughters to the homes of relatives for safety, but she herself refused to leave, as she was "caring for" a sick servant.

The fighting raged on for several hours that day, so fierce at times, say historians, that "the front lawn was covered with wounded and dying soldiers." During this period the house was used as a headquarters for Union General Wesley Merritt, and later Burnt Quarter was converted into a hospital. While the mansion was occupied, soldiers slashed the family portraits adorning the walls. One of these portraits was of Mrs. Gilliam's late husband, who had served in Congress. Bullets tore into the walls, and one cannon ball nearly demolished the great chimney at the end of the drawing room.

Exhausted by "the harrowing experiences of the day," Mrs. Gilliam retired early as the night shadows were falling. The story has been handed down in the family that a musket ball passed through the wall of her bedroom, through the pillow on which her head lay, and then out the opposite wall, "without the slightest injury to herself."

On the lawns surrounding the house, however, lay the dead and dying bodies of dozens of soldiers and horses. There is a grave marker today in front of Burnt Quarter that says: "Buried in this yard six unknown Confederate soldiers killed in Battle of Five Forks April 1, 1865."

Outnumbered by 26,000 to 7,000, the Southerners under Pickett were finally beaten back and the railroad lines Grant had sought to hold were secured. It signalled the end for Lee's Army of Northern Virginia, and a few days later the surrender at Appomattox occurred.

A few years later, several Union officers returned to the house to conduct an inquiry into the battle. As they noticed the damage to the portraits, one of the officers, General Winfield Scott Hancock, offered to pay for their restoration. Mrs. Gilliam steadfastly refused. The family had patched them up, although the slash marks still showed. Today, a visitor to Burnt Quarter can still see the pock marks of bullet holes throughout the building. There is also a size-able collection of minie-balls.

One would suspect, with so much bloodshed and suffering, that any ghosts at Burnt Quarter would surely be those of the heroic young men, from both the North and the South, who died there so close to the end of hostilities; so close to going home at last. But such is not the case.

The sole reported spirit there, instead, is believed to be an ami-able one who "never harms anybody, though her ghostly presence may be felt." It is "Nissy" Coleman, a descendent of the original owner of the house. She is said to visit — "so gentle a spirit should not be said to haunt" — her bedroom in the second floor east wing. The tradition is that "the rustle of her skirt" is heard on still nights as she ascends the stairway, enters the room, and "hovers about the bed." So strong was this presence, that even though she was known to be gentle and not to bring harm in any way, servants refused to remain in the house after dark.

CHAPTER 28

The Lone Sentinel at Sailor's Creek

(Near Amelia)

egends of Civil War ghosts abound in Virginia. Accounts of spectral soldiers run from the battlefield at Cedar Creek in the Shenandoah Valley to the rugged terrain of Ball's Bluff near Leesburg, and from the Sunken Road outside of Fredericksburg to the solemn gravesites in Richmond's Hollywood Cemetery. Often, they hold their own ghostly reenactments, still fighting, more than 130 years later.

There have been, for example, a number of witnesses who have reported sightings at one of the more important but lesser known sites of the war; a site where the Confederate's physical force, but not the spirit, was finally broken, hastening Lee's decision to surrender.

This occurred at Sailor's Creek, a small stream about 19 miles west of Amelia. It was April 6, 1865, and the proud Army of Northern Virginia was force-marching westward in hopes of escaping General Grant's charging troops, far superior in number and condition. The Southerners were exhausted to the bone. They had been marching hard for four straight days and nights, the last two without anything to eat. Officers had seen some soldiers eating raw fresh meat in the ranks - anything to quell the pain in their empty stomachs.

As they reached Sailor's Creek the Federal cordon tightened around them. Confederate General Richard Ewell described it in his official report: "The enemy's artillery took a commanding position, and, finding we had none to reply, soon approached within 800 yards and opened a terrible fire. After nearly half an hour of this, their infantry advanced, crossing the creek above and below us at the same time." At this point the over-matched Rebs, under General Anderson, launched a furious counter offensive which momentarily stunned the enemy. But the Union forces were so overwhelming in number — perhaps 30,000 to 3,000 Confederates — that the surprise attack was soon repulsed.

Still, the strong will and determination of the Southern men drew grudging respect. Said Union General J. Warren Keifer: "The enemy's rear guard fought stubbornly and fell back toward the stream . . . but then faced the murderous artillery . . . (and) were subjected to a terrible infantry fire from all sides . . . The field was covered with the dead and the dying." Keifer went on to praise the gallantry and heroism of his outnumbered foes.

"On riding past my left, I came suddenly upon a strong line of the enemy's skirmishers advancing upon my left rear," Ewell wrote. "This closed the only avenue of escape; as shells and even bullets were crossing each other from front and rear over my troops, and my right was completely enveloped, I surrendered myself and staff to a cavalry officer. . . I had surrendered . . . to prevent useless loss of life." To this, Union General Keifer added: "Flight was impossible, and nothing remained to put an end to the bloody slaughter but for them to throw down their arms and become captives."

Ewell said about 2,800 of his men were taken prisoner and 150 had been killed. A few stragglers ran off into the woods, in desper-

ate hopes to rejoin the remainder of Lee's army. Lee himself, far in the distance, had observed the rout and told an officer beside him, "That half of our army has been destroyed."

Although Ewell's surrender ended the fighting that day, and hastened the meeting of Lee and Grant three days later at Appomattox, it apparently did not end the battle for at least one dedicated Confederate ghost. This apparitional young man has been seen by a number of visitors to the Sailor's Creek battlefield, standing guard by a captured Yankee cannon.

Writer Kay Ragland Boyd, an authority on Civil War specters, wrote in a newspaper article more than a decade ago: "Not far from the Hillsman House in the sector once held by General Ewell's command are a number of field pieces — silent, grim reminders of the final battle of the War Between the States.

"One of those ancient guns is manned by a lone Confederate who stands or crouches beside his weapon awaiting the order to fire — which he may or may not have heard before he was killed in action. . . . The unknown Confederate, according to eye-witness accounts, is young, slender, with long blond hair straggling from beneath his battered forage cap. A thin boyish beard only partially conceals his face. His uniform, faded and torn, consists of a gray jacket and dark brown trousers. . . He stands to his gun . . . as though to load or fire the field piece which has not roared forth its death and destruction in more than a century.

"The young gunner appears as a three-dimensional figure, only to vanish when approached, in a bluish vapor. When thunder rumbles along the battlements of Sailor's Creek, the youthful

Johnny Reb bends to his gun. At other times he stands erect, watchfully waiting for the advancing hordes of blue coats that overpowered the remnant of the Southern command.

"Legends are known that tell of the sound of invisible horses in the area, distant, sullen gunfire, and a confused mumble of voices, together with the unmistakable tramp of marching men."

Boyd concluded her article by telling about a battle reenactment which takes place at the site in April. "It is to be wondered if, numbered among the men in gray (during the reenactment), there is a phantom gunner holding his position, silent . . . invisible except to a few who have seen him, but nonetheless manning his weapon and participating in the confusion of battle . . . hearing the Rebel yell again, the exploding shells and the gradual dying away of the battle sounds until all is quiet.

"Then the ghostly Confederate remains at Sailor's Creek, keeping his lonely vigil — forever."

* * * * * * * * * *

How devastating was the Battle of Sailor's Creek, not only to the soldiers involved, but also to the civilian population living in the area? W. A. Watson, addressing the Amelia chapter of the United Daughters of the Confederacy in 1917, gave a poignant insight. Speaking of the fact that many farmhouses were used as makeshift hospitals, he said, "These incidents show how stern and real must have been the lives of our people in that sad period of their history, how the realities of a whole lifetime could be crowded into a few short hours.

"Today, families and friends assemble in peace around the hospitable firesides of quiet country homes; tomorrow 'grim-visaged war' comes suddenly upon the scene, a great battlefield is spread out in their midst, the wounded and the dying become their guests, women become men in the service of humankind, and children grow old in the preface of life's great tragedies.

"But it is all gone now. Fifty years have passed since the sound of the guns of Sailor's Creek died away on the gentle breeze of that April day long ago. When the spring comes again, green grass and sweet flowers will wave over the last resting place of the unreturning brave of both armies, who there alike await the judgment day, but whose spirits have long since made peace on the camping ground of the brave and the just."

That is, the unreturning spirits of all but one!

CHAPTER 29

An Apparition Dressed in Gray

(Chesterfield County)

uring General Robert E. Lee's last march, westward across Virginia from Petersburg, his troops crossed land now owned by Steve LaPrade and his wife, Penny, in Chesterfield County, close to the Appomattox River. "We know there was a large encampment on our property during the first week of April 1865," Steve says. "I have about 120 acres, and the land adjoins 800 acres owned by the Boy Scouts. My brother-in-law has researched the history extensively. One thing we learned was that the old ferry used to cross the river between Dinwiddie and Chesterfield near here, and there used to be an old road, I think it was called Exeter Mill Road, that ran right down to the river."

Steve, a successful house builder in the area, says they also discovered that there was a bad storm when the Confederate soldiers crossed the Appomattox, and that as many as 300 soldiers drowned while trying to ford the raging stream.

Both he and his wife think it might be possible that some of Lee's troops still linger in the heavily wooded area that surrounds their house. "I ride horses in the woods around here and you get a feeling that you're never alone," Penny says. "It's weird, a creepy feeling, like someone is always there watching you," says Penny. "But I have never seen anything. I just get this feeling. The woods go for miles, yet it's like someone else is there with you."

"It's not really a scary feeling," adds Steve, "but like Penny says, it's like you're never alone in there. Sometimes I get the sensation that there's like a whole brigade of soldiers marching in there. And we're not the only ones who have felt it. I let some friends of mine go hunting in the woods and they said they had the same feelings.

"I can remember one time I had a bricklayer, and when I told him about it, he just scoffed and said nothing bothered him. Well, we were deep in the woods working on a little cabin one evening, and he came through the woods by himself to get there. I don't really know what happened, but all of a sudden he was a believer. He said he'd never go in those woods by himself again."

Penny says that for a while she had a difficult time feeling comfortable in the custom house they built about five years ago. "Again," she says, "it was like someone was present, someone was watching me. There are some things that have happened here that I can't explain."

Steve says their interest really got piqued when their daughter, Taylor — he calls her Bubba — started telling her mother and father that she saw a figure of a man, an old man in a gray uniform with a long beard. They didn't pay a lot of attention to her at first, even though she said she saw the vision on more than one occasion. A woman over for dinner one night said she saw someone outside the dining room window. They looked outside but found no one.

And then Steve had his ethereal experience. "It was sometime in 1992, I can't remember exactly when. It might have been October. I had been out putting up some fences, and when it started to drizzle I went back to the house. I walked into the garage, and all of a sudden I got this real cold feeling. I remember it well, because it wasn't particularly cold outside. I got a cold chill like someone had put ice down my back.

"Then I looked to my left, and there, standing no more than 10 feet away from me was a man dressed in a full Confederate uniform! He was about 5 feet 10 inches tall, and I remember noticing his belt buckle and his sword. I don't remember if he was wearing boots or not. It seemed like he had red feet, but I can't be sure of that. He might have been an officer, because it appeared that his uniform was neatly pressed and spotless. I just froze. I wasn't really scared, but I was kind of shocked. I would say he was about 30 or 35 years old, and he had a worn and weathered face, like that of a farmer.

"I can't tell you if he was a ghost. I don't know. But I can tell you he was very real, as real as it could be! I was not imagining it. I saw him." Steve says the vision lasted no more than a fleeting sec-

172

ond or two, and then the apparition disappeared. Chilled to the bone, Steve went back in the house, visibly shaken. Sometime after that, on a rainy night, Steve got out a book full of illustrations of the Civil War. He went upstairs and sat down with his daughter, then about three years old. As they flipped through the pages, he said she passed over old photographs of Abraham Lincoln and Union soldiers without comment. But when they turned to a page that had a picture of a Confederate officer, in full uniform and with a long beard, Taylor instantly pointed to it and said, "Daddy, that's the man I saw!"

It wasn't long afterwards when the skeletal bodies of three Confederate soldiers were found in shallow graves nearby. They were dug up, authentic pine box coffins were made for them, and then they were given a proper burial.

Steve says that no sightings of the mysterious Southern officer have been made since that time. Perhaps he is now, at last, resting in peace.

CHAPTER 30

The Last March of Robert E. Lee

(Amelia County, near Deatonsville)

(Author's note: A strong case could be made that the first week and a couple of days in April 1865 were the saddest in Virginia's long history. For this was when the proud Army of Northern Virginia, under the command of the brilliant Robert E. Lee, finally driven out of Petersburg after a months-long siege, force-marched across the central part of the state in a desperate, last-gasp attempt to head south and join the army of General Joseph E. Johnston, then in North Carolina.

Outnumbered by more than two to one, half-starved and exhausted almost beyond human endurance, Lee's men nevertheless trudged westward in hopes of reaching railroad lines south before the Yankees could destroy the tracks. But their hopes of uniting with Johnston were already all but dashed. The Confederates had suffered a terrible defeat at the Battle of Five Forks, Richmond had fallen, and Ulysses Grant's troops were pressing in on all sides.

"No march in the history of the Army of Northern Virginia had been as sad as this one," wrote one historian. "Defeat, utter and final defeat, weighed heavily on almost every mind." As one young Southern officer put it, "an indescribable sadness weighed upon us." Still, Lee felt if he could reach the Amelia Courthouse where he had ordered rations to be sent, he then either could turn south, or possibly move on westward to Lynchburg.

But it was not to be. When Lee's 30,000 men reached Amelia not a single ration was to be found. He was devastated. An officer wrote: "No face wore a heavier shadow than that of General Lee. The failure of supplies completely paralyzed him." Still, the crafty old warrior continued to display the charismatic command he was so noted for. He scolded a young officer for not having his uniform properly buttoned, saying, "you must avoid anything that might look like demoralization while we are retreating."

On April 6, 1865, the Confederates fought heroically at Sailor's Creek, but they were cut to pieces by northern artillery. Still, Lee moved on to the west in a drizzling rain with his famished and worn out men. With the routes south now cut off, Lee hoped to reach fresh supplies in Lynchburg. But when the superior Union forces got to Appomattox Courthouse ahead of him, he realized the end had come.

"There is nothing left for me to do but to go and see General Grant," Lee said, "and I would rather die a thousand deaths." On April 9th, he mounted Traveler and rode off to surrender at the McLean House in Appomattox Courthouse.

To all who took part in or witnessed that final march during the first nine days of April 1865, it was a tragic and sad event. But was it Lee's last march? Perhaps not. There is at least one eye-witness account that Lee's famished and battered army marched through Amelia County on its final journey at least once more — *60 years later*!

This intriguing legend is recounted by James R. Furqueron, director of the Edgar Allan Poe Museum in Richmond and is reprinted with his permission. Here is what he said:)

During the many pleasant times I spent on my grandfather's farm near Burkeville in Nottoway County, certainly the most memorable were those summer evenings when I was permitted to stay up and listen to the elders talk on my grandfather's front porch. To a young lad of nine, this was a high honor indeed with a touch of adventure to boot. On many of these occasions we would be joined by friends or neighbors, and the men would necessarily take refreshments from matters out of tall, cool pitchers. Tobacco farming was mighty hard work, and the cool of the evening (the house was right up from a creek bottom), coupled with the appropriate liquids would put the elders into an expansive and reflective mood. Talk generally centered on crops, the weather, or the damn-fool politicians.

"I remember one evening in August of 1957, my grandfather was joined by an elderly gentleman who had relocated to

Nottoway County from Amelia many years before. Even at his great age (eighty thereabout), he was still engaged in tobacco farming. On this evening (as usual) the conversation centered on the current tobacco crop. Before long, however, for reasons probably relating to the death of a mutual acquaintance, the tone turned somber and (much to my trepidation and delight) came around to a discussion of those phenomena that we generally call ghosts. To the rapt attention of a nine-year-old, these two magnificent old gentlemen passed through what surely would have constituted a volume or so of folklore and stories about the supernatural. One in particular has stuck with me all these years, largely because of the very severe manner in which the old man related it. I give it now as nearly as I can remember his words. The old man said:

"'It must have been sometime in April of '25 (1925). We was working a farm in Amelia County fornenst (near) Deatonsville. I was up an to the fields afore light and was fornst the road what run up to Rice (Rice's Station). The sky was jest beginning to lighten a bit, and it was as quiet as a tomb. I was down in a hollow jest north of the road when I chanced to look up and behind me.

"'I never heared nothing, but you know how it is when you think you are being looked at. Well, I turned around and looked up and I seen this here fellow on a horse up on the rise next to the road. I couldn't make him out real plain, but he was pictured up against the lightning sky. It warn't unusual to see a mounted man that early, but something 'bout this fellow made me right uneasy. He just sat on his horse, the two as still as a statue, and he slowly

Sword of Robert E. Lee in display case at the Museum of the Confederacy, Richmond. (Photo taken with permission of the museum.)

raised his left arm and pointed to the west. Then he reined his horse and moved back over the rise outa sight.

"'All that time I never heared one sound. Well now, I'll tell you, I was skeered good, but I reckon I was more curious. So I walked up the rise and looked out onto the road where I figured the feller had gone to.

"'There a'int no way for to describe what I seen other than jest to tell: going up that road aheadin' west and fillin' it as fer as the eye could see was *soldiers a marchin' and guns and caissons with soldiers a sittin' on top!* And I seen the flags in that dim light — Lord, they was our flags! The crossed red battle flags on the Confederate Army.

"'It was still pretty dark, but I seen 'em; thousands of men and horses and wagons a moving up that road. I was not more than 50 feet away and I never did hear one sound! I stood and I looked for ten minutes or so, and brother, it was nigh on to cold that April mawnin' and I was sweatin', yessir, I'll tell you I was. They kept on a movin' without a sound, and I knowed it was the passin' of the dead. That's what I seen, yessir, and I never did see anything else like that ever again.'"

To this, James Furqueron adds: "I remember the summer evenings on my grandparents' porch very well. The twilight, the myriad lightning bugs, and the lonely call of the whippoorwill from down in the creek hollow. And I especially remember the night the old man told about seeing Lee's army on its way to Appomattox over a half century after it had passed into history."

The Case of the Frightening Footsteps

(Somewhere in Central Virginia)

(Author's note: In researching for this series of books on Virginia ghosts — this is the eighth book in the series — I have spent hundreds of hours poring through thousands of old volumes, dog-eared and long defunct magazines, and yellowed newspaper pages.

It is best, of course, where possible to directly interview people who have personally experienced ghostly phenomena, and I do that whenever the opportunity occurs. But not all material can be compiled that way. Hidden within the covers of county histories and centennial editions, buried deep in obscure volumes, most of which have been long out of print, and gathering dust in used book stores and the musky archives of libraries great and small, one can sometimes, if one looks hard enough, find rare mentions of spectral activity. It is a laborious task which sometimes pays unexpected and highly gratifying dividends.

Such was the case one day when I was browsing at Jack Hamilton's used and rare book shop on Jamestown Road outside of Williamsburg. There, heaped in a far corner, I found a pile of 200 or so copies of a once-popular journal called "The Confederate Veteran." It was a fairly popular item in the South in the early years of the 20th century when many such veterans were still among us. I found the perusing fascinating. On the floor of the shop, I spent hours poring through the delicate, fading pages. I found some personal accounts of battles and battlefields to add to other material I had amassed.

In the last dozen or so issues I came across, in the table of contents, a reference to an article on "The Soldier Boy's Ghost."

I may have startled the young clerk when I let out what may have sounded like a Rebel yell! I was excited further when I leafed to the page and learned it was, indeed, an incident in Virginia involving a Virginian.

There are no exact details to this account. The location of the house involved is not revealed. It is only referred to as being in the central part of the state. And the witness to the phenomena is also unidentified. It was written by a woman named Mrs. B. C. Peters of Oak Hill, West Virginia, and was published in the September-October 1932 issue of the "Confederate Veteran." While the factual particulars I favor are missing, it was subtitled, "A True Story."

I include it in this collection, not only because of the confrontation with a spirit, but also because I found it a compelling narrative of what it must have been like to have been a young boy, who probably entered the war at age 16 or 17, and fought, and been wounded in the "Lost Cause." There is an understated eloquence in its simplicity. I should say no more. Mrs. Peters' poignant account speaks for itself. I have merely excerpted it a little for flow and clarity. Enjoy.)

ee was at Petersburg, and was soon to yield, having for four years warded off the attacks of the Union armies from Richmond, the citadel of the Southern Confederacy.

"On a warm April day in 1865, a young Confederate soldier walked slowly and unsteadily along a deep-rutted country road toward the west. He was as thin as a girl, and although his age was but 21, he bore the marks of a man of 40. War had seared his once youthful visage with the hardened lines of a veteran. Relieved on a furlough, he was headed toward the mountains, home, hope.

"Barely 24 hours had passed since he had been discharged from the hospital in Petersburg with a 60 days leave granted, but the officer who made out his papers had remarked, 'Things are winding up, my boy; you may not need to return.' The surgeon had said to him: 'Young man, I think you can make it home, but you must rest often and not allow yourself to go without food. When he passed out of the ward, they placed another man on his cot.

"He had volunteered at 17 and for four years had followed Pickett up and down the ravaged soil of battle-scarred states. At Gettysburg, where he was standard bearer for his company, his

reckless abandon and inspiring courage were so noteworthy his captain remarked that the only thing that saved him was that he was too thin for a bullet to hit.

"Now, as he limped weary and sore-footed, the wide expanse of an older and much larger dead brother's uniform flapped about his limbs and rendered it even more difficult for him to walk. Sometimes in his simple mind arose faint memories of his village home as it was when he left it. His mother had stood at the gate and tearfully bade him goodbye as he marched away to war, full of spirit as a gamecock. Later, when he had passed around the bend and forded the creek, he had choked back a sob. Subsequent days had brought loneliness and heartache to the boy who had never been away from home — the home that was now a distant memory. It was all so much like a dream, and he thought of the peacefulness of it all — of treasured scenes of his childhood and early manhood. But that was four years ago. He wondered if they were still there.

"The wound in his shoulder brought him back forcefully to the bitter presence of the moment. In the last hour it had commenced to bleed, and he sat down by the roadside to staunch the flow of blood. The shoulder had been struck a glancing blow by a Minie ball, and the arm hung like an iron weight, numb, devoid of feeling. The bleeding subsided and the rest strengthened him.

"Springtime abounded over the land. Wheat was knee deep and

billowy. Corn and potatoes were up, for this section of Virginia was as yet untrodden seriously by the war god. . . The scent of wild hyacinth pervaded the atmosphere. . . It was hard to believe from this peaceful scene that tragedy stalked.

"A cloud of dust on the country road was soon followed by the sound of rumbling wheels, and a cavalcade of wagons, buggies, carts, loaded with country folk and their household effects, came into view. There must have been a dozen or more. The occupants called greetings to him, but moved on hurriedly. They were fleeing from (Union General Philip) Sheridan's ravaging hosts.

"Near the middle of the afternoon he came to a bridge under which a small stream flowed deep and amber. . . Kneeling, he proceeded to satisfy his thirst. Then he plunged his head under the surface of the water several times. . . Painfully, he pulled off his worn shoes and tattered stockings, then dangled his tired, aching feet in the water. Its cooling freshness soothed his feet and brought peace to him. His attention became drawn to the shoes . . . The heels had disappeared. There were holes in the uppers and holes in the soles. No wonder he had sore feet. He grinned derisively at them and, holding them high for a last look, dropped them into the stream where they were swept under the bridge and out of sight. . . The gentle swaying of the sycamore tree lulled him into sleep.

"Hours later he awoke to the accompaniment of the crash of thunder. Overhead flashes of lightning swept across the murky sky, and the wind soughing through the branches made him shiver. . . The rain descended in torrents. The soldier sheltered himself against the bole of the tree. . . After a time (the storm) wore itself out and the broken peals of thunder sounded dim in the distance. . . The wetness had made him cold. . . Barefooted, he continued his journey.

"The day had grown dim and hunger began to assail him. How he wished for food! . . . Straight ahead, in a large open space on slightly rising ground, loomed a pretentious country dwelling. Nearer, it was seen to have a white-columned portico, shady, grassy lawns, extensive outbuildings, and all about unmistakable evidence of culture.

"The soldier, now almost famished, turned from the highway and slowly approached the mansion. . . He walked up a box-hedge-bordered path to the porch. . . All about was evidence of elegant taste, albeit the surroundings were somewhat in a state of dilapidation, something to be expected in the zero hour of Southern tide.

"A massive door stood before him as he crossed the portico,

and there was no response as he took hold of the heavy knocker and let it fall several times. Then he called loudly. Still no answer. He waited. The silence of the graveyard permeated the atmosphere. Plainly, no one was at home.

"He tried the door and it opened with ease. . . For a moment he hesitated, and stepped inside. He was in a large hallway. Doors opened to either side. Cautiously, he opened the first door to the right. Inside was a lavishly furnished parlor. Rich tapestries hung on the walls . . . The lush feel of expensive rugs was under his feet.

In an open fireplace a bright fire burned. He approached the fire to warm himself. Then he called loudly. Still there was no answer.

"Forgetting his weariness and all else, even the desolation of the mansion, in his hunger, the soldier tossed his cap, gun and knapsack upon a divan and began to search for food. At the end of the hall he found the kitchen. To his surprise, a fire burned in the fireplace there, and pots of vegetables hung from hooks in the chimney. On a table sat a pan of yeast dough. Upon shelves were some cakes and pies, and, opening a cupboard, he discovered a-cold-boiled ham and a loaf of light bread. These he seized and started to eat ravenously.

"Feeling better, he gathered an armful of wood from the kitchen pile and, carrying it to the parlor, threw it upon the fire. Then he lighted a candle, as it was now quite dark. . . Warmth crept over him, but he could not sleep. There was yet the mystery of the mansion. . .

"Suddenly, a noise startled him. It came from overhead and was like the tramp, tramp, tramp, tramp of heavy boots going from one corner to the other in the room above. He gripped himself and sat up. Then he listened steadily. Could he have been mistaken? All doubt was cast aside, when, presently, he heard the sound again, this time the walker retracing his steps to the original corner.

"He hastily seized his gun and the candle and crept quickly and silently upstairs. Three doors opened to either side of the upstairs hall. The one at the far end of the hall and to the right, he was certain, opened into the room whence the noise had issued. He would find out. Tiptoeing to the door, he opened it cautiously, and, holding the candle aloft, peered inside. The chamber was that of a young lady of that period. . . But there was no sign of life. Only the mournful call of a hoot owl to its mate came through a partly opened window. *But the room was heavy with a personality.*

"The astonished soldier took in all these details at a moment's glance. Then he hurried to the other chambers. In these, he made a circumspect examination, looking under the beds, searching the closets, and thumping on the walls. These rooms were all handsomely furnished, but devoid of life as a tomb.

"Returning to the parlor downstairs, he sat down beside the fire. In a moment he heard the noise again. The mystery walker was crossing the upstairs room again. He sprang to his feet this time, somewhat nervously, and, seizing the candle, literally ran upstairs to the young lady's chamber, throwing open the door violently. It was as empty as before. Quickly, he searched the closet, examined the bed, looked behind the pictures on the wall for a possible secret passage, but to no avail. Walking to the open window, he examined the exterior for a porch roof, tree, ladder, or trellis that might furnish footing for escape.

"No tree, shrubbery, or other avenue offered egress. . . Silence, save for the chirping of the night insects, hung over the meadow, and an even more deathlike silence pervaded the mansion. Uncertainty that hinged upon dread perplexed his brain. Though his heart was beating faster, he returned to the upstairs hall and sat down in a far corner. He had extinguished the candle, for he had ceased to think of catching the walker, and, to tell the truth, felt safer in the gloom.

"He sat in the corner for perhaps 15 minutes, listening, his dread bordering upon fear. Then he heard the walker again, this time *downstairs*, and, unmistakably, in the parlor. The footsteps began in a corner toward the front of the room and proceeded diagonally across to the opposite corner.

"The simple people of the South believed firmly in ghosts. From childhood, he had learned to fear uncanny manifestations. His perplexity had already grown into fear. He now became frightened. Little would it take to precipitate him into headlong flight. Suddenly, he heard the noise again from the parlor. The walker was retracing his steps, but had paused midway across the room, making two loud thumps with the heels of his boots, and then proceeding to the opposite corner.

"This was enough! The soldier who had dared the cannon's mouth sprang to his feet and ran at top speed down the hall to the back room, dashed to the window, and jumped out into dark space. Like a plummet, he hurtled downward and landed on the roof of a low building to the rear of the mansion. Another jump took him to the ground, and he was off like a wild man through thickets, over rocks and stubble, and up a hillside back of the house, halting on a large rock out of breath and exhausted from the terrific exertion.

"While recovering his strength, he watched the mansion below. In the black night it loomed up dark and dreadful. He half expected to see a phantom emerge from one of the doors or windows and seek the rude disturber of its placidity, yet no grim apparition came into view. . .

"He became drowsy. A soft breeze fanned his cheek. The moon rose higher in the sky and, as the soldier watched the eerie visit through half closed eyelids, he fell asleep.

"What awakened him were the pangs of hunger, and as he sat

up rubbing his eyes, the cheery rays of the sun greeted him from the east. . . He thought of the pies and cakes and the ham and light bread that he had left in the kitchen; and then of last night's ghost that had frightened him into such fast retreat to the hillside.

"At the latter incident, he roared with laughter. . . His soldier's courage had returned. As he descended the hillside, his eyes were fixed on the kitchen. Entering it, he saw that someone had been there during the night! The vegetables had been taken from the pots, the pots washed and arranged neatly upon the shelf. Rolls had been baked and laid on a white tablecloth. . .

"He ate hurriedly, swallowing his food in great mouthfuls, while his eyes roved about the place. He tried to piece together the small bits of evidence that might yield a solution of the mystery — the cozy fires of the night before in the parlor and kitchen, the strange walker, the excellent food all untouched laid out as if placed ready for some person. . .

"He would not unravel this mystery, but would leave it with the house.

"Feeling that the food in the kitchen was intended for him, he filled his knapsack with one of the pies and part of the rolls and ham, and, with a tender, thankful heart, passed into the back yard and thence, by a path, to the front yard. Pausing at the fragrant lilac bush near the front gate, he turned for one last look before departing."

CHAPTER 32

The Ghost Brigade of Centre Hill

(Petersburg)

lthough encroached upon by the trappings of the modern world, Centre Hill stands today, as it has for well over a century and a half, as the dominating architectural showpiece of Petersburg. It vividly recalls the antebellum splendor and prosperity of the old city. One early visitor to the mansion described it as a "superb" building offering a "grand and imposing view," and the wife of John Tyler, 10th President of the United States, said "the place is on a large and in some respects a really grand scale."

The grounds themselves are historic, for before the house was built, they served as a muster ground for the militia. It was, in fact, from this site that the famous company of Petersburg volunteers departed to distinguish themselves in battle in the War of 1812, and thus earn for Petersburg the title, "The Cockade City of the Union."

Perhaps this requires a little explanation, which is provided by Dr. James Bailey, city historian. "This is in reference to the fact that in the War of 1812, the volunteers marched to Ohio and fought with great valor at Fort Meigs," Dr. Bailey says. "During this period they wore cockades in their hats.

Centre Hill was built in 1823 for Robert Bolling, great grandson of the immigrant Robert Bolling, founder of a well-known Virginia family. Situated in a beautifully planted and enclosed park of over eight acres, it was constructed in "generous proportions" of oversize brick in Flemish bond, and is architecturally referred to as a "transitional Greek Revival style house."

Magnificent wolfhounds of Carrara marble guard the entrance to the columned portico, and the interior is adorned with hand-carved woodwork and lavish cornices. Remnants of a tunnel connecting the house with the Appomattox River can still be seen from the lower level of the house. It was built for the convenience of guests, mostly James River plantation owners who arrived there by barge.

Like other mansions of its size and prominence, Centre Hill has played host to its share of dignitaries over the years, including Abraham Lincoln. After the Confederate evacuation of the city, which ended the ten-month siege of Petersburg, the house became the headquarters of Major General G. L. Hartsuff, district commander for the Union. Lincoln met with him here on April 7, 1865. When the subject of rent was discussed, Lincoln said "our batteries have made rent enough here already."

It was officially opened as a Civil War era museum in 1950, and included exhibits and displays depicting the decisive and dramatic events in the history of Petersburg — Civil War portraits, uniforms, swords, pistols, shells, projectiles, rare maps, and the Confederate flag which flew above Hustings Courthouse until the day of the surrender. Centre Hill later was turned over to the City of Petersburg and today is a major tourist attraction.

With such an illustrious history, it is not surprising that the mansion is associated with some colorful ghostly legends. "Oh, yes, there are some interesting stories," says Dr. Bailey. One of the most common concerned "a beautifully dressed lady" who frequently sat at the second story window over the front door. She was seen by many passersby, but no one ever knew who she was. This occurred in the latter years of the 19th century. Once, during this time, a child living in the house told his mother of a "pretty lady" who had visited him during the night, sat on the side of his bed, held his hand, and talked to him. He indicated that he could see through her, meaning she gave a transparent appearance. The description he gave perfectly matched that of the woman others had seen in the window.

Mrs. Campbell Pryor, a direct descendent of the builder of Centre Hill lived in the house in the 1880s and 1890s, and told of the spectral playing of a little melodeon that stood in a corner of the library. "Many, many times," she said, "familiar airs have been heard played by invisible hands, as no mortal was in the room."

Her husband also experienced the strange phenomena. He once

Centre Hill

tried to use as a bed chamber a small room on the first floor near an office, but apparently the ghost, or whatever it was, felt this room belonged to it. Every time Mr. Campbell retired and the lights were turned out, "invisible hands jerked the coverings off the bed and threw them onto the middle of the floor!"

But the oddest manifestation of all was the return of the troop of soldiers, presumably Civil War veterans, who for a number of years in succession tramped through the house precisely at 7:30 p.m. each January 24th. So regular was their procession, that the house owners at the time invited friends and neighbors in to witness the eerie spectacle.

This was best expressed by Margaret DuPont Lee in her 1930 book, "Virginia Ghosts." "On that day of the year," Mrs. Lee wrote, "the clock pointing to the half hour, the door leading into the office was heard to open. Then a noise such as a regiment of soldiers marching! The clank as of sabres suggested the occupation of those tramping along the passage; up the stairs and into a room over the office. After about twenty minutes the sound was again heard descending the steps, crossing the hall, then finally the slamming of a door and all was quiet."

CHAPTER 33

The Survival (?) of John Wilkes Booth

(Caroline County)

(Author's note: In my book, "The Ghosts of Fredericksburg," I included a chapter on the legends, ghostly and otherwise, surrounding John Wilkes Booth, the man who killed Abraham Lincoln. In a further review of this intriguing case, one which encourages lively debate and controversy to this day, I discovered considerable evidence of supernatural events involving several other prominent "players." They include: Mary Surratt, suspected but never proven to be a member of the conspirators; Judge Joseph Holt, who sentenced Lincoln assassination perpetrators to death by hanging; Dr. Samuel Mudd, the physician who attended to Booth's broken leg and was subsequently accused of being a member or supporter of the plot, arguably unjustly; and Lincoln himself, perhaps the most haunted of all.

While some of these events crossed the Virginia state line into Washington, DC, and southern Maryland, I included them in order to provide a full picture of one of the most famous, or infamous, incidents in American history, and the multiple accounts of psychic phenomena which surrounded the participants in it.)

I t has been written that when he was a school boy, he once had his palm read by a Gypsy who told him he had a "bad hand, full of sorrow and trouble." The fortune teller said that he would "break hearts, but they'll be nothing to you. You'll die young, and leave many to mourn you. You'll make a bad end. . . Young sir, I've never seen a worse hand, and I wish I hadn't seen it, but if I were a girl, I'd follow you through the world for your handsome face."

The Gypsy was talking about the palm of John Wilkes Booth, the ill-fated assassin of Abraham Lincoln.

With the possible exception of the assassination and the ensuing storm of controversy which engulfed the death of John F. Kennedy, there is, arguably, no chain of historic events so shrouded in mystique and myth greater than that associated with Booth following his shooting of Lincoln at Ford's Theater in Washington.

While it has been only a generation since Kennedy's death, the confusion and contention which cloaked Booth's death — or alleged death — in a farmer's barn four miles from Port Royal, Virginia, just south of Fredericksburg, has lasted for more than 125 years and still rages today! The questions still are asked. Was Booth shot by a Yankee soldier, or did he kill himself? Was it Booth who was trapped in the burning barn, or was it someone portraying the handsome actor? Did he somehow escape the cordon of soldiers tracking him through the Virginia countryside to live out his life, as many believe, first in San Francisco and later in London? Why did the U.S. Government rush his body out of Caroline County and secretly bury it? Was this all part of a massive coverup to hide a much broader conspiracy against Lincoln and members of his cabinet?

Why was Booth's diary impounded by Secretary of War Stanton for two years after Booth's death? And why, after it finally was released, were 18 pages missing? Why were Booth's co-conspirators so cruelly treated before their trial, each shackled to a 75-pound iron ball, with his head encased in heavy canvas padded an inch thick with cotton, with one small hole for eating through, no opening for eyes or ears, and laced so tightly around the neck that speech was impossible?

Such questions were fanned for decades after his supposed death by countless reports of sightings of Booth all over this country and in Europe. As one writer put it early in this century, "Booth's ghost, a will-o'-the-wisp, has stalked the Republic, no witness sufficiently impartial and free from suspicion having been found to swear that he looked upon the disputed corpse and knew it either to be or not to be J. Wilkes Booth."

Millions of words have been written about Booth's life and death. Many authors, including immediate members of his family, have sworn that it was not Booth who was killed in Richard

Garrett's barn in the early morning hours of April 26, 1865. But if not Booth, who was it, and what happened to the one-time matinee idol?

Adding to the deep mystery are scores of strange facts and happenings:

• Booth's alcoholic father claimed to have had "ghostly experiences."

• The ghost of Mary Surratt, said to have been one of Booth's co-conspirators in the assassination plot, and the first woman ever executed for murder in the United States, haunts the Surratt House and Tavern near Washington.

• The Sergeant who claimed to have shot and killed Booth was described as being a crazy man "who talked directly to God."

• Many of the main characters involved in the Booth story reportedly died strange and mysterious deaths.

• And, 20-odd years ago, a simple Midwestern farm boy, under professional hypnosis, claimed to have been John Wilkes Booth in a past life. What made this story of reincarnation unusual was that this young man recited obscure details of Booth's life that he had no way of knowing anything about. He also said that, in fact, he had *not* died on the porch steps of the Garrett farmhouse!

Many of the circumstances of Booth's escape are well known and are fairly unchallenged. After shooting Lincoln in his box at Ford's Theater, Booth, a fairly athletic young man of 27, leaped upon the stage. However, a spur in his boot snagged a draped flag and he fell awkwardly, breaking a bone in his lower left leg. He nevertheless managed to escape by horseback with another young man, named Davy Herold. They stopped at Mary Surratt's tavern around midnight, bolted down some whiskey, and rode on. At dawn the next morning Dr. Samuel Mudd treated Booth's leg, patching it in pasteboard splints. They slept in Mudd's house until near evening. Booth shaved of his trademark mustache, and he and Herold rode off.

For the next 12 days they eluded trackers on a winding route that took them through part of southern Maryland and into Virginia. Eventually, they shot their horses, and on April 24, 1865, crossed the Rappahannock River on a ferry with three Confederate soldiers returning from the war. A short time later Booth and Herold arrived at the Garrett farm, pretending to be soldiers on their way home.

Suspicious of the visitors from the start, Garrett's sons mistakenly believed Booth and Herold were horse thieves, and they locked them in their tobacco barn. Tipped off to their whereabouts, a troop of 26 Union soldiers rode hard from Bowling Green, 13 miles away, and surrounded the Garrett farm at about two in the morning. They encircled the barn and demanded that the fugitives come out and surrender. Herold did, but Booth, playing the actor to the hilt, shouted tragedian speeches, and threatened to fight the troops with his crutch if he had to. In an effort to smoke him out, the soldiers set fire to the barn.

The objective was to take Booth alive, but as the flames began consuming the barn, an inexplicable thing happened. A single shot rang out, striking Booth in the back of the skull, oddly at virtually the same spot Booth's bullet had entered Lincoln's head. At first, soldiers who dragged Booth out, had thought he had shot himself, but then a sergeant named Boston Corbett, a former hat cleaner known as the "Mad Hatter," admitted that he had pulled the trigger of his pistol, felling Booth. When he was asked why, Corbett said, "God Almighty directed me."

Barely alive, Booth was taken to the porch of the Garrett farmhouse where his bleeding head rested on a pillow in the lap of Lucinda Holloway, a spinster relative of the Garretts. He died shortly afterwards, and she cut off a lock of his dark, curly hair, which according to a 1977 newspaper article, can still be seen at the Caroline County Historical Museum. Old time area residents said that for years afterward whenever it rained the bloodstains could still be seen on the porch. In fact, souvenir hunters so haunted the farm that the Garretts finally had to remove the boards and refloor the porch.

One of the many who claimed to have seen Booth, if indeed the man lying in Lucinda Holloway's lap was Booth, was William B. Lightfoot, a native of Port Royal who had just returned from Appomattox a few days earlier. Years later, in an interview, he told of seeing something he could never explain. "There was always one queer thing about the barn," he said. "The center post, against which Booth was leaning just before they shot him, didn't burn. Next day everything was burned up but it. It stood up there, sir, all blackened but still sound, mightily strangely, in all the ashes."

Equally extraordinary, was the highly secretive manner in which Booth's body was literally whisked from the Garrett porch, rushed back to the Washington area, and buried. The corpse was rolled into a blanket and loaded onto a cart commandeered from a Black neighbor named Ned Freeman. He was ordered to drive it northward at break-neck speed. The king bolt on a wheel snapped

John Wilkes Booth

en route causing the front end to fall, sending the dead man's body lurching forward in the red-soaked blanket. As Freeman worked on the broken bolt, blood dripped on his hands, sending him tumbling backwards screeching, "It's the blood of a murderer — it will never wash off!" Another wagon was appropriated and Freeman left his cart by the side of the road, never to use it again.

At the Potomac River, Herold and the body were transferred to the ironclad Montauk. Ironically, because of all the mystery arising from this curious action, rumors began circulating all over Washington that the body aboard ship in the middle of the river was not Booth. As dense crowds gathered on the bank, Booth's body next was lowered into a skiff and placed into a makeshift coffin — a gun-box. As the skiff drifted downstream, the crowds of spectators on the shore followed, "splashing through the shallows" to keep pace. Under the disguise of darkness, the boat turned into the great swamp behind Geeseborough Point, and the spectators could follow no further, because this area was a swampy morass into which worn out horses and mules were thrown.

At midnight the weird sojourn continued. Oarsmen rowed stealthily upstream to the old penitentiary building, where a hole had been chopped in the masonry to allow them to enter. Here, on the grounds where Mary Surratt and three other Lincoln conspirators later were hanged, Booth's body, now reposed in a white-pine casket, was buried under a warehouse floor. Everyone involved in this bizarre ritual was sworn by sacred oath never to disclose what they had seen or done, and the entrance door was bolted.

Is it any wonder, under such fantastically abnormal circumstances, that the enormous wellspring of myth and lore about Booth's death was born? It began immediately. Many believed his body had been weighted and tossed into the swamp. Grotesquely, fishermen said the body had been dissected and its parts, heavily shotted, were dropped overboard from the skiff. One newspaper reported: "Out of the darkness Booth's body will never return. In the darkness like his great crime, may it remain forever; impassable, invisible, nondescript, condemned to that worse than damnation — annihilation. The river-bottom may ooze about it, laden with great shot and drowning manacles. The fishes may swim around it or the daisies grown white above it; but we shall never know."

Soon, the myth swept across the nation that all the secrecy surrounding the burial had been maintained to hide the fact that the wrong man had been shot; that Booth had escaped. From the great groundswell of rumor came scores of reports of "Booth sightings." While the government, in the worst traditions of Watergate, stonewalled, and refused to comment, suspicion throbbed to hysteria proportions. Booth was allegedly seen in the South, in Illinois, in Canada, and on ships bound for Mexico and South America. By mid-year 1865, the staid Richmond Examiner reported in its columns, "we know Booth escaped."

One of Booth's nieces once told a news service that there were "stories" in the family of her uncle's survival after the assassination, one of which told of Booth meeting his mother in San Francisco in 1866 in which he told her how he escaped. His mother told several members of the family she had "visited" with her son.

Booth's granddaughter, Izola Forrester, wrote a book about her famous ancestor, "This One Mad Act." In it, she proclaimed that older residents in a certain area of the Telegraph Hill section of San Francisco shunned a "badly dilapidating" house they considered to be haunted by the spirit of Booth. She added that newspaper accounts published a year after the end of the Civil War mentioned a "mysterious stranger" who roamed about only after dark at this house and was described as being aloof, handsome and cloaked.

Adding to the fury, which continued to burn for years afterward, was a sequence of inexplicable occurrences quickly caressed by the superstitious. Mary Todd Lincoln, it was pointed out, died pitifully after years of insanity. Little Tad Lincoln died before reaching manhood. Major Rathbone and Miss Harris, guests in the Lincoln box at Ford's Theater on the fateful night, were caught in "the evil spell," when the Major later killed himself and Miss Harris after they were married. There were reports that all nine Union officers on the commission that had tried and condemned Mary Surratt and three others in the conspiracy, had died violent deaths, "most of them driven to suicide by remorse for having hanged an innocent woman." While at least this story proved to be fiction, Captain Willie Jett, a Confederate officer who had helped Booth on his flight, was said to have perished miserably.

Louis Weichmann, a chief government witness in the trial against Mrs. Surratt and the others, reportedly lived in fear of being avenged by either an escaped John Wilkes Booth or his ghost. Whether this is true or not is uncertain, but historians have said that when he died in 1902, "he was old and broken far beyond his 60 years."

In the years from the end of the Civil War even into the early 20th century, dozens of men stepped forward and claimed to have been Lincoln's slayer. Most were dismissed as lunatics, but the myth was kept alive, at times bordering on the ludicrous. One man in Texas who claimed to be Booth killed himself, whereupon his body was mummified and exhibited across the South and Southwest for ten to 25 cents a look.

In the late 1870s a rumor ran rampant through Richmond that John Wilkes Booth was alive and well in that city and preaching sermons every Sunday! An author, writing in "The Black Swan" magazine in June 1928, told of this belief, passed on to him by his father, when he was but a lad of eight. The man many thought to be Booth was the Reverend Dr. J. G. Armstrong, who came to Richmond in 1878 to be rector of Monumental Episcopal Church.

He was a man of "impressive presence," and a pulpit orator of "transcendent ability." The close resemblance between Armstrong and Booth "lay not alone in similarity of feature." The minister limped in the same leg which the actor broke in making his exit from Ford's Theater in Washington. Further, it was noted that Dr. Armstrong had a small scar on his neck "identical with a similar mark imprinted upon the neck of Booth."

Each man was impressive in appearance, in gesture, and in general deportment. Both wore their hair unusually long. Both men's hair was "very dark, throwing into bolder relief features as clean cut as a cameo." To add to the mystique, Armstrong frequently carried a long cape, or cloak. The effect of this garment, "hanging loosely from his shoulders, was in a sense theatric, and added emphasis to an already striking presence. He dressed in the deepest black."

Dr. Armstrong left Richmond in 1884 to accept another position "further south," but the rumors persisted. They were additionally fanned by a woman living in Richmond at the time; an English actress named Sally Partington. She steadfastly maintained, until her death, that Booth was never captured. She "never wearied" of telling the story how, while playing with a Mrs. DeBarr in a theater in St. Louis shortly after the Civil War, that Mrs. DeBarr "drew her" into a room and produced a letter she said was from Booth. "Who will now claim that John Wilkes Booth is dead?" Mrs. DeBarr told Miss Partington. "Behold the evidence of his living hand. I tell you that this letter is from him!"

Mrs. DeBarr then showed the letter to her friend. It was postmarked Australia, and the writer told how he was operating a business establishment in his "far away retreat." Miss Partington claimed that Mrs. DeBarr was in "constant communication" with Booth, and that Booth had explained to her in his letters how he had effected his escape, pawned his wife's diamond ring to a sea captain, and sailed from Norfolk in a three-masted schooner for Australia!

Still more questions and clues concerning Booth's fate arose following an episode on the network television program "Unsolved Mysteries," which included interviews with historical experts who have specialized in the Lincoln conspiracy and its aftermath. There was strong evidence that Booth was not the man shot in the Garrett barn. During part of his escape journey through northern Virginia, Booth was said to be hiding in the back of a covered wagon. Sympathizers got word to him that Union troops were nearby, and the assassin, with the help of friends, scrambled out of the wagon and hid in the woods. In the process, he lost his wallet and his personal papers.

Later, he sent a friend back to retrieve his effects and told him he would meet him at the barn. Booth arrived early, however, and again was tipped off that captors were near. He fled. So, the experts said on television, it was the friend, carrying Booth's identification papers on him, who was trapped in the barn with David Herald. In fact, when Herald came out of the barn to surrender, it was reported that the told Union troops that the man in the barn, the man Boston Corbett shot and apparently killed, was not Booth!

There was more. Lieutenant William C. Allen, assigned to the military secret service, was at the farm when they brought the body out of the barn. He saw it, and said it was not Booth because Booth had jet black hair, and this man had reddish-sandy colored hair. His statement was corroborated by two other soldiers, one who had known Booth! This man said that he knew at once the body wasn't that of Booth, because there was no injured leg. Officers told Allen and the two soldiers to keep their thoughts to themselves, and to treat the whole affair as top secret. They were to discuss it with no one. Ever!

Then there was the observation of one of the doctors who performed an autopsy on the body believed to be Booth's. His name was Dr. John F. May. He, too, felt the corpse bore little resemblance to Booth, also noting that the man had sandy hair and was freckled. He had once removed a tumor from Booth's neck and said Booth had no freckles. He was told to keep quiet. Additionally, the experts pointed out that no photographs were taken of the body. This was strange, because if it was, in fact, Booth who had been slain, the government would have photographed the body and publicized the photo across the country in an effort to quell the hysteria which arose among the public in the wake of Lincoln's killing. To the contrary, the government moved swiftly to close the book on the case and seal all documents regarding it.

And, finally there was an incident involving a man named John St. Helen, who, in 1877, thought he was dying. As he lay on his bed in a midwest state, he confessed to a friend of his that he actually was John Wilkes Booth. The friend was skeptical until St. Helen began to pour out, in great detail, the story of the assassination and escape; details only Booth could have known. Was St. Helen in reality Booth? A number of historians think this is a possibility. St. Helen took his own life by drinking poison in January 1903. Some time later, hearing of the possible St. Helen-Booth connection, doctors examined his body. They found a scar over the right eyebrow, a damaged thumb, and a right leg that had once been broken — all physically identifying characteristics of Booth!

Lastly, there is the incredible story of Dr. Dell Leonardi a hypnotist of Kansas City, who wrote a book in 1975 titled "The

Reincarnation of John Wilkes Booth," based on 73 hours of taped conversations with a young man named "Wesley." Under hypnosis — or in regression as the psychics say — he said he had been Booth in a past life. Dr. Leonardi, after painstakingly checking Wesley's comments about his former life against historical fact, came to believe that the young man indeed had lived before as the notorious assassin.

Wesley's story, as reported in book excerpts and reviews published in the mid-1970s, was that, as Booth, he had evaded his pursuers and had not been shot at Garrett's farm in 1865. He had, instead, fled to San Francisco and later lived in England where he continued his acting career, dying years later of a natural death in Calais, France.

"I have talked with the infamous John Wilkes Booth," Dr. Leonardi said. "I believe that to be a fact."

In her book, Dr. Leonardi asked was it reincarnation or was it "an entity" (Booth's ghost?) who claimed Wesley's body during hypnotic trance? She believed it to be reincarnation. Nevertheless, the question arose.

And so, it seems, the haunting mystery continues. The questions remain. In Caroline County there is an historic marker in the median strip of Route 301. It reads: "This is the Garrett place where John Wilkes Booth, assassin of Lincoln, was cornered by Union soldiers and killed April 26, 1865."

But was he?

* * * * * * * * * *

THE CRUEL FATE OF MARY SURRATT

ossibly the most pathetic figure in the Lincoln assassination aftermath was a solemn faced woman of 42 who appeared much older at the time; understandable considering the suffering, grief, and, many think, injustice she endured. Her name was Mary Jenkins Surratt, the accused co-conspirator of John Wilkes Booth. As a young girl she was sent to Alexandria to be educated by the Sisters of Charity. She became a "relentless" Roman Catholic, and developed what was described as an "abiding kinship" with the Southern secessionist movement. She married at 17, and operated, with her husband, a tavern and inn in what is now Clinton, Maryland.

When her husband died in 1862, she leased the tavern to a former Washington policeman, John Lloyd, and moved to a boarding house in the capital city. It was here that her "association" with Booth developed. It was here that she was accused of conspiring with Booth and others regarding the assassination of Lincoln — a charge that has triggered heated debate for 130 years. Many experts believe Mary Surratt had little or nothing to do with the plot and became the victim of a frenzied witchhunt in the aftermath of the President's death.

Be that as it may, what happened was that at midnight on April 14, 1865, the evening Lincoln had been shot at Ford's Theater, Mrs. Surratt was summarily rousted out of her bed and hauled off to jail without even being allowed a change of clothes. She protested her innocence to no avail. The government had made up its mind to force justice through, post haste, in an effort to calm the country. At the speedy trial, Mary was found guilty solely on the testimony of John Lloyd, who said she had told him to expect at the tavern he rented, "travelers to arrive on the night of April 14, and to provide them with supplies, including field glass and guns she had hidden in the house." The fact that Lloyd was a drunk and an unreliable witness was totally dismissed. The other evidence against her was superficially circumstantial. Tenants at her boarding house on H Street said she had met there regularly with Booth and the conspirators.

Flimsy as the case was, Mary was swiftly convicted by a military court "bent on vengeance and in satisfying a bloody national mood." She was sentenced to hang in the old District penitentiary, now Fort Leslie McNair, on the Anacosa River. It would be, perhaps, the most famous hanging in American history. No woman in the U.S. had ever been hanged before.

The date was July 7, 1865. Mary was barely able to walk when she was led to the scaffold outside the prison building — the "combined effects of debilitating fear and the shackles around her ankles." She practically had to be carried up the steps to the platform. From there she could see her own coffin below and a freshly dug hole in the ground waiting for her. She is said to have begged her executioners "Don't let me fall," seconds before the floor dropped from beneath her.

In an article published in the Washington Post in 1991, Michael Farquhar wrote, "It is said that a person who dies violently under the shadow of unresolved circumstances is remanded to a certain purgatory — a disturbed spirit in the realm of the living — waiting for a time when the truth behind his (or her) death is revealed. Mary Surratt qualifies as a ghost of exceeding prominence, as her innocence, or at least the degree of her guilt, remains stubbornly debated well beyond a century after her death. And, it is said, her spirit is restless."

Indeed, that seems to be somewhat of an understatement. Since that time, from shortly after her death to the present, the ghost of Mary Surratt has been seen and felt in three different places: the site of her hanging at Fort McNair; her old boarding house on H Street in Washington; and at the tavern in Clinton, Maryland! It is highly unusual, if not unprecedented, for a spirit to haunt more than one location. Yet there have been persistent reports of her reappearance at all three places.

Her wraith was said to frequent the boarding house almost immediately after her death. In a book titled, "Myths after Lincoln," by Lloyd Lewis, published in 1929, the author said Mary's apparition was seen within days of her death. Hearing of this, crowds gathered outside the house daily. Mrs. Surratt's daughter sold the house for a "bargain" $4,600, but the purchaser was driven away within six weeks because "his nervous system was reputedly shattered by what he had seen and heard." The Boston Post noted how other tenants came and went in "swift succession, swearing that in the dead of night, Mrs. Surratt walked the hallways clad in her robe of death."

Others who have lived in the house, or have visited it over the years have told of hearing "ominous sounds," such as mumblings, and muffled whispers coming through the walls at night. Some have even said they have heard the voices of the conspirators again going over details of the assassination. The occasional creaking of floor boards on the second floor, when no one is there, has been explained as the specter of Mary, "doomed to an eternity of pacing" until her name is cleared.

Her presence, however, may be even stronger at the site of her hanging. For example, there is an inexplicable appearance, directly beneath her gallows, of a single boxwood tree that "seemingly grew of its own accord." It has been claimed that this is her way of continuing to attract attention to prove her innocence. Another eerie and unexplained possible manifestation some years ago was the path that mysteriously appeared through a foot of snow; a path two feet wide, right down to the bare grass, maybe 300 yards long! According to Erik Swanson, a young honor guard officer at Fort McNair, the path "just appeared" in the snow; no shovel dug it.

"There are no pipes or anything else below it," Swanson said at the time. "Nothing to explain it."

The path of bare ground, incidentally, covered precisely the route Mary Surratt was forced to take from the jail where she had been held to the gallows where she was hanged!

But there have been many more strange occurrences here. In 1977, an army lieutenant saw "the apparition of a stout, middle-aged woman, dressed in black, seemingly floating through the hall-ways" of an officer's quarters. Others have heard voices and felt the sensation of being touched by "unseen hands." A major's wife said she, too, had seen a "woman in a long, dark dress floating around." She told psychic investigators it was Mary Surratt!

In the late 1980s, the Army Times did a feature on the subject. It quoted an Army Captain, Dave Osborne, who swore he heard Mary weeping and begging for help outside his window in the pre-dawn hours on Lincoln's birthday in 1989. "It started off softly crying, 'Help me, help me'," he said. "Then she began screaming, 'Oh no, help me, help me'!" He ran outside, but no one was there.

In yet another account, recorded in 1989, "Former residents of Quarters 20 at Fort McNair have reported objects moving supernaturally, drumming sounds at night, and shrieking voices outside where the Lincoln conspirators were executed." Mary Surratt was held prisoner in a first-floor apartment there! Four years earlier first lieutenant Anthony Plana said he heard "the noises of a large crow" outside of Quarters 20. He could find no source for them. Hammering, sawing, and other noises have also been heard. Several years before this, Major Bob Tonnelli and his wife brought psychics into the quarters to study the phenomena. Pool balls and flower pots had supposedly been tossed about in their apartment. Whispering voices called out to Tonnelli and his wife, and once "a bedroom unexplainably burst into flames!"

The legend of Mary's hauntings extends into Prince George's County, Maryland, the site of the old tavern in Clinton, now Surratt museum. Her specter has been sighted there on occasion "in her sweeping long black dress and tight bun in her hair." One person who has experienced Mary's "return" is Laurie Verge, historian for the Maryland-National Capital Park and Planning Commission. She used to hold meetings in the Clinton building. "When I was there at night," she recalled, "I got a very eerie uneasy feeling. The hair on my neck would stand on end. I can't explain it."

One night some years ago, Laurie and four others were meeting in a room on the second floor when they heard the front door open.

Mary Surratt

This was followed by "loud thudding footsteps, the kind that might be made by clodhopper 19th century woman's boots, a *big* woman's boots, pacing the hall, stopping in the middle of the house. Ever so cautiously, Laurie and the others crept down the stairs, but saw no one.

Joan Chaconas, a facility aide at the state-owned Surratt House museum in Clinton, told the Associated Press that she once found daisies — Mary's favorite flower — hanging from the door knob of the house. They had been left by a woman who said she had "communicated" with the spirit of Mary via an Ouija board. The woman said Mary told her she would return one night to her old home. Intrigued, Joan later gathered a group of spiritualists, including the woman who had left the flowers, and they waited one night to see if there would be a spectral appearance. Nothing was seen, but one woman cried out that "something had touched her." Joan Chaconas also said that there is a portrait of Mary in the house, facing the stairs. She called it a "creepy" portrait, with eyes that "reflect a certain unhappiness." She added that the picture's eyes "follow you everywhere you go!"

And so it appears that the sad and chagrined spirit of Mary Surratt is bound to remain restlessly wandering from Fort McNair to H Street in Washington to the old tavern in Clinton, Maryland, in a continuous quest to seek understanding and redemption.

* * * * * * * * * * * *

THE MAN WITH NO HEART!

Yet another ghostly chapter in the Booth-Surratt saga is that of Judge Advocate General Joseph Holt. He served as the U.S. government prosecutor in the trial which sent Mary to the gallows. He had insisted on the death penalty for her, and Surratt supporters say he hid from President Andrew Johnson the fact that the military commission's recommendation in the case had been to impose a life imprisonment sentence in deference to Mary's age and sex. Johnson said he never saw the recommendation.

Holt had been described as "taciturn, vindictive and ill-mannered." He also was said to be a man who "has no heart." Yet Holt became somewhat of a tragic figure himself in the aftermath of the hanging. Newspaper articles of the period say he became a recluse, and withdrew into the privacy of his home, which was only a few blocks from the old brick capitol prison where Mary had been incarcerated. One reporter said his house "was decaying, with bars on the windows and shades that never permitted the sun's rays inside."

By the 1880s, his eccentricities had become well known, and children crossed the street rather than pass by his shuttered house with its "overgrowth of weeds and tangled vines." Neighbors said "his irrevocable decision weighed heavily upon him" and he was thought to spend endless hours poring over the trial transcripts. He spent his remaining years in almost total solitude, and after he died, the new owners of the house tried to make it cheerful but, as one writer put it, "the presence of the departed 'man with no heart' is said to have chilled more than one room." For years afterward, mysterious footsteps could be heard pacing back and forth across the library in an upstairs room. People said it was Judge Holt forever questioning his harsh treatment of Mary Surratt.

Even after the old house was torn down, there were accounts of sightings of Holt, "clad in his midnight blue Union uniform, with the cape pulled tightly about him" walking toward the old brick capitol. As Mary sought vindication, the Judge sought forgiveness.

* * * * * * * * * * *

THE REDEMPTION OF DR. SAMUEL MUDD

ary Surratt was not the only victim of the Lincoln conspiracy. Another person, whom many feel was wrongly accused and punished in the questionable justice which was meted out in the days and weeks after the President died was Dr. Samuel Mudd who lived at a farmhouse in Charles County, Maryland, near Beantown. His legacy is to have become a prominent figure in one of the most controversial episodes in American history. Whether or not he was implicated in even the slightest way in the assassination plot has been heatedly argued for more than a century and a quarter and to this day has not been satisfactorily answered. It is a question that not only figuratively haunts historians, but also literally spooks his old farmhouse!

Dr. Mudd's life, and his reputation, was dramatically and inexorably shattered at about 4 o'clock on the morning of April 15, 1865, with a knock at his door. He opened it to face David Herold and John Wilkes Booth, who had broken his leg in the leap from Lincoln's box to the stage floor at Ford's Theater the previous evening. Dr. Mudd set Booth's leg and fed and sheltered the two fugitives until mid-afternoon when they rode off to destiny at the Garrett Farm in Virginia. Whether or not Mudd knew of Booth's deed the previous evening has been the subject of raging debates ever since.

Regardless of his guilt or innocence, he was summarily taken into custody several days later, subsequently tried and convicted of having been a part of the conspiracy, and sentenced to life imprisonment at Fort Jefferson on Dry Tortugas Island, Florida. Outgoing President Andrew Johnson pardoned him four years later, and he returned to his home, although it has been written that he died a broken man in 1883, never able, in his lifetime, to clear his name.

Apparently, from the beyond, he is still trying! According to Trish Gallagher, in her interesting book, "Ghosts and Haunted Houses of Maryland," published in 1988, the ghost of Samuel Mudd periodically is seen by his youngest granddaughter, Louise Mudd Arehart; a woman who has laboriously fought to vindicate him. She also has successfully restored and preserved the circa 1830 family farmhouse, which, in 1974, was listed on the National Register of Historic Places.

Mrs. Arehart told author Gallagher that in the late 1960s she began experiencing a series of strange happenings at the house. It began with phantom knockings at the front door and footsteps up the stairs and down the hall. Eventually, she began catching glimpses of an apparitional man dressed in black trousers and vest, with a white shirt, "its sleeves rolled up to the elbows." The visions lasted but a few seconds at a time before vanishing. In time, Mrs. Arehart began to realize that the figure was, in reality, her grandfather, Dr. Mudd, and that he was appearing to her for a specific reason. He was, she felt, upset that the farmhouse had fallen into disrepair, and he made it known to her that she should do something about it.

She did. She has spent the past 25 years spearheading an effort at complete restoration. The Mudd House today is open to the public as a site of national historic significance. Even more satisfying has been the paralleling effort to clear the Doctor's name; an effort that resulted in former President Jimmy Carter publicly proclaiming belief in Dr. Mudd's innocence. His spirit, at last, could now rest in peace.

* * * * * * * * * *

THE MOST TROUBLED SPIRIT OF ALL

 nd, finally, there are the ghostly legends surrounding the victim of the Booth assassination,

Abraham Lincoln himself. In one of the most famous instances of precognition ever recorded, Lincoln is said to have envisioned his death in a dream. It was a recurring dream which so disturbed him that he looked for answers in his Bible. "I turned to other passages, and seemed to encounter a dream of a vision wherever I looked," he said. "I kept on turning the leaves of the old book, and everywhere my eye fell upon passages recording matters strangely in keeping with my own thoughts — supernatural visitation, dreams, visions, etc."

At one point, Lincoln detailed his dream to his wife, Mary Todd Lincoln. He did it in a deliberate slow and sad countenance. "About ten days ago," he said, "I retired late. I soon began to dream. There seemed to be a death-like stillness about me. Then I heard subdued sobs, as if a number of people were weeping. I thought I left my bed and wandered downstairs. There, the silence was broken by the same pitiful sobbing, but the mourners were invisible. I went from room to room; no living person was in sight, but the same mournful sounds of distress met me as I passed along."

Lincoln continued: "It was light in all the rooms; every object was familiar to me; but where were all the people who were grieving as if their hearts would break? I was puzzled and alarmed. What could be the meaning of all this? Determined to find the cause of a state of things so mysterious and so shocking, I kept on until I arrived at the East Room (of the White House), which I entered. Before me was a catafalque, on which rested a corpse wrapped in funeral vestments. Around it were stationed soldiers who were acting as guards; and there was a throng of people, some gazing mournfully upon the corpse, whose face was covered, others weeping pitifully.

"'Who is dead in the White House?' I demanded of one of the soldiers. 'The President,' was the answer. 'He was killed by an assassin.' Then came a loud burst of grief from the crowd, which awoke me from my dream. I slept no more that night; and although it was only a dream, I have been strangely annoyed by it ever since."

Following Lincoln's death, Mrs. Lincoln was distraught with horror, and it is said her first coherent exclamation, was, "His dream was prophetic."

It has been documented that on the night before the assassination, Lincoln had another dream, "so troubling" that he related it the following morning at a cabinet meeting. "I had a warning dream again last night," he said. "It related to water. I seemed to be in a singular and indescribable vessel that was moving with great rapidity toward a dark and indefinite shore."

Later that day Lincoln told his bodyguard, W. H. Crook, that he had dreamed for three nights running that he would be assassinated. Crook begged the President not to go to the theater, but Lincoln said that he must go because he had promised Mrs. Lincoln. Was Lincoln psychic? Many think so. One strong indication might have occurred that evening as he was leaving for the theater. Normally, he said "good night," to Crook on such occasions. This night, however, he said "good by!"

Lincoln's ghost, too, has been reported to have reappeared over the past 130 years. At Fort Monroe, Virginia, for example, there have been numerous sightings of the President's figure in a splendid old plantation-style house facing the east sallyport known as Old Quarters Number One. He has been seen, appropriately enough, in the Lincoln Room, clad in a dressing gown standing by the fireplace "appearing to be deep in thought."

But it is in the Lincoln Room of the White House in Washington where his best known "reappearances" have occurred. In fact, "his ghost there is probably the most famous and most written-about spirit in American history. To be sure, no one had more cause to return as a lamentable specter as did this man whose life was so entwined with tragedy.

He lost his mother when he was only four years old. His first sweetheart, Ann Rutledge, died at an early age of typhoid. His sons, Edward and Willie died in childhood. Willie's death, especially, had a profound impact on Lincoln. There are newspaper accounts that he often visited his gravesite, and on at least two occasions, had the crypt opened so he could view his son. He allegedly sat there for hours and wept. There was, too, his long-troubled relationship with Mary Todd.

Additionally, there are references to Lincoln's interest in spiritualism, and to his wife's more fervent feelings about the supernatural. One encyclopedia writeup noted that Lincoln believed in dreams, and "other enigmatic signs and portents." It is known that a number of seances were held in the White House during Lincoln's term. At one session, the President is said to have asked a congressman to sit on a piano that was being levitated by a spiritualist. His added weight made no difference the piano rose and fell on command.

A National Geographic News Bulletin reported that medium J.

B. Conklin supposedly once received a telepathic message from Senator Edward D. Baker for Lincoln. Baker had been a close friend (see chapter on the Battle of Ball's Bluff), but at the time the message was received, he had been dead for two months!

There are also psychic connotations surrounding the tragic death of Lincoln's young son, Willie, in 1862. Mary Todd Lincoln screamed through the night until exhaustion finally overtook her, and the President wept for hours. Five days later, during the funeral, a fierce wind is said to have swept up under blackened skies, toppling chimneys, damaging rooves, and upsetting church steeples. Decades later, during the administration of William Howard Taft, maids and other workers in the White House told of seeing a "gossamer figure," and feeling the icy touch of an invisible hand. Taft thought the accounts were nonsense, but when some employees threatened to quit he advised his staff never to mention the incidents again.

The list of those who have claimed to have seen Lincoln's ghost in the White House reads like a celebrity Who's Who. Theodore Roosevelt once said, "I see him (Lincoln) in the different room and in the halls. I think of him all the time." Grace Coolidge, wife of President Calvin Coolidge, told a newspaper reporter she saw Lincoln dressed "in black, with a stole draped across his shoulders to ward off the drafts and chills of Washington's night air." Eleanor Roosevelt, wife of President Franklin D. Roosevelt, admitted she felt Lincoln's "presence" in the house. One of her staff members told of passing the Lincoln bedroom one day and seeing a "lanky figure" sitting on the bed pulling on his boots. She screamed and ran downstairs as fast as she could! The Washington Star once observed that a White House valet also ran screaming from the house, claiming that he had seen Lincoln's apparition.

In one widely circulated encounter, Queen Wilhelmina of the Netherlands was visiting the White House and was spending the night in the Rose Room. She heard a knock at the door late at night, got up from bed and opened the door, to see a vision of Lincoln, his "large frame taking up most of the doorway." She fainted. When she revived, the figure was gone. She later recounted this to guests at a cocktail party. Sir Winston Churchill often slept in the Lincoln bedroom when he visited Washington, although it was said he never felt comfortable there. Frequently, he would move across the hall in the middle of the night.

President Harry Truman, as no-nonsense a person as ever resided in the White House, once told his press secretary, James

Haggerty, that he often felt Lincoln's presence. He said he was awakened one night in the early morning hours by two distinct knocks at the door to his bedroom. When he got up to investigate, there was no one there, although he felt a sudden chill, and heard "footsteps trailing off down the corridor."

Lady Bird Johnson also told of a "Lincolnesque visitation" one evening as she sat watching a television special on Lincoln's death. She later told her press secretary that she felt "compelled by someone" to look at the mantel in the room. There, she saw a small plaque she had never noticed before. She felt "ill at ease" as she walked over to read it. It told of the importance of that room to Lincoln.

A number of servants in the White House said they had encountered the great man's spirit in the halls and rooms as they went about their work. Many witnesses also said they glimpsed Lincoln's apparition peering out of the office in the Oval Room. All of this caused Washington Post reporter, Jacqueline Lawrence, to write: "The most troubled spirit of 1600 Pennsylvania Avenue is Abraham Lincoln, who during his own lifetime claimed to receive regular visits from his two dead sons."

And, lastly, there is this chilling footnote to Lincoln's untimely death, and to those who may or may not have been involved. In July 1865, on the eve of Mary Surratt's execution, her daughter, Anna, forced her way inside the White House grounds and made it to the front door. She pleaded desperately for her mother's release. It has been written that on the anniversary of that occasion, some have seen Anna's spirit banging on the front door in an other-worldly plea for mercy.

So, it seems, the incredible spiritual happenings involving John Wilkes Booth, Mary Surratt, Judge Joseph Hold, Dr. Samuel Mudd, and Abraham Lincoln himself, live on, perhaps to eternity!

CHAPTER 34

The Imprisonment of Jefferson Davis

(Fort Monroe)

here are so many ghosts — famous of otherwise — at historic Fort Monroe in Hampton that it's hard to know where to begin. One can almost take his or her pick of a "celebrity specter" and chances are "it" has been sighted at some point over the past 160 years or so. The star-studded list of Civil War-era apparitions who have allegedly appeared at one time or another includes Abraham Lincoln, Jefferson Davis' wife, Varina, and Ulysses S. Grant.

In fact, the only major notable who either served or visited the Fort and has not returned in spirit form is Robert E. Lee, who as a young lieutenant helped with the engineering and construction of the facility in the 1830s.

Dennis Mroczkowski, Director of the Casemate Museum at the Fort, offers a thought about why so many spirits seem to frequent the site. "With the hundreds of thousands of people who have been assigned to the fort," he says, "there's a large population to draw from for ghosts. There have been numerous sightings of strange apparitions and many tend to repeat themselves and become identified in people's minds with the famous people who have been here."

The history of the area dates back to the time of the first English settlement in America. The hardy souls aboard the Godspeed, Susan Constant, and Discovery, saw Old Point Comfort, where Fort Monroe is located, in April 1607, at least two weeks before they dropped anchor at Jamestown. A small exploration party even rowed ashore and met with local Indians.

In 1608, Captain John Smith checked the area out and deemed it an excellent site for a fort. Consequently, a year later, Captain John Ratcliffe was dispatched from Jamestown to build an earth work fortification that was called Fort Algernourne. By 1611, it was well stockaded and had a battery of seven heavy guns and a garrison of 40 men.

The War of 1812 demonstrated the need for an adequate American coastal defense, and over the next few years plans were drawn up for an elaborate system of forts running from Maine to Louisiana.

Old Point Comfort was selected as a key post in this chain, and the assignments for building a new fort there was given to Brigadier General Simon Bernard, a famous French military engineer and former aide-de-camp to Emperor Napoleon I. Construction extended over 15 years, from 1819 to 1834, and it was named Fort Monroe after James Monroe, a Virginian, and the fifth President of the United States.

Upon its completion, the fort had an armament of nearly 200 guns which controlled the channel into Hampton Roads and dominated the approach to Washington by way of the Chesapeake Bay. In fact, it has often been called "the Gibraltar of Chesapeake Bay." It represented the highest development in the art of seacoast defense at a time when masonry works were still resistant to gunfire, and to this day Fort Monroe remains the largest enclosed fortification in the United States.

So impregnable was this bastion, and so ideally located, it was one of the few Union fortifications in the South that was not captured by the Confederates during the Civil War. It was described as an unassailable base for the Union Army and Navy right in the heart of the Confederacy. Thus President Abraham Lincoln had no qualms about visiting the fort in May 1862 to help plan the attack of Norfolk. If was here, too, in April 1864, that General U. S. Grant outlined the campaign strategy that led to the end of the Civil War.

A wide range of psychic phenomena has been experienced in a splendid old plantation-style house facing the east sallyport that is known as Old Quarters Number One. Manifestations have included the clumping of boots, the rustling of silken skirts, the sounds of distant laughter and the strange shredding of fresh flower petals in mid-winter.

It is here, appropriately enough in the Lincoln Room, where the

Varina Davis (Photo courtesy of the Museum of the Confederacy.)

image of Honest Abe himself has been seen clad in a dressing gown standing by the fireplace appearing to be deep in thought. Other residents of the house have told of seeing Grant wandering about.

And it was also at Fort Monroe that the imprisonment of Jefferson Davis, the former President of the Confederate States of America, led, many believe, to one of the first and most famous ghost stories associated with the site. Davis, who had been planning to reestablish the capital of the Confederacy in Texas with

213

hopes of continuing the war, was captured near Irwinville, Georgia, on May 10, 1865. His devoted wife, Varina, rushed forward when it appeared that a Northern cavalryman was about to shoot down her defiant husband, who also had been accused, inaccurately, of plotting an attempt to assassinate Lincoln.

Davis was taken to Fort Monroe, then the most powerful fort in the country, to prevent escape or rescue attempts. On May 23, 1865, he was placed in solitary confinement in a cell in Casemate No. 2 (a stone walled chamber), creating a painful incident which almost cost him his life and may well have provided the cause for the periodic spectral return of Varina Davis to Fort Monroe during the past century.

A day after his imprisonment, Davis was ordered to be shackled. When a blacksmith knelt down to rivet the ankle irons in place, the angered Davis knocked him to the floor. He sprang to his feet, raised his hammer, and was about to crush the Southerner's skull when the officer of the day, Captain Jerome Titlow, threw himself between the two men. Thereafter, it took four Union soldiers to subdue Davis long enough for the irons to be secured.

The next day, Dr. John J. Craven, chief medical officer at Fort Monroe, examined the prisoner and was shocked at his sickly appearance. He quickly recommended that the shackles be removed and they were a few days later. Meanwhile, the determined Varina fought hard for more humane treatment of her husband, and eventually she and Dr. Craven were successful. Davis was moved to better quarters in Carroll Hall. In May 1866, Varina got permission from President Andrew Johnson to join Davis at the fort, and she brought along their young daughter, Winnie. Jefferson Davis was released from captivity on May 13, 1867, travelled extensively in Europe, and later retired to Beauvoir, a mansion in Biloxi, Mississippi. He died in 1889 at the age of 81 and today is buried in Hollywood Cemetery in Richmond.

It is supposedly the apparition of the iron-willed Varina who has been seen on occasion at the fort, appearing late at night through the second floor window of quarters directly across from the casemate where her husband had been so harshly shackled. A number of residents have reported seeing her. One awoke early one morning to glimpse the figures of both "a plumpish woman and a young girl peering through the window." She got out of bed and walked toward them, but when she reached out to touch the woman's billowing skirt, the figures disappeared!

CHAPTER 33

A Monument to the Spirits of the Dead

(Richmond)

Here rests his head upon the lap of Earth
    A Youth, to Fortune and to Fame unknown.
Fair Science frown'd not on his humble birth,
    And Melancholy mark'd him for her own
           (First stanza of "The Epitaph," by Thomas Gray)

here are more Confederate soldiers (except for Blandford Cemetery in Petersburg) . . . more Confederate generals . . . and more Confederate tombstones and monuments at historic Hollywood Cemetery in Richmond than anywhere else in the South or in the entire United States.

There is, for example, the imposing statue of Jefferson Davis, the only President of the Confederacy. It towers over his gravesite flanked by mourning angels of stone. There is the marker for J. E. B. Stuart, the dashing general of cavalry, the charismatic symbol of the chivalry and pride of the South, who was cut short in the prime of his life by a mortal wound received at the Battle of Yellow Tavern in 1864. There is the tomb of General George E. Pickett, who courageously led a legendary charge on July 3, 1863, at Gettysburg, where thousands of Rebels fell.

And there is the dominant, 90-foot-high memorial pyramid which stands guard over the graves of thousands of Confederate soldiers. Constructed of large pieces of granite quarried from the James River, this giant monument was erected in 1869.

The first Southern soldier to be buried at Hollywood — the first Virginia casualty in the War Between the States — was 19-year-old Henry Lawson Wyatt of Richmond, who was killed at the Battle of Big Bethel near Hampton in June 1861. He was taken to Hollywood by train and interred with full military honors.

Many others followed soon after. As one witness reported at the time: "Day by day, we were called to our windows by the wailing dirge of a military band preceding a soldier's funeral. One could number these sad pageants; the coffin crowned with cap and sword and gloves, the riderless horse following with empty boots fixed in the stirrups of an army saddle; such soldiers as could be spared from the front, marching after with arms reversed and crepe-enfolded banners; the passers-by standing with bare, bent heads . . ."

As the war wore on, the formality of such events gave way to more hasty burials. The cemetery literally became swamped with bodies. There were 10,000 casualties from the Peninsula Campaign of 1862 alone, and many of the dead were dispatched to Hollywood, where a special section had been set aside for them.

For some, the long last journey home took years. At Gettysburg, an estimated 20,000 Southerners were killed, missing or seriously wounded in the fierce three days of fighting in July 1863. The Confederates had time to bury only 500 of their casualties before the battle ended. Later, Federal burial teams placed dozens, sometimes hundreds of slain men in vast pits marked only by the number of bodies thrown in. A farmer who witnessed this said that more than 200 soldiers were placed in one trench. It is believed that more than 7,000 bodies were buried on the battlefields or near hospitals at Gettysburg.

The Union moved 3,534 of their fallen to a new Soldiers' National Cemetery which was dedicated on November 19, 1863, at a ceremony attended by Abraham Lincoln. The Federal government, however, regarded the dead Confederates as traitors and made no provision for their care. Most lay at or near where they fell. The disrespect exhibited by Pennsylvania farmers toward these men shocked the South. Skeletons were ploughed up and lay "strewn about the surface." Some farmers demanded payment for the soldiers buried on their property, and one even pulled a gold dental plate from the makeshift grave of a Confederate colonel.

Amidst such desecration, a movement was started by the Ladies of the Hollywood Memorial Association to have the Southern bodies exhumed and transferred to Richmond. On June 15, 1872, nearly nine years after the battle, the first shipment of 279 plain wooden boxes, containing 708 Confederate soldiers, arrived in the Virginia capital, and thousands of Richmonders gathered at Hollywood to pay tribute to their fallen comrades. Wagons were draped in black and white and covered with flowers and Confederate flags. Throughout the city, flags flew at half mast. General George Pickett led more than 1,000 Confederate veterans in the sad march to the cemetery.

By October 1873, the remains of nearly 3,000 Southern soldiers had been exhumed at Gettysburg and transferred to Hollywood — all of those who had been killed in the battle except for about 40 men who were buried in a peach orchard.

Most of their identities were unknown.

In addition, many of those returned to Richmond were from other Southern states. They had not reached home when they were reburied in Richmond. There also are a number of Union bodies buried in the cemetery.

Is it any wonder, then, that there remain to this day witness accounts of hauntings — both at the blood-soaked grounds of Gettysburg, and at Hollywood Cemetery?

It is said, for instance, that "visitors from the beyond" gather around an old well at a site in Southern Pennsylvania along the ridge once held by the Confederates under General Armistead. Here, apparitions in gray uniforms have appeared to present-day

Confederate Monument at Hollywood Cemetery, Richmond.

onlookers on the day before the anniversary of Pickett's charge —
July 2, 1863. It is not known if they are the ghosts of Pickett's men,
but it is told that if so, they are "the visions of another time."

They are — these wispy figures — reported to be seen standing
around the well, "drinking in the life-giving waters the night before
life was to be snatched from them. They toast the next victory, or
death. They mix fine Southern bourbon with Pennsylvania well
water . . . in the dead moonlight."

Reenactors at many Civil War sites tell of having strange feelings, hearing inexplicable sounds, and sometimes seeing curious sights on battlefields. Most say such sensations occur at night, and there have been more reports of such activity at Gettysburg than at any other single location.

A group of reenactors from the Culpeper area, for example, were the first to arrive for an encampment at the historic Pennsylvania site in 1981 — or at least they thought they were the first. According to this group they were the only ones in the field, yet that evening, when it began to get dark, they noticed a fire off in the distance just beyond a stream that ran down between two ridges. Several of the Virginians spotted the fire and said they also saw a wall tent, such as the larger tents used by officers, and a table and chairs.

At dusk, a few of the reenactors decided to go over and meet their fellow troopers. They carried a bottle of whiskey with them. They crossed the first ridge and went down to the stream with the fire and tent still in view. At the bottom of the land between the ridges, they sloshed through the stream, and began walking through some tall grass. When they got to where the supposed encampment had been seen, they found nothing! Absolutely nothing! There was no tent, no table, no chairs and no fire. There wasn't even a wisp of smoke or any ashes. They carefully searched the entire area, but never found even a twig out of place, and no evidence whatsoever that anyone had been there.

Kent Brinkley, a Colonial Williamsburg landscape specialist who participates in Civil War reenactments, was at Gettysburg that same year - 1981. He tells of yet another eerie occurrence that happened then; one which is still talked about to this day. "There were a couple of fellows posted on the picket line one night," he says. "They were on the edge of the woods and it was dark, about eleven p.m. They were standing by a fire, when all of a sudden a man walked up and greeted them. He was dressed in a period uniform, but it was all dusty and dirty, with patched pants, and the man himself looked weather-beaten and worn out. The two on picket duty just assumed he was a fellow reenactor who had dropped by for a chat.

"The man asked if they minded if he sat down. They nodded. Then he said, 'our army sure took a beating today, didn't it?' The two reenactors just looked at each other, and thought to themselves, boy, this guy is really in character, isn't he. The man went on to describe the details of the fighting that had taken place during the day. He talked for about 15 minutes or so, and the two pickets were considerably impressed. This guy really knew the facts pertaining to the battle in July 1863 — down to the most minute detail. He told them he was with the 5th Corps of the Union Army.

Kent continues: "As the man started to leave, he asked the two reenactors how they were fixed for ammunition. They said they had some, but not too much. 'Well, you never can have too much,' the man said. 'I've got plenty, boys.' With that, he handed one of the pickets a box of cartridges. Then he tipped his cap and mysteriously disappeared.

"The reenactors looked at each other again," Kent says. "They said, 'that guy really knew his stuff. He must have really studied the battle.' Then they looked at the unbroken box he had given them. 'Hey,' one said, 'look at this.' They stared in astonishment. These were *real Civil War* cartridges, not recreations! They bore the original label of the Frankfurt arsenal. They had been manufactured in the 1860s!

"Such authentic cartridges can be purchased today at Civil War relic shows. However, they probably would cost in excess of $100. There was a long silence," Kent adds, "as the two reenactors again looked at each other, this time with raised eyebrows.

"The next day they checked on the units who were at Gettysburg in 1981 to participate in the reenactment.

"They were told there was no group from the Union army's 5th Corps involved!

"It was then they became convinced they had had an encounter with the supernatural."

There is an additional footnote to add to the Confederate dead at Gettysburg. Charles Bailey of Richmond is an active Civil War reenactor (23rd Virginia), as well as a member of the Sailor's Creek Preservation Committee. He tells the following: "In July 1988, we went up to Gettysburg to do a 125th anniversary reenactment of the battle.

"On July 3rd we recreated Pickett's charge. As we went up the hill toward the stone wall I couldn't help but think, here I am. It is the anniversary of the charge. It is the same hour. And we were singing the same song the Confederate soldiers sang that day in 1863 — 'Amazing Grace.' I knew my great-great-grandfather had fought in the War Between the States, and quite possibly had been at Gettysburg. It was a very moving experience for me.

"As we neared the stone wall, behind which the Union reenactors were standing, I knew it was customary, at such events, to go up and shake their hands after the charge was over. But I couldn't bring myself to do it. I said to myself, I'm not going to shake any damn Yankee hands.

"At that instant, I heard a voice. I looked around. There was no one near me. The voice sounded ethereal. It said, 'you will go up there and shake their hands!' Then it was gone. I have asked myself ever since, could it have been my great-great grandfather scolding me. I guess I will never know for sure, but I'll tell you what. I went up to that wall and shook every hand I could!"

There are recurring reports of active spirits at Hollywood Cemetery as well. Some have sworn they have heard the soft moans of wounded and dying men arising from the shadows of the Confederate Monument, and in the vicinity of Pickett's own grave.

Are they the restless spirits of Yankees and Confederates alike, non-Virginians still trying to reach the homes and farms they left more than 130 years ago when they marched off to defend their cause? Are they the unknown ghosts of families who searched vainly in the war's aftermath for some clue to the identity of their lost loved ones?

Certainly, if ever there was justification for the return of entities from the beyond, it would lie buried in the sacred grounds of Hollywood Cemetery.

"And are they really dead, our martyred slain?"
No, dreamers! Morn shall bid them rise again
From every plain, from every height
On which they seemed to die for right;
Their gallant spirits shall renew the fight
In the land where we were dreaming.

—*From "The Land Where We Were Dreaming," by Daniel Bedinger Lucas, a soldier in the Confederate Army, written in 1865.*

Author L. B. Taylor, Jr., and illustrator Brenda Goens, at a Civil War site in Newport News.

Photo by Frank Jones

About the Author

L. B. Taylor, Jr. — a Scorpio — is a native Virginian. He was born in Lynchburg and has a BS degree in Journalism from Florida State University. He wrote about America's space programs for 16 years, for NASA and aerospace contractors, before moving to Williamsburg, Virginia, in 1974, as public affairs director for BASF Corporation. He retired in 1993. Taylor is the author of more than 300 national magazine articles and 30 non-fiction books. His research for the book "Haunted Houses," published by Simon and Schuster in 1983, stimulated his interest in area psychic phenomena and led to the publication of five regional Virginia ghost books preceding "The Ghosts of Virginia," and "The Ghosts of Virginia, Volume II."

(Personally autographed copies of: "The Ghosts of Williamsburg" — 84 pages, illustrated, $6.50; "The Ghosts of Richmond" — 172 pages, illustrated, $10; "The Ghosts of Tidewater" — 232 pages, illustrated, $11; "The Ghosts of

Fredericksburg" — 177 pages, illustrated, $10; and "The Ghosts of Charlottesville and Lynchburg" — 188 pages, illustrated, $10; ($40 for all five); and "The Ghosts of Virginia" (Volume I) — 400 pages, illustrated, $14; "The Ghosts of Virginia" (Volume II) — 400 pages, illustrated, $14; are available from L. B. Taylor, Jr., 108 Elizabeth Meriwether, Williamsburg, VA, 23185 (757-253-2636). Please add $2 for postage and handling, $4 for multiple book orders. Also, please specify to whom you wish the book(s) signed.

L. B. Taylor, Jr., is available (depending upon his schedule) to speak on the subject of Virginia ghosts to civic, social, fraternal, business, school, library and other groups. Call or write about dates and details.

OTHER BOOKS BY L. B. TAYLOR, JR

PIECES OF EIGHT: Recovering the Riches of a Lost
                                      Spanish Treasure Fleet

THAT OTHERS MAY LIVE (RESCUE & RECOVERY)

LIFTOFF: THE STORY OF AMERICA'S SPACEPORT

FOR ALL MANKIND

GIFTS FROM SPACE (SPINOFF BENEFITS FROM SPACE RESEARCH)

CHEMISTRY CAREERS

SPACE SHUTTLE

RESCUE (TRUE STORIES OF TEENAGE HEROISM)

THE DRAFT

SHOPLIFTING

SPACE: "BATTLEGROUND OF THE FUTURE"

THE NUCLEAR ARMS RACE

THE NEW RIGHT

THE GHOSTS OF WILLIAMSBURG

SPOTLIGHT ON . . . (FOUR TEENAGE IDOLS)

EMERGENCY SQUADS

SOUTHEAST AFRICA

DRIVING HIGH (EFFECTS OF ALCOHOL AND DRUGS ON DRIVING)

CHEMICAL AND BIOLOGICAL WARFARE

HAUNTED HOUSES

THE GHOSTS OF RICHMOND

THE COMMERCIALIZATION OF SPACE

ELECTRONIC SURVEILLANCE

HOSTAGE

THE GHOSTS OF TIDEWATER

THE GHOSTS OF FREDERICKSBURG

THE GHOSTS OF CHARLOTTESVILLE AND LYNCHBURG

THE GHOSTS OF VIRGINIA - VOLUME I

THE GHOSTS OF VIRGINIA - VOLUME II